BIOETHICS

Latin American Perspectives

Edited by

Arleen L.F. Salles
María Julia Bertomeu

Amsterdam – New York, NY 2002

QH
332
.B45
2002

The paper on which this book is printed meets the requirements of "ISO 9706:1994, Information and documentation - Paper for documents - Requirements for permanence".

ISBN: 90-420-1517-9
©Editions Rodopi B.V., Amsterdam – New York, NY 2002
Printed in The Netherlands

CONTENTS

EDITORIAL FOREWORD

Philosophy is a powerful force in Latin America. The productivity of Latin American philosophers, considerably increased in the past decade, constitutes a substantial portion of the intellectual reality of the region. Yet, in spite of the many books that have been written about Latin America in recent years, there is not much on contemporary Latin Americans and their philosophy. Thus, many English-speaking scholars, if asked about philosophy in Latin America will, unless they are Latin American specialists, answer by asking, "Is there much philosophical activity in Latin America?" Others may be familiar with a particular philosophical current in the region, for example, philosophy of liberation, and incorrectly identify it with Latin American philosophy in general. Nothing could be more mistaken. This kind of partial and biased understanding of the thought in the region limits people's perceptions of Latin American philosophical perspectives and contributions. Contemporary Latin American thought should not be confined within narrow categories.

The Special Series *Philosophy in Latin America* represents a deliberate attempt to introduce core content of Latin American philosophy and thought to the English-speaking reader. The Special Series has been established within the Value Inquiry Book Series (VIBS), and is co-sponsored by the Society for Iberian and Latin American Thought (SILAT). Its emphasis is on philosophical works in ethical theory, applied ethics, and social and political philosophy. The Special Series has two main objectives: first, to be a scholarly forum for Latin American views and perspectives on a wide range of issues in connection with value; second, to promote comprehension and facilitate a dialogue between Latin American and North American and European thinkers.

The present book is the first in the Special Series. The chapters in this volume are on applied ethics, specifically the bioethics that is growing into an established field of study and practice in Latin America. The volume brings under one cover the labors of Latin American scholars from diverse backgrounds. The authors explore a number of questions regarding autonomy, culture, religion, rights, and justice in the context of health care in the region, and they challenge some prevalent notions about Latin Americans and their values. By emphasizing central themes and repeated contrasts, the authors provide powerful insights on Latin American bioethics while encouraging a transcultural dialogue on biomedical issues.

Arleen L. F. Salles
Special Series Editor, Philosophy in Latin America
March 2001

ACKNOWLEDGMENTS

We would like to express our gratitude to all those who helped make this book a reality. We thank the contributors who showed their enthusiasm for this project from the beginning. Their devotion and commitment to developing bioethics in Latin America have sparked the chapters in this volume.

Throughout the process of preparing this volume we have been given valuable advice from colleagues in Argentina and in the United States. We are especially grateful to Richard T. Hull, VIBS Stylistics and Format Editor, for his consistent responsiveness to our concerns and his invaluable feedback, and to Constance Perry, of MCP Hahnemann University, for her suggestions for revisions in the English-language versions of some of the chapters. We would also like to thank Robert Ginsberg, Executive Editor of Value Inquiry Books, for his ongoing support and encouragement.

Part of this work was prepared in Centro de Investigaciones Filosóficas (C.I.F.) in Buenos Aires, and we are most grateful for the support of the institution. Participants of seminars at the Masters Program in Applied Ethics of the Universidad de Buenos Aires and C.I.F. provided important impetus.

Gus Salles provided invaluable assistance in editing the manuscript. Special thanks go to him. Finally, A. L. F. S. wishes to express personal debts of gratitude to Emma and Gus for their loyal support throughout the compilation of this volume, and M. J. B. expresses her gratitude to Manuel for his encouragement and for being there.

INTRODUCTION

1. Bioethics in Latin America

Latin America is a vast and splendid territory, spreading from Mexico to Chile and Argentina, rich in cultural traditions. These traditions often vary from one country to another. Original indigenous peoples, who survived with relative purity of race in highland Mexico, Guatemala, and the Andes, have a complex cluster of attitudes, conducts, and moral and health beliefs very different from those of Afro-Americans in the Caribbean or more cosmopolitan Latin Americans, descendants from Europeans who settled in Argentina, Brazil, Chile, and Uruguay during the nineteenth century. In fact, Latin America is made up of a variety of complex societies, each of which includes a number of subcultures.

This might raise substantial concerns regarding the possibility of finding any traits that are common to Latin Americans. Yet the nations of Latin America have a considerable unity of history that allows important commonalities to emerge. Most of them started as colonies (of Spain, and in the case of Brazil, Portugal). They fought for, and eventually achieved, independence. And in many cases their independence was followed by periods of anarchy, war, dictatorships, and more recently military rule that left their imprint. While currently almost every Latin American country can claim to possess the core institutional requirements of a political system, not many of the new democracies are consolidated. Furthermore, the distribution of wealth, income, and services in the countries of the region remains far more unequal than in most developed countries, and economic growth has not been accompanied by significant or lasting reductions in poverty and inequality. In addition, the Catholic Church has played a large (and frequently controversial) role in the development of modern Latin American countries. Finally, many countries in the region have had to confront past human rights abuses, torture, and extra-judicial political executions. Even today, the violation of basic rights and liberties is still a frequent phenomenon in some places.

However, the existence of these social attitudes and political behaviors should not be allowed to obscure most Latin Americans' concern with democracy, the rule of law, and the autonomy of citizens that requires the effective realization of the rights and liberties sanctioned by the constitutions of their own countries.

The persistence of traditional institutional and social structures combined with the recognition of the importance of democracy and autonomy contributed to a great extent to the development of bioethics in Latin America. As a discipline, it emerged fairly recently, but its impact on public discourse is undeniable. If, as it has been frequently argued, Anglo-Saxon bioethics evolved as part of a wider concern about the rights of individuals, it is not difficult to understand its influence on the countries in the region. In places devastated by dictatorship, terrorism, poverty, unsatisfied needs, and the violation of basic political liberties, a discourse that focuses on rights is bound to be persuasive. The restoration to prominence in public debate of the right to self-determination, to truthtelling, to healthcare, and to confidentiality offers new opportunities not only for careful reflection but also for influencing public policy.

The present work was conceived with two objectives in mind. The first is to provide a volume of studies accessible to the English-speaking public introducing bioethical issues discussed in Latin America. The second purpose is to start reflection on the following question: Is there a Latin American bioethics, with peculiar touches? Authors in the volume suggest an answer through their work while introducing the reader to Latin American bioethics as a complex topic worthy of study.

2. This Volume

The ten chapters in the volume are by authors in three leading Latin American countries: Argentina, Brazil, and Mexico. The studies are grouped under four main sections. Arleen L. F. Salles's chapter "Autonomy and Culture: The Case of Latin America," which opens the first section, examines the physician-patient relationship in Latin America. Salles provides an analysis of the argument that holds that the notion of autonomy is incompatible with the Latin American culture. She sketches two versions of the argument: the version from preferences and the normative version. The first states that Latin Americans do not accept autonomy and respect for autonomy as fundamental values. The second claims that personal autonomy is not a Latin American value and, therefore, it should not be accepted as a fundamental value. Salles critically examines these two arguments and points to their inadequacy. The author concludes that Latin Americans should not repudiate the notion of autonomy but they should draw on aspects of the mainstream understanding of autonomy to re-conceptualize the concept from a Latin American perspective.

Margarita M. Valdés, María Victoria Costa, and Susana E. Sommer also advance the importance of self-determination in their chapters. In "Abortion and Contraception in Mexico: The Attitudes and the Arguments of the Catholic Church," Valdés discusses the issue of abortion. The chapter opens with a brief analysis of the legal status of abortion in Latin America, especially Mexico, followed by an examination of the prevalent Catholic view that abortion is immoral. Valdés confronts two important arguments that the Catholic Church provides to justify its opposition to abortion: the religious argument and the moral argument. Valdés examines them critically and concludes that the restrictive abortion laws in Latin America are rooted on prejudice. In her chapter, Valdés worries about the negative impact that the lack of options has on women and their flourishing as human beings.

Costa and Sommer's chapter examines reproductive rights. In "Women's Reproductive Rights and Public Policy in Argentina," the authors note that in Latin America debates over reproductive rights have been influenced by the approach adopted by the United Nations that relates them to well-being and thus to the importance of securing women's access to healthcare. Costa and Sommer do not deny the connection between reproductive rights and well-being, but they argue that in societies where rights are usually disrespected, the most promising way to defend reproductive rights rests on the liberal principle of respect for individual autonomy, understood as involving more than mere non-interference. The authors focus on the case of Argentina and discuss recent legislation and public policy related to this right.

The chapter by Martín Diego Farrell, "Hastening Death," has been developed out of previous material written by the author. Farrell, an Argentine legal theorist and judge, argues for the decriminalization of euthanasia. His reflections can be seen as a reaction to the prevalent conservative view on the morality of euthanasia in many Latin American countries. The issues that he discusses remain at the forefront of public and legal discussion in Argentina. In 1997, a number of legislative proposals addressing euthanasia were advanced in that country. Under those proposals, collectively known as "Death with Dignity," euthanasia would remain illegal. The proposals made no attempt to provide a definition of the practice, and they supported the view that euthanasia should remain illegal by equating natural death with a dignified death. No explanation was given in any of these proposals as to why the natural is normatively prior to the artificial. Ultimately, the views espoused in the proposals were based on allegedly shared intuitions regarding the desirability of a natural death.

Drawing on a distinction between religious and moral reasons, Farrell attempts to show that the allegedly "shared intuitions" that support the prohibition of euthanasia are based on religious reasons, and for this they lack moral valence. He advocates a kind of moral discussion that exposes implicit assumptions about what is desirable and what is not. Farrell concludes that there are no moral reasons for prohibiting euthanasia and that there are good moral reasons for respecting the wishes of those who choose to die. Therefore, euthanasia should be decriminalized.

The second group of chapters centers on one of the most urgent bioethical problems in Latin America. In countries were a considerable portion of the population lacks adequate housing and sanitation facilities, and where many of the poor live in shantytowns, health care is stratified. A careful reflection on justice and the allocation of resources is essential. The two chapters in this part focus on this topic.

Confronting the desperate poverty of forty million Mexicans, Paulette Dieterlen engages in a philosophical debate on a governmental plan implemented in México in 1997. The aim of the program is to help populations living in extreme poverty by satisfying their basic needs, thus enabling them to exercise their preferences and autonomy. One of the most prominent characteristics of this plan is its use of targeting or focalization. In her chapter "Some Philosophical Considerations on Mexico's Education, Health, and Food Program," Dieterlen acknowledges the problems raised by focalization, and does not reject in principle the possibility of a universal right to health care and other basic services. Yet she defends targeting on the basis of the extreme poverty of many sectors of the population in Mexico. She provides an interesting critical reconstruction of the concept of "basic needs" and rejects any allocation policy based solely on preference satisfaction.

The chapter by María Julia Bertomeu and Graciela Vidiella, "Moral Person and the Right to Health Care," analyzes the right to health care understood as a capability intimately connected to the exercise of autonomy. Their defense of an equal and universal right to health care is grounded on two things: a particular conception of the moral person and the basic human capabilities, and a multicausal definition of health. The authors reject that idea that the right to health care is a special good. They link it to the recognition of social and economic rights. They argue against targeting and in favor of a universalistic approach to healthcare. Yet they accept that targeting might be necessary in extreme cases, and, in this sense, they agree in general with Dieterlen's view.

The next section in the volume focuses on human experimentation and vulnerable populations. In "Research in Developing Countries: The Ethical Issues," Florencia Luna examines the ethical problems posed by clinical research carried out in developing countries. Luna takes as a starting point the international collaborative studies carried out in Sub-Saharan Africa, the Dominican Republic, and Thailand, places that cannot afford treatments routinely used in the United States and Europe. The aim of this kind of research is to test a cheaper therapy better adapted to the resources of those countries. Luna critically examines the arguments against and in favor of the research and argues that two things should be considered when designing international multicentered trials in developing countries. First, the possibility of systemic corruption. Second, the vulnerability of the people in those countries. Luna cautions that economic reasons may underlie some of the standards currently regulating this kind of research, and she contends that researchers from developed countries should apply the same high ethical standards and norms for appropriate treatment that they observe in their own countries.

José Roberto Goldim's chapter, "Bioethics and Research in Brazil," reviews the historical evolution of human experimentation and regulative attempts in Brazil. In his chapter, Goldim reconstructs local and national regulations that have been an important step not only toward controlling research and testing on human beings but also toward the consolidation of bioethics in Brazil. Goldim is optimistic about the role that these regulations can play in the structuring and development of bioethics in his country.

The final section of the book is concerned with allocation and commercialization of organs for transplantation. In his chapter, "What Is (Exactly) Wrong with Selling Your Body Parts?", Eduardo Rivera López discusses a particularly contentious issue: the sale of human organs. Given that demand for organs currently exceeds supply, and that so many people live in conditions of extreme poverty in the world, the sale of organs could flourish in the absence of legal and ethical controls. Probably because of this, the commercialization of organs has been widely condemned. In his chapter, Rivera López is concerned with the social contexts within which organ sales might be an issue. The author acknowledges that there are no reliable reports denouncing organ sales in Latin America, yet he observes that in many Latin American countries the conditions that would favor such a market exist. Rivera López attempts to show that the mere prohibition of organ sales constitutes no significant moral improvement. Instead, he argues that governments should target the forms of exploitation and inequality that generate the practice.

The final chapter in this volume, María Graciela de Ortúzar's "Interdisciplinary Ethics Committees for Determining Criteria of Organ Distribution," discusses how kidneys for transplant should be allocated. The author provides an overview of this topic taking into account the relevant legislation in force in Argentina. She proceeds by considering international and national kidney distribution protocols and by examining the values underlying those protocols. De Ortúzar contends that social utility values underlie the medical values supposedly used to allocate organs. The author argues in favor of interdisciplinary ethics committees that will guarantee equal access to healthcare to formulate and assess protocols for organ allocation.

These ten contributions are diverse in subject matter. They have, however, one primary pattern of concern. The chapters suggest that beyond cultural differences there are universal standards that are independent of particular practices. They underscore that while there might be distinctive Latin American issues emerging from specific historical situations and different cultural traditions, we have reason to expect a shared moral ground in some bioethical issues.

One of the recurring themes is the importance of autonomy. The emphasis on autonomy makes clear that the common assumption that Latin Americans find this notion to be inhospitable is often the result of a cultural bias or a frame of reference that determines what is seen when looking at the people in the region. We also see an interest in examining the range of options that are socially and culturally available to persons to exercise their autonomy. In explaining this connection, many authors draw on a popular account in Latin America: the capabilities approach developed by Martha Nussbaum and Amartya Sen. Another theme that some of the authors develop is the importance of making a distinction between religious and moral considerations when discussing the moral status of practices.

The studies in this volume by no means attempt a comprehensive account of the topic named in its title. Instead, they take some important bioethical issues and raise questions to open rather than conclude the discussion. The intention is to stimulate readers to begin a careful examination of a discourse that is beginning to play an important role in Latin America.

The Editors

PART I

AUTONOMY AND THE RIGHT TO MAKE DECISIONS

One

AUTONOMY AND CULTURE: THE CASE OF LATIN AMERICA

Arleen L. F. Salles

1. Introduction

Respect for the autonomy of patients is a recurrent and increasingly prominent theme in American bioethics. For the past thirty years, this discipline has identified the competent patient as the decisive moral agent, the right to choose overriding the beneficence of physicians and their interests to do what is medically best for the patient. Today, few people would deny that in the United States bioethics has been and still is dominated by what is known as the "autonomy paradigm."

It has been said that the notion of autonomy and the principle it grounds is too contaminated by American or Eurocentric values; thus, the autonomy paradigm is not appropriate for the Latin American medical context. In Latin America, it is argued, citizens are neither able nor willing to exercise their autonomy, and this notion is at best just a derivative concern. In this chapter, I state and critically analyze one of the main ethical arguments typically offered by those who argue that autonomy concerns should play a secondary role in Latin American medical practice: the argument from cultural differences. I believe that this argument rests upon a faulty interpretation of the nature and role of autonomy, and on a simplistic view of Latin Americans and their values. I also believe that the argument is dangerous. When offered by Latin Americans, it fosters the idea that cultural traditions are immune to rational criticism. When stated by bioethicists and scholars from developed countries, it avoids the arrogant view that other cultures are backward, but is too condescending and fails to recognize the distinction between normatively justifiable criticism of other cultures and mere stereotyping.

I start by providing a brief characterization of autonomy and outlining some major criticisms to the traditional understanding of the notion. Then I turn to an examination of two versions of the argument from cultural differences. I end with a brief analysis of two additional considerations commonly used to reject the importance of autonomy in the Latin American medical practice.

But first a preliminary note. There is not much data on autonomy in Latin America derived from published studies of this topic. Much of what I discuss here is drawn from my experiences as a Latin American ethicist who regularly teaches bioethics in the United States and in Argentina, delivers lectures on these issues, and attends ethics committee meetings in various countries. I also draw from informal questionnaires and conversations with bioethicists, physicians, lawyers, and women's health advocates from Latin America.

2. Autonomy and Respect for Autonomy

The importance of the principle of respect for autonomy has been advanced in various ways by bioethicists. The notion of autonomy that supports this principle is arguably one of the most treasured values of Western civilization, at least since the Enlightenment.

What is autonomy? Literally it means self-determination. However, it is in the very specification of this idea that so many practical problems center. Although a few bioethicists have made a distinction between several senses of autonomy in order to clarify some of the issues raised in the medical encounter,[1] initially autonomy seemed to be solely associated with the liberal ideal of independence and individual choice. That this conception of autonomy was generally adopted is understandable, for the notion emerged out of concerns about abuses of physicians and researchers. That such abuses actually happened made it relevant and significant to understand in what sense the ideals of independence and freedom of choice and action implicit in the notion of autonomy support a set of rights that ground opposition to all kinds of authoritarianism, tyranny, and abuse of power.

However, embracing an individualistic understanding of autonomy made the notion vulnerable to criticism. And criticism came from many quarters. In political theory, communitarians complained that liberal thought assumes a metaphysically and epistemologically problematic conception of the self, whose interests are primary and independent of the construction of any social bond with others.[2] Some feminist writers have charged that the conception of autonomy implied by liberal thought has been conceptualized in terms of traits that suggest an anti-female bias, and that it bypasses concerns about the situations of people and attachments to others.[3]

In bioethics writings, critics have taken issue with the markedly legalistic tone evident in the language of rights and privacy frequently used to discuss autonomy and infringements of autonomy. They also note that the rights encompassed by the concept of autonomy are of the negative sort, focusing on the right of the individual to freedom from undue interference and the satisfaction of individual preferences rather than the positive right to health care. Other critics argue that this notion and the model it shapes is too abstract, theory driven, and at odds with the everyday experience of both doctors and patients.[4] According to them, the dominant North American bioethics identifies the notion of autonomy mostly with detachment. The autonomous self is defined against others and lacks essential connections to them. It thus promotes an atomistic approach to morality, an approach that does not recognize the historical and social nature of human beings. Traditional bioethics, it is argued, has buried historical human beings under abstractions, losing track of the flesh and blood individuals actually involved in the medical encounter.

Yet, while the lack of justification for accepting overly simplistic or stereotypical understandings of autonomy provides good reason for criticism of those conceptions, it does not provide reasons for thinking that the notion itself is irremediably contaminated by those understandings. The notion of autonomy is vital. This is why the predominant tendency for philosophers writing about autonomy in the late 1980s and 1990s has been to reexamine and reconstruct the notion, avoiding stereotypical traits and validating aspects of it that are particularly helpful and should be retained. Champions of autonomy have tried to show that the right to autonomy allows people to make their own choices and does not deny them the choice to share with others or to acknowledge their dependency to others.

Mainstream conceptions of autonomy are procedural: they take autonomy to be the capacity that enables people to critically reflect on their motivational structure. In his classical theory, Gerald Dworkin characterizes autonomy as a "second order capacity of persons to reflect critically upon their first order preferences, desires, wishes, and so forth and the capacity to accept or attempt to change these in light of higher order preferences and values."[5] Yet Dworkin places no constraints on the content of people's choices. He states, "in my conception, the autonomous person can be a tyrant or a slave, a saint or sinner, a rugged individualist or champion of fraternity, a leader or follower."[6] In his view, shared values and beliefs may still be fully chosen as one's own.[7] Insofar as people subject their motivations to the appropriate kind of critical reflection, autonomy and social relations can be reconciled.[8]

Some feminist thinkers have drawn on aspects of the feminist critique of autonomy to propose a relational conception. While sharing the idea that autonomy as self-determination is crucial, they argue that autonomy is essentially social; social ties are not just contingently tied to a person's self understanding. For example, according to Diana T. Meyers's procedural account, autonomy is a competency that allows people to critically reflect on their conduct and to live in harmony with their authentic selves. However, the self is dynamic. Who one is, is an open question. The values and commitments that people have and with which they identify when exercising their autonomy are the result of socialization.[9] In Meyers's account, people's social relations make autonomy possible, and autonomy does not entail a necessary isolation from the influence of others. Instead, only in the context of social relationships and practices can autonomy competency be developed.

Criticisms to the notion of autonomy notwithstanding, autonomy has hardly lost its importance in bioethics. Appeals to patient autonomy figure prominently in debates about the moral permissibility of the new reproductive technologies, euthanasia, and the analysis of the patient-physician relationship. And so they should, for the notion of autonomy provides the basis from which pressures and oppression can be resisted. What recent work on autonomy shows is that we can break away from a narrow understanding of autonomy closely associated with the achievement of separateness, and include an understanding of the development of the ability to be autonomous, which can be defined in terms of relationships and values that people engage in when making choices. Autonomy does not have to be about believing in individualism rather than the community. People do not have to evade their own social history of personal development. But people need the ability to reflect on their values, norms, and relationships, and to consider which should be reshaped, changed, and promoted. Becoming autonomous in the procedural sense involves this ability. In turn, respecting it expresses something deeply important about human beings that we should be reluctant to give up.

3. Autonomy and the Physician-Patient Relationship

In the United States, the vindication of autonomy against traditional physician paternalism provided a strong foundation for an alternative view of the patient-physician relationship: one based on a contract. The contractual relationship aims at conceiving both the physician and the patient as responsible moral agents capable of making major decisions. Autonomy provides a natural conceptual justification for the informed consent requirement and for the moral obligation of physicians and all health care professionals to respect the values of patients and not to let their own values unduly influence decisions about treatment.

In Latin America, the Hippocratic tradition prevails. The patient-physician relationship is premised mainly on a paternalistic model and reinforced through a system of medical education that emphasizes beneficence-based obligations and suppresses the obligations that flow from respecting the wishes and goals of patients.[10] Nonetheless, it is true that discussions concerning the significance of respecting a patient's autonomy have increased in the last few years.[11] Recent codes of ethics of professional medical organizations in several Latin American countries, including Brazil, Argentina, Chile, and Perú, generally state that the consent of the patient is of consequence and even necessary in some cases.[12] However, in practice, respect for the patient's autonomy is not standard in Latin America. In Argentina, law 17.132 establishes that health care professionals must "respect the will of patients on refusal of treatment or institutionalization, except in cases of mental incompetence and alienation."[13] This suggests some kind of legal recognition of the value of consent as an expression of the will of the patient. Yet informed consent in the country is still either mostly discussed in the context of malpractice lawsuits or considered no more than a formality. All too often physicians tend to rely on implicit consent, except in critical care. This is partly due to the fact that many well-intentioned health care practitioners still believe that respect for patients' autonomy is not a goal to be sought. And many times they support this view by claiming that "Latin patients do not want to make decisions" or that "autonomy is a North American value."

This raises a host of issues, but mainly the following: could it be that autonomy and respect for the autonomy of persons is no more than a social construct? Is it the case that the emphasis on autonomy reflects just the North American or Western European way to do bioethics? The argument from cultural differences offers a positive answer to these questions.

4. The Argument from Cultural Differences

This argument begins with observations about differing worldviews, values, and beliefs. The right to individual liberty, it is argued, is a long-standing American and Western European value that cannot be separated from sociopolitical systems that take as a starting point the belief in the worth, uniqueness, and sovereignty of the person. The notion that the individual person comes first results in the fact that the principle of beneficence is constrained by the obligation to respect individual rights, interests, and autonomy.

Taking this as a starting point, two variations of the argument from cultural differences can be distinguished. The first, which I call the argument from preferences, is an empirical argument that could in principle be settled in terms of the empirical evidence available. It invites us to accept the following claims: In countries such as the United States, the concept of autonomy is central to the understanding of ethical health care. In contrast, in Latin America, people are generally more attentive to the quality of their relationships with their physicians than to their rights to be informed and make autonomous decisions, less concerned with having their autonomy respected than with finding a doctor they can trust.[14] Diego Gracia, a leading Spanish bioethicist, states,

> Latin people are profoundly uncomfortable with rights and principles. They are used to judging things and acts as good or bad, instead of right or wrong. They prefer benevolence to justice, friendship to mutual respect, excellence to rights.[15]

Taking this as a starting point, some people argue that Latin Americans do not, as a matter of empirical fact, accept or even understand autonomy and respect for autonomy as a fundamental value. Thus, those principles are not morally binding for those acting in the Latin American context.[16]

The second variation of the argument from cultural differences is concerned with more than preferences, it goes beyond the empirical claim to hold a more normative one: Latin Americans should renounce commitment to norms and standards that may be radically at odds with cultural conventions and customary practices. Alien values should not be accepted. They are considered to be unwelcome incursions upon a society's way of life. The acceptance of those values is seen as the result of an imposition and a form of cultural subordination to other societies.

In what follows, I examine the argument and its variations in more detail.

5. The Version from Preferences

Is the version from preferences persuasive enough? I believe that it has three apparent weaknesses.

First, it justifies the prevailing lack of respect for patients' autonomy by attributing concrete preferences to Latin Americans. But if we assume that Latin Americans in fact have those preferences, and we make the concepts of negative liberty and autonomy co-extensive, it is not clear to what extent this is an argument against the importance of respecting the autonomy of patients. That is, if physician paternalism were the result of the recognition that patients do not want to be autonomous, then this would not be at odds with the recognition of the value of respecting their autonomy (at least at the basic level of liberty of action). Making decisions on behalf of patients because they prefer not to make those decisions does show respect for their autonomy. So those who argue along this line are really in favor of respecting the preference autonomy of patients.

The second weakness of the argument is that the notion of autonomy that supports it is not one that has a claim to our respect as an ideal, for on this conception there are no substantive requirements about the way preferences develop over time. Minimally, autonomy requires that people's preferences and choices be arrived at in a way that is free of coercion and manipulation. This means that not all preferences should be accorded equal credence. Jon Elster, among others, argues that people's preferences can be manipulated and that respectable preferences must have been formed through a process over which the agent has sufficient control.[17] A person or a group's preferences are not quite the basic data that the argument from preferences assumes if they are not subjected to the appropriate kind of reflection. Preferences may be distorted by mistaken expectations—as to what the role of the physician is— by lack of education, by the absence of accurate information, by pervasive social teaching—for example, instilling the belief that people cannot decide for themselves or that autonomy has to be mediated by the teachings of a particular religion—or by Latin Americans' own (sometimes justified) fear of questioning authority. This possibility has to be seriously examined, considering that typically the principle of respect for autonomy has not been weighty in social and individual behavior in Latin America. Societies could have preferences deformed by a number of factors, including a history of intolerance and authoritarianism. This is not to say that the desires of people who prefer not to be autonomous should be necessarily dismissed or are necessarily irrational. However, the possibility of preference deformation should be seen as a strong reason for skepticism about the merits of the view that in Latin America people prefer not to exercise their autonomy in the medical context.

But so far, we have been assuming that Latin Americans prefer not to make those decisions. A third weakness of the argument from preferences is that it takes as a starting point a surprisingly idealized model of Latin American culture that oversimplifies its complexity. Latin American culture is not monolithic or static. It is diverse and characterized by plurality, and it has evolved over time. Furthermore, even people within a particular cultural context do not necessarily agree on the status of particular practices. Just as North Americans have had substantial disagreement about how to understand autonomy in the medical context and how to respect it, Latin Americans have their disagreements as well.

In fact, the degree to which standards of behavior are shared within the group varies with socioeconomic status, region, and generation. There are considerable differences in the living conditions of Latin Americans in different classes, and this often leads to differences in values relevant to medical decision-making, and how they are applied. For example, affluent Latin Americans tend to be more concerned with autonomy than those who are poor. Yet not all those who belong to a same class can be regarded as similar in lifestyle and values, because a person's values are also a reflection of the person's particular background, ethnicity, place of birth, and residence. The ethics of autonomy plays a more significant role in places such as Buenos Aires and Porto Alegre, cities where the people are almost exclusively of European descent, than in poorer and underdeveloped cities. Thus, if we are going to focus on preferences, we must first define which particular group of people we are talking about.[18] This is partly the reason why it is almost impossible to talk about what Latin Americans prefer, for even if most of them do not want to be autonomous it is a fact that some do.[19] Those who value autonomy argue that they prefer to make decisions consistent with their beliefs and principles, and want explanations that they can understand so that they can make those decisions. They systematically note the difficulties that they have when communicating with their physicians, and complain about the failure to receive adequate explanations of their condition. The resounding message is that they want their autonomy respected. The views of these people, even if they are a minority, must be taken into account.

A common assumption is that we are all to some extent influenced by the cultural context in which we live, that it determines in large part the values and attitudes that we embrace, and that each of us represent and express cultural attitudes and values in different forms of conduct. However, in virtue of the difficulty of making generalizations about people and the serious and delicate nature of the issues involved, health care practitioners should be sensitive to diversity and allocate decisional authority on a case by case basis. Without denying the importance of culture, it is necessary to individualize its meaning for "culture is only meaningful when interpreted in the context of the patient's unique history, family constellation, and socioeconomic status."[20] An approach that uses ethnic background or culture as a predictor of beliefs may lead to harmful stereotyping of patients.[21] But an approach that is grounded in the idea of respecting the autonomy of people will support individuals who want to make decisions as much as those who do not.

6. The Normative Version

This variation of the argument from cultural differences addresses the transcultural applicability of the notion of autonomy. It takes the position that the claim that autonomy ought to be respected in non mainstream Western medical practice amounts to an oppressive moral and cultural imperialism that undermines the legitimacy of other ways of life. Those who hold this view are not overly concerned with whether Latin American people would accept the validity of the principle of respect for autonomy. Instead, they argue that Latin Americans should not accept such a principle for it reflects an alien value superimposed on the cultures of the region. As far as I am aware, there is no detailed articulation of this view within the field of bioethics. However, it underlies many of the criticisms to autonomy in the Latin American medical context.

To do justice to the view, three aspects need to be considered. First, the reasons for holding this view should be addressed. Second, the underlying assumptions of this view should be uncovered. Finally, an internal critique should be conducted to look for the shortcomings internal to the argument. I will take up each of these points in turn.

Reasons: Two groups of people suggest this view, and for different reasons. In the first group, we find a few well-intentioned bioethicists from developed countries who have expressed interest in bioethical practices in other cultures. Often they try to avoid moral criticisms of foreign practices.[22] Now, the eagerness to validate other cultures' moral practices is not necessarily misguided. Mainstream Western culture's attitude to others has been problematic, often justifying economic and political intervention by attributing uncivilized behaviors to others. Many Latin Americans consider their own developing nations to be too dependent on developed nations and as economically, politically, and culturally subordinate to them. When bioethicists from developed countries assume a respectful but uncritical attitude toward designated practices in other cultures, they may be trying to avoid contributing to this view and to negative stereotyping. In practice, this often leads to avoiding subjecting Latin American medical practices to the kind of analysis to which Anglo-Saxon medical practice is subjected.

Still, this is problematic for precisely the same reason that an idealized understanding of Anglo-Saxon bioethics is problematic. Lack of criticism cannot and should not be identified with respecting a culture and its traditions, for respect requires a critical and discriminative attitude. It is well known that many Latin American societies have not been committed to treating their members fairly and respectfully. The strong penchant for centralist authority embedded in the Spanish political tradition during the centuries of rule over Latin America was transmitted to the colonies and later to independent Latin American nations, and it has militated against personal freedom. Ultimately, it has resulted in a tendency towards authoritarianism in medical and non-medical contexts. Yet authoritarianism should be morally criticized rather than excused. Regarding authoritarian practices as traditional and deserving of respect is no more than a poor substitute for any thought about their validity. Thus, even though the lack of criticism is aimed at enhancing the dignity and rights of historically marginalized societies, it ends up doing the opposite, for dignity and rights are not enhanced when one declines to engage in the kind of moral dialogue necessary for discussing crucial issues.

The second group of people who hold this view is formed by some Latin Americans who suggest that values like autonomy are not typically Latin-American and that their acceptance leads to betraying, and possibly losing, one's cultural identity.

This position stems from a poor understanding of the value system in Latin America, and from a confusing notion of cultural identity and the possibility of preserving it. Contrary to what many people think, the value system of many Latin Americans is not much different from the value system of many Western Europeans and North Americans. This has a lot to do with the fact that the roots and values of modern Latin Americans lie not only in indigenous thought and in the region's Iberian Catholic heritage, but also to a great extent in the French, German, and British Enlightenment. Ideas spread in Europe during that time reached different Latin American countries by many channels, and were discussed by *criollos* in Mexico City, Buenos Aires, Bogota, and Lima. The international exchange of ideas during colonial times was particularly significant for the independence movements in the region. In Latin America, country after country based its declaration of independence on claims to natural rights of which each complained it had been unjustly deprived by the mother country. Yet the acknowledgment of the influence of international intellectual currents should not be allowed to obscure the fact that the longing for autonomy arose out of the distinctive experience of Latin Americans themselves, and it was the result of concrete social struggles.

The normative version of the argument from cultural differences, which concludes that autonomy concerns should not be important in the Latin American medical practice, depends on the assertion that autonomy is a foreign value and oppressive in this context. But if it is true that the notion of autonomy is not alien, its acceptance is not incompatible with preserving the Latin American identity.

However, for the sake of argument let us assume that autonomy is not a Latin American value. Does it follow then that it should not be weighty in Latin American medical practice? The issue here is, what consideration should be given to the notion of cultural identity in the construction of a normative moral order, and to what degree does preserving one's cultural identity undermine any basis for the cross-cultural importance of values like autonomy?

Let us start with the issue of cultural identity, for the preoccupation with the search for a Latin American identity and its preservation is one of the most pervasive characteristics of Latin America social thought in the nineteenth and the twentieth centuries.[23] The Mexican thinker Octavio Paz asked: "What are we, and how can we fulfill our obligations to ourselves?"[24] This question is in the mind of many who look for that something essentially Latin American that can give a meaning and unity to the Latin American people. Can the elusive Latin American identity be preserved if supposedly alien values are accepted? If we consider that cultural identity in Latin America has been conceptualized as a problem that arises out of the condition of marginalization and dependency, it might very well be that rejecting alien values is essential for preserving the Latin American cultural identity.

The notion of cultural identity has undergone a great deal of rethinking among Latin American philosophers in recent years.[25] Mexican philosopher Luis Villoro, for example, warns against the view that a group's cultural identity and corresponding values can be easily discovered by stripping back layers of allegedly alien influences. Villoro rejects an essentialist view of identity and claims that "there is no essence to be discovered," no primordial foundation.[26] For Villoro, cultural identity is not to be identified with singularity but with authenticity. And cultural authenticity can only come about through a process of addressing collective needs and desires and articulating the beliefs and values of people.[27] Thus, cultural identities are projects and, as such, fluid, dynamic, historical, and the result of a plurality of influences. The cultural identity of a community is always in a state of evolution or transformation.

Instead of defining cultural identity in opposition to external influences, in Villoro's account cultural identity is to a great extent made possible by those influences. The meaning of cultural identity does not emerge from culturally bounded values but flows through global interconnections. So Villoro suggests that we have two options. The first is to accept the elasticity of the notion of cultural identity, which should lead us to skepticism about the possibility of preserving intact one's cultural identity. The second is to resort to the view that one's cultural identity is to be found in inherited traditions.

But this seems to imply that tradition has some kind of collected moral wisdom in it and ought to be uncritically accepted. Yet to defend something just because it happened in one's culture is no moral achievement.[28] If one has to accept one's traditions because they are one's traditions, one has to give up any attempt to rationally defend and justify them. This is problematic for two reasons. The first is that it makes it impossible for anybody to try to change or reform those traditions. The second is that it makes it possible for those unquestioned traditions to be used as tools to vindicate a particular political morality. As Villoro argues "the unreflective repetition of inherited conventions is as strong an alienating factor as is blind imitation of [foreign] ways of life."[29] Cultural alienation does not result from being receptive to the ideas of others but rather from uncritically accepting them, without debating their merits. Thus, cultural autonomy is not incompatible with the acceptance of foreign values. But it is incompatible with blind imitation, for this requires subordination.

It is true that the preservation of the culture is a necessary condition for the exercise of the autonomy of the individual, for it is within a culture that the individual makes choices. However, too strict a paradigm of cultural identity may exert a stifling effect on positive change and development in a given region.

Assumptions: An assumption apparently shared by the two groups of people who hold the normative version of the argument from cultural differences is that all values have equal weight. There is no rational basis for establishing across cultures that one set of culturally accepted values is right and the other is wrong.

Yet this relativistic position is not beyond criticism. Martha Nussbaum, for example, has recently argued that it is not the case that all values are culture specific. She proposes an approach according to which we can assess the moral status of a particular value by assessing the degree to which it promotes or obtrudes functioning capabilities that are essential to a flourishing life.[30] Her list of capabilities includes, among others, bodily health, living out a normal lifespan, and the ability to "form a conception of the good and to engage in critical reflection about the planning of one's life."[31] Thus, Nussbaum concentrates on the functioning of individuals in areas regarded central to their quality of life, and argues that on the basis of these functionings we can examine and criticize local and traditional practices.[32]

Mainstream philosophical work on this topic by leading Latin American thinkers tends to agree that even if some values are internal to some traditions, it can be shown that some of them are still necessary for any society or culture to exist.[33] Human beings have universal basic physiological and psychological needs, confront a common fate, and suffer the same daily limitations regardless of race, religion, and ethnicity. If this is true, and I believe it is, not all values have equal weight. Some values, for example those that do not protect human beings' central capabilities or that harm others, are not worth preserving. Similarly, values that have to do with a full development of a moral personality must be honored universally.[34]

The argument when applied to autonomy: The normative version of the argument from cultural differences is untenable for one main reason: it rejects the notion of individual autonomy as supposedly too Eurocentric by endorsing the notion of cultural autonomy which supposedly is not. However, while it is true that cultural and personal autonomy are not the same, it is impossible to make sharp distinctions between them. The values underlying the right to cultural autonomy—the values of equality, authenticity, and tolerance—are the same values that underlie personal autonomy. The notions of cultural autonomy and respect for autonomy do justice to the uniqueness and diversity of cultures and their right to express that uniqueness in the desired way. Similarly, the notion of personal autonomy does justice to the diversity and uniqueness of individuals and their right to express it as they wish. But, why accept the significance of self-development and self-determination as the ultimate touchstone for justifying the right to expression of cultural heritage and not for justifying the right to have one's own opinions and to act upon them? Why affirm the notion that cultures should be free from controlling interference by others and not accept that individuals should remain free to determine their destiny? Should we reject autonomy for individuals and see it as an ideal for groups only? What is the argument for this? Ultimately, the problem of this view is that it is not aware that in order to defend the notion of cultural autonomy it has to resort to the values that it finds objectionable when it comes to individual autonomy.

It is misguided to think that practices that broaden the rights and liberties of members of a community are intrusions of foreign cultures on one's own. Cultures ask and answer questions about real needs, wants, and concerns of people. They should respond to those needs and concerns, and they should not be used to block the expressions of their members. Thus, cultures cannot ignore the context in which persons themselves and their capabilities are formed, nor can they dismiss as unimportant the individual values of their members.

None of the versions of the argument from cultural differences justifies repudiating or being skeptical about the value of autonomy in Latin America. Moreover, the argument preserves a view that in practice has not been beneficial to Latin Americans: that there is a distinctive "Latin American way," one that is more communitarian, family-oriented, and virtue-oriented, and at odds with the "imposed" value of autonomy with its focus on the individual. This view has led people to overlook some of the most profound practical problems that Latin Americans have: the lack of respect of basic freedoms and rights. This becomes particularly problematic in the medical context where starting with the presumption that autonomy is a foreign notion limited to a particular nation or cultural group entails separating a group of people, patients, from what many times is their ultimate source of comfort and protection. If their dignity is to be respected, their perspectives on the meaning of life and desirability of treatment, whether based on religion, personal philosophies, or notions of dignity, must be recognized and honored regardless of their cultural background.

7. Two Additional Concerns with Autonomy in Latin America

To conclude, I will comment briefly upon two other objections to autonomy in Latin America with which I disagree.

The first I call the argument from justice. It suggests that Latin Americans should not be overly concerned with respect for autonomy because other more serious bioethical problems exist. These concern the issue of macro-allocation of health care resources. As is the case in many Western countries, in Latin America some sectors of the population enjoy the best kind of health care, while many others receive only basic health care and services. Thus, it has been argued that a focus on the autonomy and interests of the person means concentrating on only a sector of the population—those people who actually receive good health care—and leads people to ignore the problems of the needy, most of whom have no access to adequate health care and for whom "autonomy concerns are without meaning."[35]

That concerns about social justice are essential is not under discussion. It is true that the persistence of mass poverty is a problem in Latin America. Economic growth in the region has raised the standards of living, but gains usually go to upper income groups. Thus, a focus on justice and an appreciation of the unequal social conditions that leave many people more vulnerable is a priority in Latin America, and a concern about rectifying increasingly divisive inequalities at the social level is essential. However, the question is: is it true that in countries where social and cultural inequalities are common autonomy concerns are less consequential?

I think that, on the contrary, a focus on autonomy reveals a myriad of ways in which the rights of some sectors of the population are just not taken into account precisely because they are poor, vulnerable, and "illiterate."[36] What generally may be no more (and no less) than medical paternalism for the patient who can pay and has access to the best kind of treatment, becomes medical authoritarianism for the patient who lives in extreme poverty. A focus on autonomy may be used as an antidote to this kind of paternalism and authoritarianism. Thus, I believe that we have to be careful not to overstate possible tensions between respect for autonomy and justice. Rather than saying that respect for autonomy should not be a main concern in Latin America, it is better to say that justice and autonomy must be considered as inextricably linked.

Finally, I turn to an additional consideration being offered to support the view that Latin Americans are better off without worrying about autonomy: the argument from authority. People familiar with Anglo-Saxon bioethical theory usually advance this argument. They oppose an emphasis on autonomy in Latin America on the grounds that the notion of autonomy is being challenged and criticized by those who have historically been its main defenders: North American bioethicists. This perspective is illustrated by a comment made by a physician in a bioethics class in Buenos Aires. Following an examination of the nature and justification of autonomy in the context of home health care, he stated, "Americans have created a monster, and now they do not know what to do with it." Part of my aim in this chapter is to prove this statement wrong.

First, if a monster exists, Americans did not create it. Two key sources concerning the importance of autonomy come from Germany and England. Arguably, Immanuel Kant's most significant contribution to ethics is his claim that autonomy is the foundation of human dignity and the source of all morality; John S. Mill defended the ability to make free choices on consequentialist grounds. The notion that persons have worth and that their decisions ought to be respected is not originally American.

Yet what is crucial is not the origin of the notion of autonomy but its transcultural value.[37] Ultimately, the Latin American, like the North American and the European, needs to solve practical problems that arise in the medical setting. Some disputes between doctors, patients, and family members do not have many precedents in terms of traditions and shared experiences that can be used to ground ethical decision-making. Accordingly, what is essential to our theorizing on these issues is the existence of these problems, not the origin of the principles that can be used to solve them.

Second, it is apparent that Americans know what to do with the monster: they do not want to kill it, just tame it. However, we should not forget that, contrary to what many people think, the triumph of autonomy in countries such as the United States is still extremely precarious. Despite all the attention paid to autonomy in bioethics, evidence exists that even in the United States the existing health care system does not afford adequate protection to those who wish to act autonomously respecting their health.[38]

However, all of this holds only if autonomy is the monster. And even if some American bioethicists occasionally depict the notion as such, most would agree that the notion of autonomy is defensible and needs to be preserved. The notion of autonomy and the principle of respect for autonomy have been so widely accepted in Anglo-Saxon bioethical theory for a good reason. Since no broad societal consensus exists about the aims and goods toward which health care ought to strive, respecting autonomy and people's conception of the good is the only plausible response. But even if such consensus existed, it would be possible to argue that respect for individual autonomy is necessary insofar as it is grounded in human and moral rights that all human beings have.

This leads to one considerable difference between North American and Latin American criticisms to the autonomy model. Most bioethicists who argue against the primacy of autonomy in the United States still recognize that it is a value not to be overlooked. Yet this is not the case for many who oppose it in Latin America and criticize it *a priori*. In Latin American countries, with a long history of authoritarian governments, terrorism, and widespread intolerance, many people still need to understand that autonomy is not an American monster but a notion that supports a set of rights that provide the basis to oppose unwanted interference from others and has the potential to enhance the patient-physician relationship

No one among Latin Americans should be prepared to abandon freedom nor give up on the capacity for making decisions and choosing life plans. But as mentioned before, this does not mean ignoring the social nature of the self and the importance of social relationships to people's projects. Thus, continuing to invoke ostensibly discredited values like autonomy and respect for autonomy is vital in Latin America. This is not a call for exporting North American or European standards without thinking them within the configuration of the specific communities where they will be used. But it is a call for recognizing that autonomy is a special tool to be applied in many of the moral problems Latin Americans face, and for laying the groundwork for an understanding of autonomy that is compatible with the specific reality of Latin America.[39]

NOTES

1. See Bruce Miller, "Autonomy and the Refusal of Lifesaving Treatment," *Hastings Center Report*, 11:4 (1981); David Thomasma, "Freedom, Dependency, and the Care of the Very Old," *Journal of the American Geriatrics Society*, 32:12 (1984).

2. See, *e.g.*, Alasdair MacIntyre, *After Virtue: A Study in Moral Theory* (Notre Dame, Ind.: University of Notre Dame Press, 1981), pp. 232-233.

3. See Lorraine Code, "Second Persons," *What Can She Know? Feminist Theory and the Construction of Knowledge* (Ithaca, N.Y.: Cornell University Press, 1991).

4. See, *e.g.*, Carl Schneider, *The Practice of Autonomy* (New York: Oxford University Press, 1998); Daniel Callahan, "Autonomy: A Moral Good, Not a Moral Obsession," *Hastings Center Report*, 14:5 (1984), pp. 40-42; Daniel Callahan, *Setting Limits* (Washington: Georgetown University Press, 1995); Bruce Jennings, "Last Rights: Dying and the Limits of Self-Sovereignty," *Depth: A Journal for Values and Public Policy*, 2:3 (1992); Hilde Lindemann Nelson and James Lindemann Nelson, *The Patient in the Family* (New York: Routledge, 1995); James Lindemann Nelson, "Taking Families Seriously," *Hastings Center Report*, 22:4 (1992).

5. Gerald Dworkin, *The Theory and Practice of Autonomy* (Cambridge, England: Cambridge University Press, 1988), p. 20.

6. *Ibid.*, p. 29.

7. Marilyn Friedman, "Autonomy and Social Relationships," *Feminists Rethink the Self*, ed. Diana T. Meyers (Boulder, Col.: Westview Press, 1997).

8. See Thomas Hill, "The Importance of Autonomy," *Women and Moral Theory*, eds. Eva Kittay and Diana T. Meyers (Totowa, N.J.: Rowman and Littlefield, 1987); Osvaldo Guariglia, "Identidad, autonomía y concepciones de la buena vida," *Isegoría*, 20 (1999); Tom Beauchamp and James Childress, *Principles of Biomedical Ethics* (New York: Oxford University Press, 1994); Dan Brock, *Life and Death: Philosophical Essays in Biomedical Ethics* (New York: Cambridge University Press, 1993), esp. p. 29.

9. See Diana T. Meyers, "The Socialized Individual and Individual Autonomy: An Intersection Between Philosophy and Psychology," *Women and Moral Theory*; Anne Donchin, "Understanding Autonomy Relationally: Toward a Reconfiguration of Bioethical Principles," *Journal of Medicine and Philosophy*, 23 (1998); Anne Donchin, "Autonomy, Interdependence and Assisted Suicide: Respecting Boundaries/Crossing Lines," *Bioethics*, 14:3 (2000); Susan Sherwin, "A Relational Approach to Autonomy in Health Care," *The Politics of Women's Health*, eds. Susan Sherwin, *et al.* (Philadelphia: Temple University Press, 1998).

10. See, *e.g.*, José Alberto Mainetti, "Bioethical Problems in the Developing World: A View from Latin America," *Unitas*, 60 (1988); José Alberto Mainetti, "History of Medical Ethics: Latin America," *Encyclopedia of Bioethics*, ed. Warren Reich (New York: Simon and Schuster, Macmillan, 1995); Miguel Kottow, "Esbozo multicultural del principalismo bioético," *Cuadernos del Programa Regional de Bioética*, 2 (1996). See also the chapters by María Victoria Costa and Susana E. Sommer, Florencia Luna, and María Graciela de Ortúzar in this volume.

11. See recent articles in the following Latin American bioethics journals: *Cuadernos de Bioética* (Chile), *Bioética* (Brazil), and *Perspectivas bioéticas de las américas* (Argentina).

12. In Brazil, see articles 46 and 56 of the *Ethics Code of Conselho Federal de Medicina*. In Argentina, see *Código de Etica Médica de la Confederación Médica de la República Argentina*, art. 15. In Chile, see *Normas y documentos del Colegio Médico*

de Chile II, article 15. In Perú, see *Código de Etica Profesional del Colegio Médico de Perú*, art. 49.

13. Elena Highton and Sandra Wierza, *La relación médico-paciente: el consentimiento informado* (Buenos Aires: Ad-Hoc, 1992), p. 72.

14. Diego Gracia, "The Intellectual Basis of Bioethics in Southern European Countries," *Bioethics*, 7:2-3 (1993).

15. See Diego Gracia, "Hard Times, Hard Choices: Founding Bioethics Today," *Bioethics*, 9:3-4 (1995).

16. See, *e.g.*, Dorothy C. Wertz, "International Research in Bioethics: The Challenges of Cross-Cultural Interpretation," *Bioethics and Society*, eds. Raymond Devries and Janardan Subedi (Upper Saddle River, N. J.: Prentice Hall, 1998), p. 154.

17. Jon Elster, *Sour Grapes: Studies in the Subversion of Rationality* (New York: Cambridge University Press, 1996); Martha Nussbaum, *Women and Human Development* (New York: Cambridge University Press, 2000).

18. See Diego Gracia, "The Historical Setting of Latin American Bioethics," *The Journal of Medicine and Philosophy*, 21 (1996).

19. See, *e.g.*, Charles M. Culver and María Julia Bertomeu, "Results of a Survey on Informed Consent in La Plata, Argentina," *Clinical Ethics: Practice and Theory* (18-19 March 1994).

20. Barbara A. Koenig and Jan Gates-Williams, "Understanding Cultural Difference in Caring for Dying Patients," *Western Journal of Medicine*, 163 (1995), p. 244.

21. *Ibid.*

22. See, however, Ruth Macklin, "Ethical Relativism in a Multicultural Society," *Kennedy Institute of Ethics Journal*, 8:1 (1998) and Ruth Macklin, *Against Relativism* (New York: Oxford University Press, 1999).

23. See Jorge J. E. Gracia and Iván Jaksic, *Filosofía e Identidad Cultural en América Latina* (Caracas: Monte Avila Editores, 1988).

24. Octavio Paz, *The Labyrinth of Solitude* (New York: Grove Press, 1961).

25. Fernando Salmerón, "Etica y diversidad cultural," *Cuestiones Morales*, ed. Osvaldo Guariglia (Madrid: Editorial Trotta, 1996); Leon Olivé, *Multiculturalismo y Pluralismo* (México: Paidós, 1999); Leon Olivé, ed., *Etica y diversidad cultural* (México: Fondo de Cultura Económica, 1993).

26. Luis Villoro, "Aproximaciones a una ética de la cultura," *Etica y diversidad cultural*, ed. Leon Olivé, p. 133.

27. Luis Villoro, *Estado Plural, Pluralidad de Culturas* (México: Paidós, 1998).

28. Carlos Pereda, *Crítica de la Razón Arrogante* (México: Taurus, 1999).

29. Luis Villoro, "Aproximaciones a una ética de la cultura."

30. Martha Nussbaum, "Non-Relative Virtues: An Aristotelian Approach," *The Quality of Life*, eds. Martha Nussbaum and Amartya Sen (New York: Oxford University Press, 1993); Martha Nussbaum, "Human Functioning and Social Justice: In Defense of Aristotelian Essentialism," *Political Theory*, 20 (1992), pp. 202-246; Martha Nussbaum, "In Defense of Universal Values," *Women and Human Development*.

31. Nussbaum, "In Defense of Universal Values," p. 79.

32. In this volume, see the chapters by Margarita M. Valdés, Paulette Dieterlen, and María Julia Bertomeu and Graciela Vidiella.

33. See Ernesto Garzón Valdés, "El problema ético de las minorías étnicas," *Etica y diversidad cultural*, ed. Leon Olivé; Eduardo Farrell, "El alcance (limitado) del multiculturalismo," *Universalismo y Multiculturalismo*, eds. María Julia Bertomeu, Rodolfo Gaeta, and Graciela Vidiella (Buenos Aires: Eudeba, 2000).

34. See Larry Gostin, "Informed Consent, Cultural Sensitivity, and Respect for Persons," *Journal of the American Medical Association*, 274:10 (September 1995); Edmund Pellegrino, "Is Truth Telling to the Patient a Cultural Artifact?", *JAMA*, 268:13 (October 1992).

35. Diego Gracia, "The Historical Setting of Latin American Bioethics," *The Journal of Medicine and Philosophy*, 21 (1996).

36. See Florencia Luna, "Paternalism and the Argument from Illiteracy," *Bioethics*, 9:3-4 (1995), p. 607.

37. Edmund Pellegrino, "Prologue: Intersections of Western Biomedical Ethics and World Culture," *Transcultural Dimensions in Medical Ethics*, eds. Edmund Pellegrino, Patricia Mazarella, Pietro Corsi (Frederick, Md.: University Publishing Group, 1992).

38. See "Study Shows Doctors Are Lax in Giving Information to Patients," *New York Times*, (22 December 1999). Also Clarence Braddock III, *et al.*, "Informed Decision-Making in Outpatient Practice: Time to Get Back to Basics," *Journal of the American Medical Association*, 282:24 (1999), pp. 2313-2320.

39. For helpful and detailed comments on earlier versions of this chapter I am very grateful to María Victoria Costa, Constance Perry, Elizabeth Millán-Zeibert, Christopher Herrera, and María Julia Bertomeu.

Two

ABORTION AND CONTRACEPTION IN MEXICO: THE ATTITUDES AND THE ARGUMENTS OF THE CATHOLIC CHURCH

Margarita M. Valdés

1. Introduction

Human capabilities and functionings, in the sense introduced by Amartya Sen and Martha Nussbaum to discuss what is relevant for assessing the quality of a human life, are a good starting point for an argument in favor of the importance of women's access to contraception and abortion.[1] This is the case especially when the concern is women's well-being and the quality of their lives. If we believe that what makes a human life good is its functioning and its having distinctive human capabilities to function in different areas of human experience, it is possible to see how women's access to contraception and abortion enhances their capabilities and improves their lives.[2]

While it has frequently been noted that unwanted maternity can be an obstacle to the flourishing of a woman and to her fulfillment as a human being, as a person, the reasons why this is so are usually left implicit. Maternity can seriously interfere with the plans that a woman may reflectively have chosen for her own life. Moreover, and especially for poor women with many children, maternity can become such a heavy burden that it precludes any possibility of doing anything other than taking care of their progeny and of heavy household work. This can enormously restrict both their capabilities and the scope of their functionings.

Let us consider briefly some of the consequences of unplanned maternity, especially in the lives of poor women in poor countries. Unplanned maternity generally increases women's poverty, and lowers their levels of health and nutrition. It favors a gendered division of work, insofar as women who do not control their fertility assume more easily than others their role as caretakers of the children and the home, thus renouncing the possibility of getting a full time job outside the home or participating in other community activities. In Mexico, according to official statistics, only 25 percent of women older than fourteen have a paid job, and the percentage of married women with a paid job is just 13 percent.[3] Women who never had a paid job have considerably more children than those who do.[4]

The mere possibility of unplanned maternity diminishes women's opportunities of getting a job. It is a well-known fact that most employers prefer to hire men than to hire women, for they run the risk of unplanned pregnancies. Moreover, in countries where women are employed in informal paid labor, they are often fired from their jobs when they get pregnant.[5] Family dynamics change as well. Women who do not control their fertility and cannot get a paid job become economically dependent on men. They are considered less economically valuable than men, notwithstanding the fact that women are responsible for all unpaid work in the household. The lack of a paid job and women's economic dependency on men make them poorer and diminishes their bargaining position in their relationships with men when their mutual interests conflict. This promotes women's subordination and inequality in the context of the family. Susan Moller Okin offers an excellent description of how all these negative factors are interwoven in women's lives.[6]

From an educational standpoint, in countries where women do not have access to effective means of family planning, they get much less schooling than males. Women tend to see their lives as predestined to motherhood and wifehood, and consequently tend to become mothers very young. In Mexico in the early 1980s, 11 percent of women with children were illiterate, 50 percent of women of reproductive age had had at most six years of schooling,[7] and 8 percent of women younger than fifteen and 56 percent of women between fifteen and nineteen were already married or cohabiting.[8] The general result is that women's prospects for functioning in many areas characteristic of human life, and thus their opportunities for genuine flourishing, are severely diminished when they cannot control their own fertility.

If we consider the basic human capabilities proposed by Nussbaum, we can see how women's well-being is also impaired by the lack of access to contraception and abortion. The rate of premature female mortality is considerably increased.[9] Furthermore, women's and children's health problems, lack of shelter, and undernourishment are commonly consequential upon women having more children than those they reflectively choose to have. Undesired pregnancies are a painful experience for women and their families: women with unwanted children are less educated and have less time to imagine, think, and engage in critical reflection in order to plan their lives. Unwanted children generally promote parental negligence; women unable to control their own fertility have less time to play and to enjoy recreational activities. In short, women who do not have access to effective means of family planning do not live their own lives, but lives imposed upon them. Once we become aware of this, it is not exaggerated to say that the capability (in the sense of positive freedom) to control their fertility is essential to women's flourishing.

In this chapter, I examine some of the problems concerning women's access to abortion and contraception in Mexico and Latin America. First, I focus on the social and legal problems surrounding abortion and contraception in Mexico, including the obstructive attitude of the Catholic Church to any efficient family-planning program. I focus on Mexico, but I assume that the country can be taken to be representative of other Latin American countries. Second, I provide a brief history of the doctrinal teachings of the Catholic Church on abortion and contraception. Next, I present and discuss the Catholic Church's arguments against abortion and contraception. I conclude with some general considerations concerning the consequences of the view I defend for legislation on abortion.

2. Contraception and Abortion: Mexico and Latin America.

Contraception and abortion represent two different problems in Latin American countries. Contraception is not only legally permitted but also encouraged by some Latin American governments. Yet induced abortions continue to be illegal. In Colombia, Chile, Panama, and the Dominican Republic, abortions are absolutely illegal.[10] In Argentina, Brazil, and Mexico, abortion is generally illegal but restricted exceptions exist in cases of rape or when the life of the mother is seriously threatened.[11] Venezuela and Nicaragua reportedly do not accept abortion in cases of rape. Bolivia, Ecuador, Honduras, Perú, El Salvador, and Uruguay have less restricted exceptions: abortions can be legally performed for health or eugenic reasons.[12] Only in Cuba and Puerto Rico is induced abortion legal.

In the early 1970s, given the high fertility rates officially admitted in Latin America (2.9 percent) and the dangers of overpopulation, the United Nations recommended Latin American governments to implement family-planning programs. These were supposed to cover the free distribution of contraceptives and the education of people in demographic and reproductive questions so that they could effectively and knowingly decide to avoid pregnancies. In 1974, the Mexican Government created the National Population Council to take charge of family-planning and birth control programs. A Constitutional amendment granted the right to every person to get all the relevant information concerning different means of family planning and to choose freely and responsibly the number of children desired and the temporal spacing between them. In 1976, the Population Council invited a group of multidisciplinary and ideologically pluralist specialists to study the problem of abortion in Mexico and to make recommendations concerning its legal status. This group concluded that the range of circumstances in which abortion could be legal should be broader to include economic, eugenic, and medical considerations relating to the physical or mental health of the mother.[13] The reaction of the Catholic Church was quick and telling. In 1978, a Pro-Life committee linked to ecclesiastical authorities was created, and its members immediately started a well-organized media campaign. They mobilized several sectors of the Catholic population—in Latin America 80 percent of the population is Catholic—to denounce the "abominable crime"[14] whose legalization the government was considering.[15] As a result, the Mexican government decided to separate the issue of family planning and the use of contraceptives from that of abortion. The government and the church seemed to have reached a compromise. The church would not protest, at least not so frequently and not so violently, against the ambitious governmental campaign encouraging the use of contraceptives; the government would not touch the Federal Penal Code dating from 1931 that made abortion almost without exception a crime.

Since the late 1970s, Mexican women have increasingly used contraception to control their fertility. In 1976, the percentage of women of reproductive age using some contraceptive method was 30 percent, in 1982 the percentage reached 47 percent, and in 1987 the percentage was 63 in urban areas and 38 percent in rural areas, for an average of 51 percent.[16] Between 1980 and 1990, the birth rate descended impressively from 37.56 to 25.77 *per* one thousand people. The total fertility rate descended from 6.31 children in 1973 to 3.84 children in 1986.[17] Through its efforts, the government was ultimately effective in giving women the capability to reduce the size of their families, and contribute not only to their own well-being but also to the control of demographic growth.

Yet, if we compare the total fertility rate with the number of children that Latin American women declare they want to have, we appreciate a considerable difference.[18] In 1986 and 1987, Mexican women of reproductive age with an average of 3.8 children claimed that they desired to have an average of 2.1. Mexican women in those years were having an average of 1.7 undesired children. This shows that even though they had relatively easy access to contraception (contraceptives in the countryside are not easily available in Latin America[19]) women were not controlling their fertility according to their reproductive intentions and declared desires.

Three partial explanations for this phenomenon exist. First, the traditional "macho" ideology in Mexico and Latin America—according to which virility is partially measured by the number of children a man has—and the traditional submission of women to their partners in family matters. Second, the Catholic Church's opposition to effective contraceptive methods forces a great number of Catholic women who want to control their fertility to use "natural" but unreliable methods—15 percent of all Mexican women using contraceptive methods are in this situation. Third, the absolute prohibition of abortion by the Catholic Church, and the illegality of the practice means that in cases of unwanted pregnancies women do not have the option to choose a safe legal abortion.

I do not focus here on the ideology of male Latin Americans since this is a topic for another study. In the next section, I concentrate on the arguments and the attitudes of the Catholic Church as regards contraception and abortion. The rest of this section examines the legal situation concerning abortion in Mexico, and the political and social obstacles for its legalization.

Abortion in the Mexican Federal Criminal Code is considered a crime. Women who consent to an abortion may be punished with one to five years in prison. Those who perform abortions may get one to eight years of prison. For physicians or trained midwives, the additional penalty is suspension from practice from two to five years.[20] Two things are worth noting. First, the man co-responsible for the unwanted pregnancy (and in some cases even for the abortion) is not mentioned in the Mexican legislation. Second, because of the additional penalty to doctors and medically trained people, the law favors an underground industry of illegal abortions practiced by medically incompetent people, without any health control.

However, despite the illegality of abortion in Mexico and Latin America, abortion is widely practiced. The World Health Organization estimates that six million abortions are performed every year in Latin America.[21] It is difficult to get an exact idea of the dimensions of illegal abortion in Latin American countries because they do not appear in any official health record. The most conservative reliable estimate is eight hundred thousand illegal abortions in Mexico, but liberal and feminist literature puts it at two million each year. In 1980, in one of the largest public obstetrical hospitals in Mexico, 8 percent of all deaths were due to medical complications after an illegal abortion.[22] Moreover, it is estimated that at least one percent of Mexican women die as a result of illegal abortions. This means that according to the most conservative estimates, eight thousand women die every year in Mexico due to the illegal status of abortion. These women prefer a risky and unhealthy abortion to an unwanted child. Of those women, 52 percent have an abortion because they have too many children already, 27 percent have an abortion because of economic problems, 12 percent due to serious problems with their partners, and the rest for social or therapeutic reasons.[23]

The illegal status of abortion is especially unjust to some women. Wealthy and informed women who decide to have an abortion can arrange a safe and not so unpleasant one by travelling to a country where abortion is legal, or can arrange one by a private doctor in an expensive private hospital. In contrast, poor and uninformed women are forced to risk their lives in sordid and unhealthy places where they are physically and morally harmed, and even face the danger of being sent to jail. The physical and emotional effects of abortion are certainly much worse for the second group of women than for the first.

We can say that given the statistics of illegal abortion in Mexico, abortion laws are not successful as a deterrent. They do not discourage people from having abortions. Furthermore, the state does not seem to be strictly enforcing the law. In 1988, only fifteen women were prosecuted and six convicted; in 1989, there were only fourteen accusations of illegal abortion and seven persons were ultimately imprisoned.[24] Thousands of women continue to have abortions, and neither the law, nor the repeated condemnation of abortion by the Catholic Church has succeeded in dissuading those who decide to have one. Why do we still have such a law? A look at the reactions to recent attempts by the Mexican government and by leftist and feminist groups to reform or repeal the legislation on abortion might help us to understand the problem and the difficulties involved in finding a socially acceptable way of solving it.

In 1976, the Mexican government made a first attempt to reform the abortion law by widening the range of exceptions under which abortion would be legal. The Catholic Church protested with energy in the press accusing the government of trying to legalize homicide. In the major national newspapers, 66 percent of the articles on abortion were against its legalization, only 33 percent were in favor.[25] A National Pro-Life committee closely linked to the Catholic hierarchy was founded in 1978. When Pope John Paul II visited Mexico in 1979, the Catholic community displayed all its power; this encouraged the church in its confrontation with the state. At that point, the government had to retreat.

The second attempt to change the law came in 1980 when a coalition of left-wing representatives agreed to submit to the House of Representatives a bill elaborated by several feminist groups on "Voluntary Maternity." The bill had several purposes. First, to affirm the right of women to decide questions concerning their lives. Second, to repeal all abortion laws in the penal code, introducing instead a health regulation for surgical abortions. Finally, to state the obligation of the public health system to practice abortion on demand especially in the case of poor women. At this juncture, criticism came not only from the Catholic Church, the pro-life movement, and the most prominent right-wing political party. The ruling political party protested as well, for the government did not want to repeal the law, just reform it. Left-wing representatives questioned the right of the church to intervene in political matters, given that at that time according to the Mexican legislation the church lacked any legal character. The discussion led to the issue of the relationship between the state and the church.

The third attempt to reform abortion legislation came in 1983. The Mexican president announced his decision to submit to the House of Representatives a new criminal code that included a change in the abortion law. According to the new code, eugenic considerations and serious economic difficulties of the mother would also be considered sufficient reasons for a legal abortion. The Mexican Bishops Conference replied with a Pastoral Letter on "Abortion and Legalization." They presented three considerations. First, abortion is the worst injustice a human being can commit given that personhood begins at the moment of conception, and abortion violates the right to life of an innocent person. Second, a society that does not defend the most vulnerable people is doomed to disintegration; if abortion is legally accepted, then there will be no stop to crime. Finally, a state should not only dictate laws to guarantee the rights of all people, it should enforce them efficiently. A nation in which the breaking of the law is not followed by the corresponding penalty is "bound to destruction."[26] The Pastoral Letter had a big social impact. Two-thirds of the articles on abortion in the Mexican press were against the legalization of abortion.

By the end of 1990, the last attempt to reform abortion laws came from the State Legislature of Chiapas, a state in the southeastern part of Mexico. A bill was presented and passed by the majority legalizing abortion for family-planning pregnant single women. The church, pro-life groups, and the most powerful right-wing party argued then that the legislation in question represented a human rights violation. The debate became so intense that in January 1991 the Chiapas legislature declared that the law would be suspended until the National Commission on Human Rights gave an opinion on the disputed question.[27] We are still waiting for that opinion.

What seems to emerge from this history is the refusal of the government to directly confront the Catholic Church on the issue of abortion. I do not try to explain the reasons for this refusal—the history told brings to light the enormous political power of the church in Mexico. However, while the Catholic Church presents its position as "the only truth" derived from religious and moral Catholic principles, the present monolithic position of the church has been much more fragmented in the past than is usually known.

3. The Catholic Church on Abortion and Contraception: A Historical Review

In 1992, the official position of the church on abortion and contraception seemed clear. The Encyclical *Humanae Vitae* dictated by Pope Paul VI in 1968 declared that both practices are sinful and immoral. However, the *prima facie* immoral character of contraception can be overruled in some personal cases, when the confessor authorizes a woman to use contraceptives for medical reasons. There are no general exceptions to the immorality of contraception. Exceptions to the general prohibition should always be casuistic. A Catholic woman desiring to control her fertility has to prove she has a health problem in order to obtain a special permission from a priest to do so. Thus, the Catholic Church's opposition to contraception is less radical than its opposition to abortion. However, in public documents the ecclesiastical authorities always defend the view that the use of contraceptives is immoral given that the only admissible purpose of having sexual intercourse, according to the church, is reproduction.

The official doctrine is clear on the issue of abortion: it is always a sinful immoral act. Even therapeutic abortions are considered criminal. The only moral way of stopping a pregnancy when the life of the mother is endangered is when abortion is "indirect," where the direct intention of the doctor is not to kill the embryo or the fetus but where its death is a foreseen effect of the doctor's action.[28]

However, the present orthodoxy of the church is a historical result of an interesting succession of several views on abortion and contraception that have prevailed at one or another time in the history of the moral theology of the church.

There is just one passage of the Bible where abortion is mentioned, *Exodus* 21: 22-24. The Septuagint translation of this passage states that if someone causes an abortion resulting in a non-formed fetus, the punishment will not be severe. However, if the fetus is formed, the abortion will be considered homicide and the one causing abortion will pay life for life. The Greek translation of the Hebrew Bible was accepted as the official one in early Christianity and used by the fathers of the church to support their views in the discussion over ensoulment. St. Augustine and St. Jerome considered that something lacking sensibility and a human form could not have a human soul. According to St. Augustine, "there cannot be said to be a live soul in the body that lacks sensation when it is not formed in flesh and so no yet endowed with sense."[29] St Jerome states, "Seeds are gradually formed in the uterus, and it is no reputed homicide until the scattered elements received their appearance and members." [30]

Abortion in itself is rarely mentioned as a moral issue during the first centuries of Christianity.[31] The canon law did not determine whether abortion in itself was a wrongful or sinful act. When it was mentioned as something morally wrong it was generally in connection with adulterous behavior or with prostitution, and the laws usually distinguished between aborting animate and inanimate fetuses, assigning different punishments in each case.[32]

In the Middle Ages, Yves de Chartres in 1000 emitted an act establishing that the death of an embryo is not a homicide because the soul is not infused into the body until the fetus is already formed. In 1140, the Gratian's *Decretum*, which soon became the basic text for all professors of canon law at the universities, followed the position of Yves de Chartres, and so did Peter Lombardus.[33] Bonaventure, quoting Aristotle, maintained that a soul cannot exist in the embryo before this is adequately organized.[34] Albert the Great, in his *Summa de Creaturis,* held that the soul is not infused by God into the body until its members are formed, forty days for males and ninety days for females.[35] Following Aristotle, Aquinas maintained that "the soul is united to the body as its form," so that a human soul requires a body already formed. He adds, the embryo has first of all a soul which is merely sensitive, and when this is removed, it is supplanted by a more perfect soul which is both sensitive and intellectual.[36]

Elsewhere Aquinas states,

the soul is in the embryo, the nutritive soul from the beginning, then the sensitive soul, and lastly the intellectual soul. [...] the intellectual soul is created by God at the end of human generation.[37]

For these philosophers, the distinction between ensouled and non-ensouled fetuses was not only significant in itself but also crucial for determining the moral status of abortion. Aborting a non-ensouled embryo was not a mortal sin or a homicide. Yet they usually disapproved of it (as of contraception) because it went against the natural laws of generation given by God.

By the end of the sixteenth and the beginning of the seventeenth centuries, the historic period where Michel Foucault locates *la mise en discours du sexe*,[38] abortion became a more important moral issue in treatises on moral theology. Tomás Sánchez and Paul Laymann, two outstanding moral theologians in this period, dealt with the morality of abortion. They accepted the distinction between an ensouled and a non-ensouled fetus. According to Sánchez, direct abortion when the fetus is not ensouled is permissible in four cases: for therapeutic reasons, for pregnant single women who run the risk of being killed by their family, for betrothed women who cannot avoid by any other means a bastard child not accepted by a future husband, and in cases of rape.[39] For Sánchez, the loss of "the unformed matter" was not "such a great loss" as to be a mortal sin. He is one of the firsts to use the doctrine of double effect, and he accepts the abortion of an animate fetus when its death is not sought intentionally but is produced "incidentally." Paul Laymann made a strong defense of abortion when the fetus is yet not formed. When the embryo threatens the life, the honor, or the freedom of a woman, it can be considered an innocent aggressor and abortion is permitted "if there is no other means of defense."[40]

Although the distinction between an ensouled and a non-ensouled fetus continued to be accepted by the majority of Catholic theologians by the end of the seventeenth and beginning of the eighteenth century, there was an increasing interest in the distinction between "direct" and "indirect" abortion. The Catholic doctrine on abortion started to change. The majority of theologians concluded that direct abortion should not be permitted when there is doubt as to whether the fetus is ensouled. Given that determining ensoulment is so difficult, direct abortion was no longer permitted. Indirect abortion was only permitted when the life of the mother was in danger.

All through the first half of the nineteenth century, the discussion continued to be centered around questions concerning the probable dates of ensoulment of the fetus and the casuistic discussions on the doctrine of double effect. Some defenses of the doctrine of immediate ensoulment of the fetus, apparently grounded on the false biological hypothesis that the spermatozoon is literally an homunculus, started to appear in the second half of the nineteenth century. In 1869, Pope Pius IX declared that those practicing abortion would be excommunicated *ipso facto*. He did not refer to the distinction between ensouled and non-ensouled fetuses. The 1917 Canon Law reiterated the penalty of excommunication for all those who induce an abortion,[41] and adhered to the theory of immediate animation when it established the obligation to baptize any fetus no matter the degree of its development.[42]

In the twentieth century, the distinction between ensouled and non-ensouled fetus has tended to disappear. Of the twenty-six contemporary ecclesiastical authorities in canon law and moral theology who have an opinion on abortion, seventeen defend the doctrine of immediate ensoulment and absolutely condemn direct abortion as a kind of homicide.[43] Seven are skeptical about the possibility of knowing the exact time when ensoulment takes place, but all the same consider abortion at least as an "imperfect" or "anticipated" homicide and, therefore, seriously immoral. Only Antonio Lanza and Pietro Palazini defend the doctrine of "retarded ensoulment" on the basis of an Aristotelian and Scholastic argument: being the substantial form of the human body, the soul must be the end and not the beginning of the human generation.[44] According to Lanza and Palazini, only the doctrine of retarded ensoulment is supported by sound philosophical arguments. In their opinion, the doctrine of the immediate infusion of the soul at the time of conception is either the consequence of assuming erroneous scientific hypotheses or a practical expedient to solve some difficult moral matters. Yet they consider that abortion of a non-ensouled fetus is morally wrong for the same reasons that contraception is wrong: it is an illicit violation of the divine order, but not a violation of a person's right to life.

In 1961 in the Encyclical *Mater et Magistra,* Pope John XXIII declared the sanctity of the human life from its very beginning insofar as it presupposes the action of God. The document *Gaudium et Spes,* emitted by the Vatican II Council, addressed the question of responsible procreation and the duty of every couple to decide conscientiously the number of children they have. The document did not take a stand on contraception, but repeated the absolute condemnation of direct abortion, which together with infanticide is considered a horrendous crime. Given the proliferation of artificial contraceptive methods in the early 1960s, in *Humanae Vitae* Pope Paul VI approached not only the question of abortion but also that of contraception. Direct abortion is morally impermissible even for therapeutic reasons, and only natural contraceptive methods are morally permissible. Since then, all the official organs of the Catholic Church have reiterated the same doctrine, stressing the absolute prohibition of abortion.

Latin American bishops have not been an exception to this general rule. In their official documents they usually refer to the fetus at any stage of development as a "child," "innocent person," and "helpless creature," thus implying that they give the fetus the moral status of a born baby. In 1973, in a document on abortion, the bishops of El Salvador declared that "it is forbidden to kill a child as a means to save the mother's life.... One can never take intentionally the life of an innocent."[45] The Colombian Bishops in a Pastoral Letter dated 1975 stated that "abortion is a transgression against a helpless innocent life ... [and so] the worst violation against the dignity of the person."[46] The Conference of Mexican Bishops in 1975 declared that "abortion is a cruel and wrong decision to destroy a helpless creature who claims her right to life."[47]

This history can be interpreted in more than two ways. It can be viewed, as many Catholics do, as a kind of moral progress, in the sense of achieving recognition of a moral value that had been hitherto overseen.[48] But it can also be interpreted as a moral regression. It may be seen as a process of making up allegedly "new values" whose main function is to control women's lives, and to neglect some moral values in the life of women on the basis of a very dubious conception of non-ensouled fetuses as persons. Following Foucault's line of thought, and given the connection between aborting and having had sexual intercourse, one might view the history of the doctrine of the church on abortion as the history of an invention whose purpose has been to increase the control on women's consciousness by putting into operation one of the many forms available to the *dispositif de la sexualité*. Or yet, from a more clearly political perspective, this history might be understood as the result of a political struggle of the church against the state to control human lives. But independently of how we interpret this history, underlying the discussion is a deep philosophical problem: who is right, those who consider the unformed fetus to be a moral person or those who consider it to have no moral claims on us? This question is significant not only in itself but also as a way of assessing the grounds on which the Catholic Church bases its absolute condemnation of abortion.

4. The Arguments of the Catholic Church

In the writings of the Catholic Church, two kinds of arguments against abortion can be distinguished: a religious and a moral argument. Although they are not disconnected, it is possible to isolate them so as to be able to appreciate the corresponding force of each.

A. The Religious Argument

What I take to be the religious argument has many variations, and it can in principle be shared by non-Catholics. The argument says that nature is the work of an almighty and infinitely good being, and since human life is a gift from God, it is intrinsically good, and human beings should always revere it and accept it with hope and joy. On this view, human epistemic and moral faculties are limited and frequently biased. This is the reason why sometimes human beings focus on secondary matters such as the dangers of overpopulation, the advantages of having small families, and the possible interference of a pregnancy with the plans of a woman, instead of appreciating the intrinsic value of a new human life. Honesty and humility will make us grasp the sanctity of life. Once we see that life is sacred we will also see that it is morally wrong to interfere with the natural process of generation. Prevention and interruption of pregnancy are obvious ways of interfering with this natural process; therefore, contraception and abortion are morally impermissible.

Two difficulties with this argument I do not address. The first has to do with what counts as interference with the process of human generation. The second is the possibility of extending the argument to all natural processes.[49] Instead, I am concerned with a key point. The whole reasoning depends on the acceptance of a premise that both presupposes a belief in God's existence and expresses a religious way of seeing the world. For this reason, it is not the kind of premise for or against which one can conclusively argue. When people disagree about the premise, little (if any) probability of reaching a consensus through objective rational discussion exists.

It has been pointed out to me that it is difficult to give an acceptable account of what an "objective rational" discussion would amount to in general.[50] The assumption underlying this objection is that different parties in a discussion could count different things as "objective" and "rational." I doubt that this can be so, but still my claim here is more modest. All I require is that the participants in the discussion do not appeal to any religious convictions nor draw any clearly invalid or unreasonable conclusion. As Roger Wertheimer suggests in his excellent article, acceptance of the premise has to do with a belief that is neither true nor false.[51] It is no more than an expression of a way of seeing the world, of a personal outlook from which the world makes sense. If this is so, an "argument" for this premise can be at most an invitation to see the world in a way considered valuable by the person who has the belief in question. But we can think of many other equally valuable ways of viewing the world that allow people to make sense of it. To suggest without begging the question that one way of seeing the world is superior—morally superior—to the rest is implausible. In this respect, the religious argument cannot convince others by means of a purely rational and objective dialogue. The core idea is that religious belief goes beyond what reason can establish by itself and that faith is a gift. The appeal to authorities not accepted as such by both parties in the discussion is useless.

Giving a religious argument to establish the immorality of abortion and contraception has its advantages and disadvantages for the purposes of the Catholic Church. It has a tremendous strength for those already having the religious worldview presupposed in the argument. This is not a trivial matter when we think of the Catholic Church addressing Latin Americans on abortion and contraception. Yet, if this were the only argument advanced by the Catholic Church against abortion, it should not have any influence on public legislation. The reason is that it is based on religious convictions, and since freedom of religious belief is consecrated in most contemporary political constitutions, accepting it—or any other religious belief—would be a private matter.

Furthermore, the principle of the sanctity of life involved in the religious argument is open to several interpretations. On a broad interpretation, it would apply to all kinds of human life: the life of a fertilized human ovum and the life of people in vegetative state, among others. On a much narrower interpretation, it would apply primarily to the life of rational conscious human beings, and only derivatively to other sorts of human life. On an intermediate interpretation, it would properly apply only to sensitive living human organisms. So, accepting the principle of the sanctity of life does not settle the question. Moreover, people have to support their understanding of the principle and explain why their interpretation is better than others. And the reasons for choosing one or another interpretation of the principle must appeal to moral considerations.

This takes us to the second kind of argument used by the Catholic Church to condemn abortion: the moral argument.

B. The Moral Argument

In this argument, an essential use is made of the notion of a "person" or of a "human being." When articulated in terms of rights, the argument says: all innocent persons (or human beings) have the right to life, fetuses are innocent persons (or human beings) from the moment of conception; therefore, fetuses have the right to life from the moment of conception.

The argument can also be cast in terms of actions that are morally wrong. It says: intentionally killing innocent persons (or human beings) is morally wrong, fetuses are innocent persons (or human beings) from the moment of conception; therefore, it is morally wrong to intentionally kill a fetus at any stage of its development. Here, I assume that both those who consider that abortion is morally impermissible and those who consider that it is sometimes a morally acceptable practice agree on the major premise; therefore, I will not discuss it.[52] The problem is with the minor premise. Are fetuses innocent persons or human beings? For something to be an innocent person it has to be a person; so, are fetuses persons? Assuming the truth of the major premise, the answer we give to this question will determine whether we accept the conclusion. The issue of abortion has many aspects, and I do not mean to say that the only one morally relevant is the issue of the personhood of the fetus. However, as we are examining the moral argument of the Catholic Church for rejecting abortion, it is inevitable to deal with this question.

Some writers have emphasized that the notion of a person used in arguments like the one above is not empirical, in the sense that no amount of empirical information is sufficient to settle the question. The underlying assumptions are: (1) asserting that something is a person is making a value judgment, and (2) there is a distinction between facts and values, so that through the relevant empirical information we can come to an agreement regarding facts but not regarding values. I will argue that these writers are partially wrong. In order to give a reasonable answer to the question of whether fetuses are persons we must distinguish among four notions of personhood usually intermingled in the discussion on the morality of abortion.

(1) In some discussions, personhood or humanity is equated with the notion of biological humanity, with having the genetic code characteristic of the species *homo sapiens*. On this view, being a human being or "a person" amounts to nothing more than being the offspring of the union of two human gametes. According to this perspective, a human embryo, like any born person, is a "human being" because it has the genetic code of a *homo sapiens*.

The genetic make-up of the embryo is an empirical fact, a verifiable one that is often brought into the discussion to support the minor premise in the Catholic argument. However, arguing that the possession of a certain genetic code is sufficient for personhood in the morally relevant sense, and that it exerts a moral claim on us, is begging the question. A fertilized human ovum has indeed a human genetic code but is not at all in many other morally important respects like an actual human being. Moreover, having the human genetic code is not even a necessary condition for being a person. If we found other biological entities with genetic material different from that of *homo sapiens* but whose functioning and, perhaps, whose appearance were identical or very similar to those of full-fledged human persons, we would value them and count them as genuine persons. Hence, the fact that a human embryo has the genetic code it has does not exert by itself a moral claim on us, and is not even necessary for an entity to be a person.

I am not denying that in some contexts the mere fact of an embryo having the genetic material it has may exert some moral claim on us. Think of cases where we might be concerned with the preservation of the human species or the increase of the human population; in those contexts, the fact that an embryo has a human genetic code may be considered instrumentally valuable, as a means to achieve a valuable end. Consider also the case of a pregnant woman who reflectively desires to have a child; she would certainly value the fact that her fetus has the necessary genetic material for becoming a human being. But not even in these cases would the genetic code be considered intrinsically valuable. More generally, when we grant value to something having the genetic code of *homo sapiens* this is always because we know that a full-fledged person may develop from it, and because we value certain capabilities and functionings in full-fledged persons.

This makes two things clear: first, we can value some empirical features, for example, the possession of a genetic code; second, we can value them because we value other empirical things, some characteristic functionings and capabilities in born human beings. What I mean by saying that we value some human capabilities and functionings, such as intelligence or being friendly, is not simply that we happen to like them or that we just desire to have them. I mean that our desire to possess them is, using Thomas Nagel's terminology, a "motivated desire."[53] Thus, having a genetic code is not something valuable in itself. A genetic code does not have intrinsic moral worth, but at most it has a derivative one. Embryos and fetuses have the genetic material necessary for becoming actual persons, and given that we grant intrinsic value to certain features in actual persons, the genetic constitution of fetuses can make them derivatively valuable. If fetuses are considered valuable it is because they are seen as "potential" or future human persons.

(2) What is a potential human person? Let us say that a potential human person is something with a human genetic code (an "originative source of change," in Aristotle's words) that has already started a process of development so that if no one interferes with it, it will develop into an actual person or human being. In cases of miscarriage it may not develop into anything at all even if no one "interferes" with it. So we have to change "will" for "can" in this characterization of a potential person, thus holding that in principle a fetus is both a potential person and a "potential non-person." To claim that if a fetus does not develop into a person then it is "a potential non-person" might seem incorrect, for "non-persons" do not form a kind, and what teleologically explains the make-up of a fetus is what is needed to become a person.[54] My purpose, however, is to stress the difficulty involved in valuing a fetus that by hypothesis fails to become a person; thus, "is a potential non-person" may be read as "fails to become a person."

This coincides with Aristotle's view on potential entities in his *Metaphysics*.

Every potency is at the same time a potency of the opposite; for ... everything that is capable of being may not be actual. That, then, which is capable of being may either be or not be.... . And that which is capable of not being may possibly not be.[55]

Even if we were ready to attribute derivative moral value to a potential person, the attribution of value to something that is a potential non-person, something that will fail to become a person, is strange. By the same token, the attribution of moral value to something that has "at the same time" the potency for becoming a person and the potency for the opposite is even stranger. Applying this to the question of abortion, we can say that the attribution of derivative moral value to an embryo that will never come to be a person is strange, for from where is its value going to be derived? Similarly, the attribution of moral value to an embryo that may or may not become a person is even stranger.

However, we can speak of a potential person in a stronger sense, where it does not fail to become a full-fledged person. This is the case of those fetuses that are the causal antecedents of actually born human beings. Potential persons, in this stronger sense, are future persons or persons to be, and can be derivatively valuable. However, we can consider a fetus a potential person, in this stronger sense, *a posteriori,* once the fetus has developed into an actual human being. We can think, for example, of the fetus of Albert Einstein as a potential person of the actual man, and make the backward-looking judgement that it was a valuable fetus owing to the worth of the life of Albert Einstein. A fetus seems to be valuable just to the extent that it actually develops into a full-fledged person, and more so when it develops into an autonomous human being with a worthwhile life. It is because we value the actual human capabilities and functionings of a child or of an adult that we derivatively value their respective fetuses. This, as Jonathan Glover points out, strongly suggests that "what the person [a fetus] will become is what is really valued."[56] So, if there is no actual person causally connected with the fetus from which the fetus could gain its worth, its life seems to be void of moral meaning. How could an early fetus failing to become an actual person have some intrinsic moral worth? If someone argues that its intrinsic moral worth derives from the principle of the sanctity of life this would take us back to the religious argument examined above. Appealing, as Jonathan Glover does,[57] to a possible future worth-while life which never takes place (in the case of abortion) seems to me most puzzling, for how are we to determine whether such a non-existent but possible life was really worth living? Or, should we consider that any life is worth living? This would take us close to the principle of the sanctity of life which Glover so strongly criticizes.

(3) Persons are peculiar particulars in the world around us. What is the trait that distinguishes persons from other things? In the recent literature on the metaphysics of persons, we find proposals for different conditions which, it is maintained, must be satisfied by something if that something is to be a person in the metaphysical sense of the word. These conditions refer to a diversity of properties, instances of mental or psychological properties, and the discussion has frequently centered around the question of which are necessary and sufficient for something to be a person.

P. F. Strawson approaches the problem from a different angle. Instead of looking for the set of psychological properties necessary and sufficient for something to be a person, he raises a question concerning what is distinctive of the concept of a person, what are the traits that make persons different from any other particulars.[58] According to Strawson, the concept of a person is among our primitive concepts in that it cannot be analyzed in any way. Persons are not a mixture of different things. We cannot think of a person, for example, as a compound of a consciousness and a body. Persons are peculiar kind of basic particulars to which we can ascribe states of consciousness and corporeal characteristics. That is, persons have two different kinds of properties. Some they share with material bodies, for example, being at a certain place or having a certain weight. But only persons can possess some other properties, such as the belief in God, perception of the environment, going for a walk, or being in pain.

There is something deep in Strawson's theory of persons. It captures a universally shared intuition: we do not recognize as a person (in any sense of this term) something that lacks or is not able to have any psychological properties or the ability to perform any kind of intentional action. People do not attribute personhood to things that have only material properties, such as a tree or a stone, unless, perhaps, they hold a religious or a poetic view of those things, and hence attribute some sort of mental property to them.

Another interesting aspect of Strawson's theory is that it suggests that determining whether something is a person is an empirical matter. Either we attribute a state of consciousness or an intentional action to something, or we do not, and the attribution of a state of consciousness or an intentional action is always ruled by public empirical criteria.

I believe that if something is not a person in Strawson's sense but merely a material object, we lack any grounds for attributing any intrinsic moral value to any aspect of it. Furthermore, normally we would not think that this kind of object imposes any non-derivative moral claim on us. In contrast, the empirical fact that something has states of consciousness and is capable of functioning in distinctive human ways does seem to impose moral claims on us. For example, anything capable of feeling pain or hunger can impose a moral claim on us. Although Strawson's notion of a person allows for all kinds of gradualism, it does not admit the possibility of a person who is not able to have any of the properties peculiar to persons. If this is so, it is evident that all born human beings are metaphysical persons, whereas fetuses in the first months of gestation are not persons in this metaphysical sense of the word; we cannot ascribe to them any of the mental properties distinctive of persons. However, a fetus capable of feeling pain or cold would have some of the properties distinctive of persons, and so it must be counted as a person. Given that the Strawsonian notion of a person is not committed to "speciesism," for the notion of a person is not identical to that of a biological human being, it seems that some animals and sufficiently developed fetuses are metaphysical persons. In contrast, embryos and immature fetuses cannot be counted as persons in the metaphysical sense of the word; therefore, there are no grounds at all to subsume an embryo into the concept of a person.

Advocates of the moral argument against abortion can still argue that they have a different concept of a person, and that under their metaphysical concept of a person fetuses are persons from the moment of conception. But if we are to understand what they say, they have to explain what they mean by metaphysical person. If they really have a concept different from ours this must be because, as Wittgenstein says, they see "certain very general facts of nature to be different from what we are used to." Only if they can explain what those general facts are will "the formation of concepts different from the usual ones ... become intelligible."[59]

At this point, advocates of the moral argument can do one of the following. They can appeal to the premises in the religious argument and try to explain how they see the world and how, within their view of the world, God "infuses souls" into embryos from the moment of conception, and how this act of God makes them into genuine persons. Or they may not want to appeal to a religious conception of life and embryos to defend their argument but instead to two other concepts, that of a "potential human person" and that of a "moral person."

If they choose the first alternative, their notion of a person will depend on a religious conception of the world that, as already shown, needs not be universally shared. It seems just that some happen to have it and that some do not, and that seems to be the end of the matter. So, although one may understand to a certain point the theological view supporting the idea that fetuses are persons from the moment of conception, there is no reason why it must be accepted under pain of irrationality. If they choose the second alternative, then they may argue that a fertilized human ovum is a potential person, but as already shown, this move is ineffective. So, next I say something about the notion of a moral person.

(4) All metaphysical persons can be moral persons, and there is a rationale for this: the fact that something has properties distinctive of persons can exert a moral claim on us. So, for example, we should be morally sensitive toward something capable of having desires or beliefs, or of feeling hunger or pain. Cruelty toward an animal can be in some cases as morally blameworthy as cruelty against a human being. By the same token, once a human fetus has developed enough to feel sensations of comfort and discomfort, of hunger or pain, it becomes a moral person in the sense that it can exert some moral claims on us. But a fetus in the early months of gestation, incapable of feeling, does not seem to be something in relation to which we can behave morally or immorally. For this reason, abortion during the first two months or so of pregnancy is not in itself morally right or wrong; it is not a moral matter at all.

It may become a moral matter only to the extent that the act of aborting is placed within the field of other human relations of the pregnant woman. It can, for example, be an act of disloyalty, selfishness, or generosity; it can be an act of self-aggression or something forced upon the pregnant woman. To that extent, aborting a very immature fetus can acquire a moral value, can be judged as right or wrong. But the mere fact of aborting it is neither morally good nor bad.

Thus, there is a point to the distinction made by ancient philosophers and theologians between "animate" and "inanimate" fetuses. The distinction captures a deep intuition concerning what are the characteristic traits of persons and moral persons. If this is so, the question concerning the morality of abortion when the fetus is not "adequately organized" or not yet "formed" is a piece of non-sense or a groundless social construction, an ideological invention. So, returning to the debate with those who defend the Catholic moral argument, they carry the burden of argument. They must provide an explanation of how it is possible for something that is not a person in the metaphysical sense of the word to be a moral person, of how a merely material object can exert moral claims on us. I suspect they have no explanation, except, perhaps, one that appeals to their religious worldview.

All the concepts of a person intermingled in the discussion of the morality of abortion are empirically grounded. This, however, does not preclude the possibility of granting moral value to things falling under some of them, even in virtue of their falling under them. The valuing is based in all cases on empirical considerations. On the other hand, given the kind of grounding that we have found to support the metaphysical and moral concepts of persons, these concepts appear to admit and even imply some kind of gradualism. At one end of the scale are born adult human beings capable of performing a variety of distinctive human functionings. At the other end are particulars capable of experiencing some simple sensations to which we naturally attribute value or disvalue, such as being in pain, being hungry or undernourished, and feeling comfortable.[60] Born human beings are the metaphysical and moral persons *par excellence*.

But another good reason for considering born human beings moral persons is that we naturally recognize them precisely as persons or human beings. Our capability for recognizing something as one of us makes that something, through the mere fact of being so recognized, a human being and, by the same token, a moral person. As Nussbaum points out, in this case the conceptual, the empirical, and the evaluative seem closely linked. We naturally recognize human beings, and our concept of a human being is precisely shaped by what we find ourselves able to recognize, but at the same time, recognizing something as human is a kind of evaluation.[61] When we recognize someone as a human being we naturally feel, as Nussbaum remarks, "a sense of affiliation and concern" for her or for him.[62] Recognition of others as human beings is grounded on the recognition of human bodies as distinct from other bodies, as well as on the recognition of distinctive human functionings closely linked to the capacities and needs of the body. Hence, the importance of the human body and of having a recognizable human form for being part of the human moral community. Our natural emotions and reactions to a body having a human form can be taken as a cognitive response to what is there, in front of us. In this context, Wittgenstein's remark: "The human body is the best picture of the human soul" is profound.[63]

If we apply these intuitions to the case of abortion, we have to conclude, as Aquinas and others did on the basis of Aristotle's ideas, that aborting a "formed" fetus is morally different from aborting an unformed one. Only in the first case can we recognize in the fetus a human body, can we see it as one of us in some relevant respects. Moreover, in order to be recognizable as a human body, the formed fetus should also possess some of the properties distinctive of persons (in the metaphysical sense of the word); thus, the two criteria we have mentioned for considering that something is a person and that it may exert moral claims on us are satisfied by sufficiently developed fetuses.

I am aware of the many difficulties facing this conclusion, but there are no quick and easy recipes for solving moral problems. The notion of a "formed" or "sufficiently organized" fetus does not have clear-cut boundaries and, perhaps, does not permit a "yes" or "no" answer in every case. But this is one of the distinctive features of moral problems: difficult, borderline cases always exist.

The moderate position I defend concerning the morality of abortion has the advantage of coinciding not only with the profound intuitions mentioned above but with significant attempts to systematize these intuitions into elaborate theories of personhood and of human beings. Yet it has the disadvantage of having lost "prestige" owing both to its intrinsic difficulties and to the fact that it has been the focus of repeated criticisms. To conclude, I address one criticism that has been frequently advanced and has consequences for legislation on abortion.

Many philosophers have pointed out that part of the difficulty of dealing with the problem of abortion has to do with the different intuitions that human beings have towards different entities. Our intuitions about a blastula or an early embryo are different from those about a fully developed fetus or a newborn baby.[64] We do not want to treat them alike. Furthermore, some of these philosophers hold that, since the development of the fetus is continuous, drawing any boundaries to determine the point at which abortion starts being morally reprehensible is arbitrary, for what is the difference between a ninety-days-old fetus and a ninety-one-days-old fetus?

We have to concede not only that in this case there is no great difference but also that we will never find a significant difference if we compare embryonic stages separated by short temporal spans. However, if we take larger temporal spans—if we compare, for example, a thirty-days-old fetus with a six months fetus or with a fetus about to be born—the differences are considerable, and moreover, they are morally relevant. We cannot be cruel toward a blastula, but we can be cruel toward a six-months-old fetus, or even more so toward one about to be born. We should not require moral reflection on abortion to provide mathematically exact dates within which abortion is morally innocuous, but we must demand that it give some reasonable directions to guide our decisions. The fetus's development is a question of degree, and like many other questions of degree, the most we can do is to draw more or less rough boundaries and give good reasons for drawing them where we do. These reasons must be empirical in that they must appeal to public scientific criteria. For example, a focus on the development of some parts of the fetal nervous system is relevant because, according to widely accepted scientific theories, they are sufficient for having basic capabilities or functionings, such as the capability for feeling cold or pain, for being hungry or feeling "unprotected," for moving by itself, and perhaps for crying. These reasons, in turn, may serve as a rationale for the legislator to dictate the appropriate laws. Perhaps we shall feel very uncertain about whether a sixteen-weeks-old fetus should be considered as exerting some moral claim on us, but we will have no doubts concerning a blastula or a seven-months-old fetus. Empirical information concerning the normal development reached by a sixteen weeks old fetus may help us achieve a reasonable answer. Our aim should not be that of giving indisputable answers, but reasonable ones—reasonable in that they make our own moral judgments intelligible, or perhaps even acceptable, to others.

What consequences does this view on abortion have for the law? Most abortion laws claim to be justified on moral grounds. By revealing the philosophical mistake or the religious or ideological prejudice on which some abortion laws are grounded, the view defended here supports a complete liberalization of abortion laws in cases of early pregnancies. The legislator should decide with the aid of specialists on fetal development where to draw the line, keeping in mind that embryos have to be treated as what they are and not as what they might be. This legal recommendation would have the additional advantage, mentioned by Mary Warnock, that even if it fails to reflect the feelings of all people, it should not outrage the feelings of too many of them.[65]

I have not discussed here other considerations which may certainly be brought to bear on the morality of abortion practiced at later stages of fetal development, for example, questions concerning the so-called conflict of rights between a formed fetus and the potential mother. My main purpose in this chapter has been to show some of the obscurities underlying the belief that a person or a human being begins to exist at the moment of conception. This has been the core of the Catholic doctrine on abortion, and has been used to justify some actual abortion laws that have a tremendous social and human cost.

5. Conclusion

In the first two sections of this chapter, I described the ways in which the lack of full access to contraception and abortion has affected women's capabilities and quality of life. I subsequently examined the obstructive attitude of the Catholic Church when faced with any efficient family-planning program and any attempt to legalize abortion, focusing especially on the Mexican case. I admitted that behind the Catholic Church's refusal to accept abortion there are arguments worth considering. I examined those arguments and tried to show in the case of early abortion the insuperable difficulties faced by the Church in establishing the crucial premises of its argument by any objective, rational, or "dialogical" means. Early abortions were described as those in which the fetus is still incapable of having any of the properties or functionings distinctive of persons and does not have a human form, that is, a body that we could intelligibly recognize as that of a human being. I argued that early abortions are neither intrinsically moral nor intrinsically immoral; they simply are not the kind of act that can be morally evaluated.

Laws that make abortion a crime at any time of pregnancy are based on arguments similar to the moral argument of the Catholic Church. If this is so, these abortion laws lack adequate moral grounding and, therefore, can be considered the result of mere prejudice or, worse still, a consequence of a submissive attitude of the state to other political forces. Both alternatives involve politically and morally unacceptable considerations. Moreover, if the laws in question are the cause of the death of so many women and of a serious reduction in their capability to function in distinctive areas of human life, then, far from being beneficial to the community, these laws are politically harmful. Their actual result is not that of increasing the quality of women's lives, but that of diminishing it under the cloak of bad moral argument.[66]

NOTES

1. See Amartya Sen, "Equality of What," *Tanner Lectures on Human Values*, vol. 1, ed. Sterling McMurrin (Cambridge, England: Cambridge University Press, 1980); Amartya Sen, "Rights and Capabilities," *Morality and Objectivity*, ed. Ted Honderich (London: Routledge, 1985); Amartya Sen, *Commodities and Capabilities* (Amsterdam: North Holland, 1985); Amartya Sen, "Well-Being and Capability," *The Quality of Life*, eds. Martha Nussbaum and Amartya Sen (Oxford: Clarendon Press, 1991); Martha Nussbaum, "Nature, Function, and Capability: Aristotle on Political Distribution,"

Oxford Studies on Ancient Philosophy, Supplementary Volume (1988); Martha Nussbaum, "Aristotelian Social Democracy," *Liberalism and the Good*, ed. R. Bruce Douglas, Gerald Mara, and Henry Richardson (New York: Routledge, 1990); Martha Nussbaum, "Non-Relative Virtues: An Aristotelian Approach," *The Quality of Life*, ed. Nussbaum and Sen; Martha Nussbaum, "Human Capabilities: Female Human Beings," paper read at the Conference "Human Capabilities: Women, Men, and Equality" of the World Institute for Development Economics Research (WIDER), Helsinki, Finland, August 1991.

    2. Nussbaum, "Aristotelian Social Democracy," pp. 219-227.

    3. See *La salud de la mujer en México* (México: Secretary of Health, Dirección General de Salud Materno Infantil, 1990), p. 27.

    4. See *Encuesta Nacional Demográfica* (México: Consejo Nacional de Población, 1982), pp. 55, 133-134.

    5. See Rose Marie Muraro, "El aborto y la fe religiosa en América Latina," *Mujeres e Iglesia*, ed. Ana María Portugal (Washington: Catholics for a Free Choice, 1989), esp. p. 92.

    6. See Susan Moller Okin, "Inequalities between the Sexes in Different Cultural Contexts," *Women, Culture, and Development: A Study of Human Capabilities*, eds. Martha Nussbaum and Jonathan Glover (Oxford: Clarendon Press, 1995).

    7. See *Encuesta Nacional Demográfica*, p. 19.

    8. *La salud de la mujer en México*, pp. 31-39.

    9. *Ibid.*, p. 24; and *Evaluación del decenio de la mujer 1975-1985* (México: Consejo Nacional de Población, 1985), pp. 46, 48.

    10. Portugal, *Mujeres e Iglesia*, p. 139.

    11. *Ibid.*

    12. *Ibid.*

    13. See "Informe del grupo interdisciplinario para el estudio del aborto en México," (México: Typescript not published, 1976).

    14. *Gaudium et Spes*, document issued at the II Vatican Concilium; Luís De la Barreda-Solórzano, *El delito del aborto, una careta de buena conciencia* (México: Miguel Angel Porrua, 1991), pp. 76-79.

    15. María Luisa Tarrés, Gabriela de Ita, and Alicia Lozano, "Actitudes y estrategias de diversos agentes sociales y políticos en el debate sobre el aborto en la prensa mexicana 1976-1989" (manuscript, El Colegio de México, 1991).

    16. *Evaluación del decenio de la mujer 1975-1985*; and *La salud de la mujer en México*.

    17. *Ibid.*

    18. See Elza Berquó, "O crescimento da população da América Latina e mudanças na fecundidade," *Direitos Reproductivos*, eds. Sandra Azeredo and Verena Stolche (São Paulo, Brasil: Fundação Carlos Chagas, 1991), esp. pp. 66-69.

    19. *La salud de la mujer en México*, p. 34.

    20. See *Código Penal de los Estados Unidos Mexicanos*, articles 329, 330, 331, 332.

    21. See Portugal, p. 4. Also quoted in De la Barrera-Solórzano, *El delito del aborto*, p. 72.

22. See Manuel Mateos-Cándano, "Aspectos médicos y de salud," *El problema del aborto en México,* ed. María Luisa Leal (México: Miguel Angel Porrúa, 1980).
23. See Marie Claire Acosta, Flora Bottom-Berlá, and Kyra Nuñez, *El aborto en México* (Mexico City: Fondo de Cultura Económica, 1976), p. 18.
24. See De la Barreda-Solórzano, *El delito del aborto,* p. 85.
25. See Tarrés, *et al.,* "Actitudes y estrategias."
26. *Conferencia del Episcopado Mexicano* (México, Ediciones Paulinas, 1988), pp. 17-21.
27. See Kristin Luker, *Abortion and the Politics of Motherhood* (Berkeley, Cal.: University of California Press 1984), esp. chs 4, 5, 6.
28. Phillippa Foot, "The Problem of Abortion and the Doctrine of the Double Effect," *Oxford Review,* 5 (1967), Included in her *Virtues and Vices* (Oxford: Blackwell, 1978).
29. St. Augustine, *Questionum in Heptateucum,* II, 80 , PL XXXIV, 626, Quoted in Germain Gabrie Grisez, *Abortion: The Myths, the Realities, and the Arguments* (Washington: The World Publishing Company, 1970).
30. St. Jerome, "Epistle to Algasia," quoted by John T. Noonan, "An Almost Absolute Value in History," *The Morality of Abortion,* ed. John T. Noonan (Cambridge, Mass: Harvard University Press, 1970), p. 15.
31. Noonan, "An Almost Absolute Value," pp. 11-14.
32. See Grisez, *Abortion: the Myths,* pp. 230-235.
33. Both quoted in *ibid.,* p. 237.
34. Bonaventure, *Sententias II,* 31, 1, 1. Quoted by Héctor Rogel, "El comienzo de una vida humana," *Libro Annual del ISEE* (Instituto Superior de Estudios Eclesiásticos: Seminario Conciliar de México, 1977), p. 306.
35. Quoted in *ibid.,* p. 306.
36. Thomas Aquinas, *Summa Theologica* (Madrid: Biblioteca de Autores Cristianos, 1957) art I, Q.76, Art.3.
37. *Ibid,* part I, Q. 118, Art. 2.
38. Michel Foucault, *Histoire de la Sexualité* (Paris: Gallimard, 1976), vol. 1, p. 21.
39. See *De sancto matrimonii sacramento* (Anvers, 1614), ix, Disp. 20, 7-9. Quoted in Grisez, *Abortion: the Myths.*
40. See Paul Layman, *Theologia Moralis* (Venice, 1630), Book 3, pars 3, chs. 3, 4. Quoted in Grisez, *Abortion: the Myths.*
41. Canon 2350.
42. Canon 747.
43. See Rogel, "El comienzo de una vida humana," pp. 312-315.
44. See Antonio Lanza and Pietro Palazini, *Principios de teología moral* (Madrid: Rialp, 1958), vol. 2, pp. 265-273.
45. See Angel Fandiño-Franky, *El aborto: 45 documentos del Magisterio* (México City: Ediciones Paulinas, 1975), paragraphs 822-824.
46. *Ibid.,* paragraph 563.
47. See Episcopado Mexicano, *Gazeta Oficial* (1975), n. 9-10, 1975.
48. See, *e.g.,* Noonan, *The Morality of Abortion,* esp. pp. 40 and 58.
49. I thank Anthony Price for calling my attention on this matter.

50. David Crocker, in a reply to a previous version of this chapter.

51. Roger Wertheimer, "Understanding the Abortion Argument," *Philosophy and Public Affairs,* 1:1 (1971), pp. 88-89.

52. Jonathan Glover, *Causing Deaths and Saving Lives* (London: Pelican Books, 1977), esp. chs. 3, 4, 5.

53. See Mark Platts, *Moral Realities. An Essay in Philosophical Psychology* (London: Routledge, 1991), esp. ch. 3.

54. I thank Anthony Price for this observation.

55. Aristotle, *Metaphysics*, 9.8.1050b, 8-12. Translation of W. D. Ross.

56. Glover, *Causing Deaths and Saving Lives,* p. 122.

57. *Ibid.,* esp. chs. 4 and 11.

58. P. F. Strawson, *Individuals* (London and New York: Methuen, 1959), see esp. ch. 3.

59. Ludwig Wittgenstein, *Philosophical Investigations* (Oxford: Basil Blackwell, 1953), Part 2, 230e.

60. Nussbaum., "Aristotelian Social Democracy," p. 221.

61. *Ibid.,* pp. 221-222.

62. *Ibid.,* p. 222.

63. Wittgenstein, *Philosophical Investigations,* Part 2, 178e.

64. See Foot, "The Problem of Abortion," p. 19; Glover, *Causing Deaths and Saving Lives,* p. 137; Wertheimer, "Understanding the Abortion Argument," *passim*; Donald Marquis, "Why Abortion is Immoral," *The Journal of Philosophy,* 86 (1989), *passim.*

65. See Mary Warnock, *A Question of Life, The Warnock Report on Human Fertilization and Embriology* (Oxford: Blackwell 1984), p. xvi.

66. A previous version of this chapter was read at the Conference "Women, Equality, and the New Reproductive Technologies" organized by Martha Nussbaum and Jonathan Glover for the WIDER Institute, Helsinki, Finland, August 1992.

Three

WOMEN'S REPRODUCTIVE RIGHTS AND PUBLIC POLICY IN ARGENTINA

María Victoria Costa and Susana E. Sommer

1. Introduction

Reproductive rights were one of the main topics of international political debates in the 1980s and 1990s. Interest in this issue seems to have arisen together with the recent explicit acknowledgement of women's rights in the international realm.

Yet, in these debates and in the literature that they inspired, appeals to "rights" often involve ambiguities. One has to do with whether they are considered to be institutionally sanctioned rights with juridical force or moral rights that can precede legal enactment. Another is related to the fact that the term has been employed to refer both to rights to engage in activities leading to reproduction, and to rights to take a variety of measures to avoid reproduction. The notion of "reproductive rights" has been used to support claims to non-interference by governmental and public institutions, and to support claims to assistance by governmental and public institutions in facilitating or preventing reproduction. Moreover, it has not been clear who the bearers of these rights are.

In the present chapter, we do not attempt to provide an exhaustive discussion of reproductive rights. Instead, we defend the moral right of women to control their fecundity and, consequently, we defend the legal sanction of this right. Although it is plausible to hold that both men and women have a right to choose whether to reproduce, men and women are not in the same situation in this respect in contemporary societies. Reproductive decisions affect women's lives more than men's, not only because of the physical and psychological effects of pregnancy and childbirth, but also because of existing social arrangements for childrearing in most societies. The acknowledgment of reproductive rights at the international, national, and local level is far more relevant to the lives of women than to those of men—to their agency, their well-being, and their status as equal citizens.

Since women's rights to control their reproduction have not been completely guaranteed in Argentine legislation, we begin by providing a moral defense of this right. After examining some theoretical alternatives supporting this right, we assess its relevance to public policy in Argentina. We argue that the most promising way to defend this right rests on the liberal principle of respect for individual autonomy, understood as involving more than mere non-interference. We discuss recent legislation and public policy related to this right, in connection with the ideological and religious views held by different sectors of Argentine society. Because disputes about the moral status of fetuses make the debate on abortion more difficult, we discuss the right to abortion separately from access to contraception and voluntary sterilization.

2. The Basis for Reproductive Rights

To clarify the notion of reproductive rights it may be useful to begin by analyzing the notion of reproductive freedom. Reproductive freedom can be understood formally as "freedom in activities and choices related to procreation."[1] To develop a substantive account of reproductive freedom, it is necessary to determine the activities and choices that men and women are morally—and legally—allowed to do and make. Some of the choices relevant to reproductive freedom are: whether to reproduce (or to engage in activities leading to reproduction), when to reproduce, with whom, by which means, in which context (as a single parent, in marriage, with an heterosexual or homosexual partner), how many and what kind of children to have (to select the sex or other genetic features of children).[2] This list of reproductive choices developed by Dan Brock illustrates the wideness of reproductive freedom, which has been increased by the development of new contraceptive and reproductive technologies. By these technologies, we refer to the great variety of means developed to control human reproduction. They include means to prevent or end pregnancy, means to monitor and intervene in pregnancy (such as fetal monitoring and surgical deliveries), and means to facilitate conception and to control the quality of the embryos produced.[3] The availability of reproductive technologies makes possible options (such as preimplantation genetic diagnosis) previously unavailable.[4] It also gives another meaning to previous options by providing more efficient means to control reproduction. The reproductive options open to men and women in a society depend not only on the existence and availability of technological means to control reproduction, but also on the existence of a social and cultural environment favorable to them. Alternative accounts of reproductive freedom and reproductive rights can be constructed depending on the types of activities and choices related to reproduction one considers to be morally permissible.

In this chapter, we focus on women's right not to reproduce, understood in terms of the rights to voluntary access to contraception, sterilization, and abortion. We argue that the right not to reproduce is basically a right to a type of freedom. However, this right has also been defended in terms of other basic rights: in particular the right to health.[5]

The main way of grounding reproductive rights on the right to health is by pointing out that denying women the right to control their fertility may have a negative impact on their health. Tying reproductive rights to the right to health may have some political advantages in the short term. It is a way to defend women's rights to control their reproductive capacities in societies—such as Latin American societies—where citizens' freedoms are not always widely acknowledged.

This may help explain the approach adopted by the United Nations in recent documents on reproductive rights:

Reproductive health is a state of complete physical, mental, and social well-being, and not merely the absence of disease or infirmity, in all matters relating to the reproductive system and to its functions and processes. Reproductive health therefore implies that people are able to have a satisfying and safe sex life and that they have the capability to reproduce and the freedom to decide if, when, and how often to do so. Reproductive rights rest on the recognition of the basic right of all couples and individuals to decide freely and responsibly the number, spacing and timing of their children, and to have the information and means to do so, and the right to attain the highest standard of sexual and reproductive health. It also includes their right to make decisions concerning reproduction free of discrimination, coercion, and violence, as expressed in human rights documents. Sexual health enhances life and personal relations, and does not merely involve counseling and care related to reproduction and sexually transmitted diseases.[6]

This characterization of reproductive rights is connected to the notions of freedom and health. The document mentions the right to make free decisions concerning reproduction, and the right to attain the highest standard of sexual and reproductive health. Yet the document puts more emphasis on the idea of reproductive health, for reproductive rights are analyzed in the context of a discussion of the problem of securing women's access to health.

The notion of reproductive health is quite broad, and it is equated with well-being in all matters relating to the reproductive system. However, this equation is theoretically misleading. It is possible for people to be healthy and, at the same time, to experience dissatisfaction or lack of well-being, perhaps because of hardships suffered by loved ones. It is also possible for people to suffer some chronic health condition and still experience well-being, in part as a result of being able to deal with their situation. The possibility of being healthy and lacking well-being on the one hand, together with the possibility of experiencing well-being without being healthy, on the other hand, show that health and well-being are different notions.

Admittedly, reproductive rights are connected to individual health and well-being, since restrictions on reproductive rights may have a negative impact on individuals' well-being and health. But characterizing reproductive rights in terms of health and well-being is misleading because lack of well-being in these matters does not always imply lack of reproductive health. Nor does a lack of reproductive health always imply a violation of reproductive rights. For example, the lack of a satisfactory sexual life may be the result of a voluntary choice to join a religious community that requires a vow of chastity, or the result of not finding an adequate partner. In this sense, an enlarged concept of reproductive health is not theoretically precise even if it is politically advantageous. Politically, it may justify a variety of progressive social policies under the general banner of promoting reproductive health. It may help justify education against the discrimination of women. Furthermore, in many societies the relevant policies that guarantee reproductive rights are administered by the health care system. However, the notion of reproductive health is not useful to challenge existing prejudices and lack of respect for women's choices.

Yet this notion has had a prominent place in public debate on reproductive rights in Latin American countries, and it has inspired wide empirical research.[7] According to Lucila Scavone, feminist groups introduced the notion of reproductive health into public debate as part of an effort to publicize issues generally regarded as private, such as sexuality and reproduction.[8] The idea of reproductive health was thought to be a useful theoretical tool for the promotion of women's self-knowledge and for the appropriation of their bodies. Reproductive health was originally bound up with the struggle for women's reproductive autonomy, and it was used in an effort to question the idea that maternity is woman's biological destiny. Reproductive health was meant to involve free choice of maternity, which implies knowledge about one's body, control of contraception, and the possibility of accepting or rejecting one's pregnancy. Vindication of reproductive health in Latin America was tied to political struggles for a public policy that would secure access to free contraception and abortion services, though these struggles have had only moderate success. Now, due to the widespread use of the notion of reproductive health by international and governmental organizations in the 1990s, much of the initial radical implication of this notion has been lost.[9]

We believe that although reproductive rights receive further support from their contribution to health and well-being, they can be better justified in terms of personal autonomy. It is true that in many societies, including most Latin American societies, lack of reproductive freedom is connected to deficient health. Restricted access to contraception and to safe abortions associated with low income have a big impact on maternal mortality and morbidity. However, in cultures where respect for women's right to self-determination is not a primary concern, a focus on the right to health to defend women's access to contraception and abortion suggests that the only issue at stake in public discussions of social policies is women's health. This is mistaken. Women's reproductive freedom is, in fact, the central issue.

Stressing the connection between women's reproductive rights and their health and well-being is less problematic when a social and cultural environment that is respectful of women's autonomy is predominant. Such an environment is lacking in most Latin American societies, which have a history of violations of citizens' basic constitutional rights, and a tradition of authoritarian and paternalistic social structures (including the health care system).[10] In this context, holding that women should be granted reproductive rights in order to attain reproductive health might lead to imposing paternalistic restrictions on their reproductive freedom in the name of women's health. A woman's considered decision to get a surgical sterilization may be rejected in the name of her health, by claiming that sterilization interferes with the natural functioning of the body, or that in the future she may seriously regret this decision and this would affect her mental health. In fact, women should be free to make decisions about their reproduction, even if these decisions involve some risk to their health. Given that risks to health do not automatically justify paternalistic restrictions on reproductive freedom, appeals to the right to health cannot be the main way to defend reproductive rights.

Another difficulty with defending reproductive rights just in terms of well-being is that some restrictions on women's reproductive freedom might seem acceptable if such restrictions do not affect women's health significantly. For example, restrictions on women's access to contraceptives might seem justified in order to promote population growth, as long as such a measure poses no significant threat to women's health. We do not deny the relevance of the right to health in ethical and political arguments on reproductive rights. But we want to stress the importance of providing independent arguments based on the idea of respect for women's freedom or autonomy.

Instead of relying on a notion of reproductive health, it is more promising to defend the idea that women have a right to make decisions to control their fecundity in order to avoid undesired pregnancies. A wider acceptance of this liberal principle in Latin American societies would not only help increase the scope of women's control of their reproduction, but would also improve the quality of their lives. The fact that in our societies there has not been much acceptance of respect for women's autonomy does not show the inadequacy of this principle. Instead, it suggests a direction in which current values and attitudes might be challenged. The idea that women have a right to make reproductive decisions presupposes that these decisions are personal matters about which individuals should be free to make up their minds. Reproductive decisions are similar in relevant respects to decisions about whether to get married, or to profess a religion. They should not be imposed on anyone but should be freely adopted. Because of the relevant similarities between these types of decisions, a principle of tolerance about decisions to avoid procreation is just as appropriate as it is for other personal matters.

The analogy between reproductive decisions and other personal choices, such as whether to get married or to join a religion, may be more convincing for defending access to contraception and to voluntary sterilization than for defending access to abortion, because some people assign embryos and fetuses an independent moral status. It is beyond the scope of the present chapter to determine the moral status of embryos and fetuses. This is a controversial issue on which different positions exist, from granting them the highest value from the time of conception, to denying them all value, or granting them increasing value with their development according to different criteria. In the absence of consensus on this issue, we provide an argument in support of granting women the authority to make decisions about whether or not to carry their pregnancies to term. Our argument does not attempt to solve all the moral concerns raised by abortion, but proposes, instead, a political method for designing policy in a pluralist society. Restrictions on personal reproductive decisions that try to impose a conception of the good—such as a religious view that holds that human sexuality should be always "open" to the possibility of procreation—are morally unjustified. They fail to respect women's rights to decide about personal issues affecting their plans of life in a significant way.

The ability to control fertility is part of a woman's capability to develop a life plan according to her convictions, and it increases her chances of attaining a satisfying life. Decisions about whether, when, and with whom to have children are significant decisions, which have a considerable impact on women's and, to a lesser extent given current social arrangements, on men's plans of life. Having and raising children—like getting married—may be an important part of women's projects, but it may not be. It may be a source of self-fulfillment, but it also may become a heavy burden that causes significant harm, or interferes with other projects and interests at particular stages of their lives. For this reason, the right to make decisions about one's reproduction should not be understood merely as a right to non-interference. A right to non-interference can guarantee freedom of choice only to those people who already have enough knowledge and resources to allow them to make use of this freedom in a meaningful way. Having children should be a matter of decision, instead of being something that happens to women and their partners due to a lack of adequate information and resources. In other words, laws and public institutions should be designed to empower women to make effective decisions about their lives, including decisions as to how to control their fecundity. In this respect, access to adequate information and to contraception and abortion does not imply that they will be used. Nevertheless, it provides women, especially those with less income, with the means to make reproductive choices according to their values.

The principle of respect for women's autonomy in matters of reproductive choice also has implications for the way in which related medical services should be provided. Despite the existence of slightly different accounts of the principle of respect for autonomy in medical ethics, it is generally understood as the acknowledgement that patients have authority to make decisions about their health care, and that the physician's role is to provide adequate information and to offer recommendations about possible treatments and alternatives.[11] The adoption of a principle of respect for autonomy may promote women's control of their reproductive decisions in the health care setting. Nevertheless, the mechanical use of this principle in informed consent situations may also be criticized because, given the influence of patterns of power and authority, it does not always favor the exercise of women's autonomy. Feminist bioethicists have pointed out the need to develop a deeper understanding of the forces that interfere with patients' autonomy and to take into account the impact that social and political structures have on the lives and opportunities of individuals.[12] The approach that they propose has the advantage of reminding us of material restrictions, including limited economic resources and lack of educational opportunities, that limit the options available to patients. These sorts of considerations will be brought to bear in our discussion of the practice of contraception in Argentina.

Taking women's (and men's) rights to control their reproductive capacities seriously also has wider implications. It involves adopting a critical attitude toward population policies designed by governmental and international organizations. It leads to a careful assessment of their impact on the promotion, restriction, or violation of individual reproductive rights. According to research conducted in the late 1980s by the United Nations, 56 percent of U.N. members countries hold that they have a "population problem," defined as "a government's perception that its fertility is either too high or too low."[13] On many occasions, governments and international institutions have aimed at increasing or decreasing population growth. Accordingly, they have outlined policies without assessing their moral permissibility, without seriously searching for alternatives, and without considering the needs and interests of individual citizens. Rights violations, for example, involuntary or coercive sterilization of men and women and coercive or deceptive application of sub-dermal implants on women, have been reported during the implementation of antinatalist policies in the poorer populations of some countries. These antinatalist strategies are unfair because they fail to respect the rights of individuals to make informed decisions about reproduction. Furthermore, underlying these policies is the idea that collective goals override individual rights. But, as Amartya Sen points out, there are ways of reducing fertility rates while respecting individual rights and promoting the empowerment of women.[14] Pronatalist strategies that prohibit the use of contraception and criminalize abortion are similar to antinatalist strategies, in that they also fail to respect basic rights. In the next sections, we discuss the pronatalist policies that were set up in Argentina, based not only on population goals but also on a religious view of human sexuality and procreation. This discussion is meant to show the importance of a wider public recognition of the principle of respect for individual autonomy, not only at the national law and policy level, but also in the health care setting.

3. Public Policy in Argentina and its Background

Historically, Argentina has had a rather low fertility rate compared to other Latin American countries, and its public policy has had a pronatalist orientation.[15] An early decline in fertility rates occurred between 1880 and 1910. This suggests that women used the scarce knowledge available about contraception and abortion to maintain a small family size. Persistently low fertility rates together with the perception that the country needed to be more populated, led to different governmental policies aimed at increasing the size of the population. These policies included the encouragement of European immigration between 1880 and 1930. During the 1930s, bills were passed to protect pregnant women. In the 1940s, various subsidies and loans for housing stimulated marriage, and childbearing was encouraged by campaigns, laws to protect pregnant women, and severe repression of abortion. Salary increases and tax exemptions based on number of children were some of the measures taken in the following decades.

In the 1970s, with the rise of the "Ideology of National Security," population growth was declared a strategic national goal, supposedly leading to political, economic, and social development. These same ideas were the basis of the first coercive measures against the use of contraception during Isabel Perón's government. In 1974, her Minister of Welfare, José Lopez Rega, issued a decree that forbid all activities intended to control fertility, introduced strict regulations on the purchase of contraceptives, and ordered an educational campaign to teach the "risks" of contraceptive practices.[16] For the purchase of oral contraceptives, this decree required a prescription in triplicate, which is the usual practice for dangerous and narcotic drugs. Although this requirement was not strictly obeyed for long, the decree was effective in dismantling family planning services that had been offered by public hospitals to women with low income. These services had been established at the end of the 1960s and the beginning of the 1970s through the initiative of health care professionals and with the support of the private sector, especially the Argentine Association of Family Protection (AAPF). This association had promoted contraception since 1968, but after 1974 its activities were seriously restricted. In 1982, conditions became critical when a group that opposed fertility control on ideological grounds bombed the AAPF building.

With the military *coup d'état* of 1976, one of the bloodiest periods of Argentine history began. It resulted in the kidnapping or "disappearance" of roughly 30,000 men and women. The consequences of state terrorism on the lives of the Argentine people during that time and afterwards are many, and will not be analyzed here. The military government restricted the use of contraceptives. Once again the argument was that Argentina had a large territory with too many areas of scarce population, and that this put Argentina at geopolitical disadvantage.[17] The decree claimed that in view of the importance of the "country's growth and the fundamental reasons of national security, which require a better relationship between population and territory," fertility control had to be eliminated.[18]

This geopolitical argument, employed to justify restrictions on a woman's right to use contraception, has four weaknesses:

(1) The notion of an ideal population size is too vague. It involves many empirical uncertainties.

(2) An increase in population is mistakenly presented as a necessary condition for social growth, and as the way to secure national sovereignty. But a simple comparison of present societies demonstrates that no strict and clear correlation exists between the size of a population and its level of social development or national sovereignty.

(3) The mere statement of collective goals is presented as an adequate reason for restricting a woman's access to contraception. This argument assumes that collective goals always have priority over the freedom and well-being of individuals. In fact, the argument shows no concern for individual rights, and this is consistent with other serious violations of human rights that took place during the same period.

(4) Even if population growth is needed, other ways to attain such a goal exist. The alternatives should be carefully assessed, considering their impact on the promotion, restriction, or violation of individual reproductive rights. Alternatives such as the promotion of immigration do not interfere with reproductive freedom. Thus, they are not morally problematic and should be adopted if population growth were needed.

During Raúl Alfonsin's government, the first democratic government after the military dictatorship, the discussion of human rights in general also brought out the issue of reproductive rights. In 1986, a presidential decree ended the prohibition on offering contraceptive services in public hospitals. This decree did not appeal to population goals, and it asserted the right of citizens to make free and responsible decisions about their reproduction.[19] Yet the possibility of free and responsible reproductive decisions was still not guaranteed to all citizens, because the decree did not include any provision for public funding of contraceptive methods.

The United Nations Conference on Population and Development (Cairo, 1994) and the Fourth World Conference on Women (Beijing, 1995) gave new force to public debates on reproductive rights promoted by feminist and other progressive groups in our country. During these international conferences, the Argentine government aligned itself with the Vatican in matters such as the absolute value of human life from the moment of conception and a condemnation of abortion, and favored the inclusion of several reservations in the final documents. Yet, despite Argentina's official position at international meetings, several bills were afterwards presented to the national, provincial, and council legislatures to set up programs on "Reproductive Health." By January 1998, six provinces had passed bills favorable to women's reproductive rights, and other provinces and various town councils were discussing similar bills. In June 2000, the city of Buenos Aires passed one such bill.[20]

However, a bill for a national law on "Responsible Procreation" did not pass due to the pressure of Catholic groups. Legislators belonging to these groups lobbied to include several restrictions in the law, among them, the possibility of conscientious objection by physicians unwilling to provide contraceptive services, the requirement of parental consent or parental notification for teenagers seeking contraceptives, and the exclusion of intrauterine devices (IUDs) based on the claim that they are abortive. Ultimately, the bill did not pass. Its initial advocates held that a restrictive law would be worse than the *status quo*, because of its interference with existing programs and the development of new ones.[21]

From a democratic point of view, the position expressed by Catholic legislators in these public debates is inconsistent with the views and behavior of the vast majority of Catholics in Argentina. They use contraceptive methods other than the "natural" ones authorized by their church. Thus, it is the case that

> the procreative and contraceptive behavior of Roman Catholic individuals and couples ... seems to suggest that there is a growing separation between Papal doctrine and practical behavior of Catholics, who find ways of circumventing Papal authority and make decisions according to economic, cultural, or religious reasons.[22]

We believe that the difficulties in passing bills to secure access to fertility control programs in Argentina are due more to ideological opposition than to a lack of economic resources for providing adequate services. The influence of the Catholic doctrine is apparent in many aspects of the legislation related to reproductive issues.

Regarding voluntary sterilization, the law holds that even when a competent adult has consented, it is forbidden for physicians to perform interventions that provoke sterilization if there is not a clearly established therapeutic recommendation and if there are other ways to retain the reproductive organs.[23]

In order to allow sterilization, the law requires the written consent of the patient, a precise therapeutic reason for performing the surgery, and that all alternative procedures be exhausted. If the reason for performing sterilization is only to avoid procreation, the physician's intervention is not legally justified and may be considered harmful, leading to criminal punishment.[24] The only legal justification for sterilization is grounded on something like the doctrine of double effect. According to this doctrine, aiming at sterilization as a contraceptive method is wrong, but sterilization may be justified when it is performed for a "good" reason, such as to save the life of the patient by removing a cancerous uterus. Although the requirements of a "therapeutic reason" and "lack of alternatives" could be interpreted so that they authorize most requests for sterilization, the spirit of the law gives priority to the preservation of the "natural" function of the reproductive system, and discourages the recourse to sterilization as a means of fertility control. The law assumes that sterilization causes harm comparable to the amputation of a limb, which cannot be justified by the mere consent of the patient.

However, this comparison is misleading because the importance to a person of keeping his or her reproductive capacities intact depends on a desire or interest in becoming a parent in the future. Many considerations, among them the need to prevent abuses, favor setting legal limits on sterilization practices. But such legal restrictions cannot be grounded on a natural-law view of the proper use of a person's body. Such a view would misplace the boundary between permissible and unlawful procedures. Recent bills on reproductive health presented at the national, provincial, and local legislatures only considered reversible contraceptive measures. Although this narrowness was probably part of a strategy to attain consensus on the bill, it is consistent with a pattern of imposing "authorized views" of the proper goals of human sexuality that deny women's needs and rights to decide by themselves about these issues.

Leaving aside the debate on abortion, which we examine later, there have been other public debates that exhibit a similar pattern. Since 1990, there have been discussions on the regulation of human-assisted reproduction in Argentina, but no bills were passed. Settling on a proposal for a law on assisted reproduction has faced many obstacles, primarily because it is difficult to devise regulations that are acceptable both to the medical establishment and to the Catholic Church. Allowing the production of several embryos and their freezing seems to undermine the value assigned to embryos, and it could open the door to a less restrictive abortion law. Catholic legislators proposed legal protections for embryos, both inside and outside a woman's womb, and rejected their freezing as something against their "intrinsic dignity." On the other hand, physicians working on assisted reproduction have been lobbying for a somewhat more flexible law, in order to provide more chances for success in fertility treatments. Instead of challenging the excessive concern with embryos, physicians tend to talk about "pre-embryos" to avoid open discussions. Lee M. Silver notes, "the term 'pre-embryo' has been embraced wholeheartedly by in vitro fertilization practitioners for reasons that are political, not scientific."[25]

In Argentina, lack of consensus on the status of embryos has resulted in the fact that presently assisted reproduction takes place without the necessary legal regulation and adequate control.[26]

There have also been obstacles to the introduction of sexual education as a compulsory subject in primary and secondary schools in our country, and to the setting of public campaigns to prevent HIV infection. This is partly explained in terms of a lack of separation between church and state. But given the controversial nature of religious views on human sexuality, such views are not an acceptable ground for the law and public policy of a pluralist society, which should respect its citizens' rights to be informed and to decide about their sexual and reproductive behavior. We develop this general claim in the next section, contrasting the normative requirement of respect for women's capacities to make informed decisions with the practice of contraception in our country.

4. Contraception: Limits to Access and Informed Choice

Contraception can contribute to a woman's freedom and well-being, allowing her to enjoy sex without having to procreate, and to time her pregnancies according to her ability to parent a child alone, with a partner, or with the help of others. In order to contribute to women's ability to choose when to become pregnant, contraceptives should be easy to use, should have minimal side effects, and should never be imposed on a woman against her wishes. However, as some feminists have noted,

> the history of contraceptives is a tale not only of scientists developing increasingly safer and more effective means of birth control but also of women being used as non-consenting research subjects.[27]

Moreover, contraceptive research is not always oriented toward finding methods that increase individual reproductive autonomy. Instead, such research is sometimes aimed at the ultimate goal of controlling population growth in an efficient way. Given their potential for abuse, the development and testing of contraceptive vaccines and of substances like quinacrine for non-surgical feminine sterilization raise serious concerns.[28]

In Argentina, oral contraceptives and the IUD were introduced in the market by the end of the 1960s, but women's access to these "modern" methods has been restricted because of ideological and economic factors. As mentioned above, due to geopolitical "needs" and religious doctrine, women's use of contraceptive methods was first prohibited, and later discouraged by lack of public funding. According to the information available today, contraceptive use by women of fertile age in urban areas ranges from 73 percent to 53 percent.[29] Although surveys indicate that most women from different social backgrounds hold that they have the intention to use contraceptive methods to regulate their fertility, the percentage of women using them is higher in the middle and upper classes than in the lower classes. In areas where health care services provide information and free contraceptives, their use by women is much higher than in areas where those services are scarce. Statistics provide some evidence that contraceptive use is not the result of a choice made by all women, but it is severely restricted by social and economic factors. Together with the difficulties in obtaining free contraceptives, poorer women also have difficulties in getting adequate information, counseling, and medical check ups, and for these reasons their contraceptive behavior tends to be less effective.

In our country, the procedures that precede the voluntary choice to use contraceptives are often problematic when viewed from the perspective of informed consent. When considering the moral requirements of informed consent, as related to contraceptive choice, most bioethicists agree that health care providers should do the following:

(1) discuss the risks as well as the benefits of any recommended contraceptive with the patient and, if possible, the patient's partner;

(2) explain how the recommended contraceptive works, urging the patient to ask questions and taking the time to answer them;

(3) present alternatives to the recommended contraceptive;

(4) encourage the patient to report any problems she has with the recommended contraceptive, and to discontinue its use if she finds that it does not suit her specific needs; and

(5) ascertain that the patient has understood items 1 through 4, requesting her to repeat in her own words, if necessary, the gist of the communicated information.[30]

The requirement to provide written information in clear non-technical language could be added to this list, in order to improve the process of understanding and consent. Questions about timing and language, about what true consent is, and about how much information patients need for the process to be adequate must also be considered.[31] Even if these requirements impose too high a standard for current medical practice, they are useful to analyze how services work in a particular area.

Informed consent is not a common practice in our country—except in highly specialized areas such as assisted reproduction, genetic counseling, or organ transplantation, where it is understood mainly as a legal practice. Physicians are trained in a paternalistic tradition that denies that informed consent is part of good medical practice, or supposes that it is an unrealistic goal. Hence, most physicians do not have the training that would enable them to be sensitive enough to find out which contraceptive method is the most suitable for a woman or a couple, according to their particular characteristics and circumstances. Physicians' confidence in their knowledge about what is in the best interests of their patients imposes limitations on the variety of the methods they offer. Moreover, some physicians deliberately omit to mention some methods because of their religious views, as in the case of IUD and emergency contraception. Also, a shortage of alternative contraceptive methods available for free in public hospitals has an impact on the recommendations of physicians and on the final "choice" of patients.[32] Finally, the availability of products in the Argentine market is limited.

Contraceptive methods currently available in the Argentine market include a variety of oral contraceptives, different injectables, intrauterine devices, and barrier methods such as male condoms, diaphragms, and spermicidal products. Female condoms are imported, but they are expensive and not marketable, and they are difficult to obtain. Sub-dermal implants such as Norplant were never introduced in Argentina, but research conducted in other developing countries suggests that they have significant side effects and present serious risks to health.[33] As far as emergency contraception goes, copper IUDs and some oral contraceptives can be used for this purpose, and a specialized product is also available. Despite its availability in the market, most women do not know about the possibility of using emergency contraception, nor is it widely recommended by physicians when it is necessary.[34] Although not a contraceptive, the sale of the pill RU 486 is prohibited in Argentina, as it is in other countries with a restrictive legislation on abortion.

Because of the nature of the legislation on sterilization, access to this practice both for men and women tends to be difficult. The Argentine situation is rather peculiar in this respect, since in nine other Latin American countries feminine sterilization is the most common contraceptive method used by women with a permanent partner.[35]

It is true that there should be strict regulations on the practice of male and female sterilization. Such regulations are needed to prevent abuses and to secure adequate mechanisms of informed consent. Nonetheless, sterilization should not be legally precluded as a contraceptive option. Although some physicians perform sterilization, many physicians are afraid of lawsuits and refuse to perform them. Other physicians request a judicial authorization, which may or may not be granted depending on the opinion and values of the judge assigned to decide the case. Thus, the legislation on sterilization and the legal procedures for its authorization transfer the ability to make decisions from individual women to medical and legal experts.

5. Abortion: Legal Restrictions and Moral Concerns

In Latin America, excepting Cuba and Puerto Rico, legislation on abortion is highly restrictive. In Argentina, the law forbids abortion and prescribes criminal punishments for people who perform abortions and for women who bring about their abortion or consent to have one. The Argentine law states that abortion is not punishable in only two cases:

(1) if it is done to avoid a danger to the life and health of the mother, and this danger cannot be avoided in any other way;

(2) if the pregnancy was caused by rape or indecent assault of a mentally disabled or insane woman.[36]

According to the law, physicians are allowed to perform an abortion when this is the only way to save the life of a woman or to avoid a danger to her health. The wording of the second legal exception is ambiguous, and there have been discussions about the scope of the first "or." On one interpretation, all abortions in the case of rape would be legally allowed, as would be abortions for incompetent women not considered able to give valid consent to sexual relations. On the other interpretation, only abortions of mentally disabled or insane women would be allowed, whether pregnancy was the result of rape or of a non-coerced sexual activity.

Despite the existence of clause (2) above, in practice, women can only get a legal abortion when the pregnancy threatens their lives. This situation can be explained by the influence of the Catholic doctrine, which justifies an abortion only if it is performed to save the life of the pregnant woman. This exception is generally defended by means of the doctrine of double effect. Following this doctrine, medical procedures aimed at saving the life of a woman are allowed, even though they may cause the death of the fetus as an "unintended" and inevitable effect. The official Catholic doctrine does not consider that a woman's health or the psychological suffering caused by rape and subsequent pregnancy are significant enough to justify an abortion. Because of these views, requests for legal authorization of abortions in the case of incompetent women, or of pregnancies caused by rape, tend to be denied by judges. An illegal abortion becomes the only actual recourse for women seeking to terminate their pregnancies, even in those cases that are authorized by law.

Despite restrictive laws and the difficulties for obtaining legal authorization for abortions, an estimated 350,000-500,000 illegal abortions are performed each year in our country—which yields a ratio of about one abortion every two births. These numbers suggest some sort of social acceptance of abortion, confirmed by the fact that almost no attempts to enforce the law have been made. The present legal restrictions on abortion stand in opposition to the intuitions of many people in Argentina about the moral permissibility of this practice. Even though not everybody agrees with a law that would allow unrestricted access to abortion, many people consider abortion to be permissible under a variety of circumstances, for example, in cases of rape, when the mother has physical or mental health problems, and when fetal anomalies are found. In other words, there is a wide consensus that the law should allow for several exceptions. But, on the other hand, it is true that bills in favor of more permissive laws have failed to pass.

The practice of prenatal diagnosis is a good example of the tension between the content of the law and the moral intuitions of a significant number of people in our country. The law does not allow abortion when a serious fetal condition is discovered through prenatal diagnosis, but many couples seek to obtain this information in order to decide whether to continue a pregnancy. According to the *Guidelines on Ethical Issues in Medical Genetics and the Provision of Genetic Services*,

> professionals who offer prenatal diagnosis have an ethical obligation to provide referrals for safe, affordable abortions, preferably within the nation, if the woman desires it after unfavorable findings.[37]

In Argentina, doctors who offer prenatal diagnosis tend to overlook this problem, and most of them are reluctant to make suggestions about how to obtain a safe and affordable abortion. Some doctors minimize the relationship between prenatal diagnosis and abortion, holding that prenatal diagnosis actually contributes to childbirth. They claim that people who would not dare to have children because of their age or some genetic condition in their family decide to have them when they are aided by this service.[38]

The restrictive nature of the present law does not seem to have a deterrent effect on the performance of abortions, but it affects the conditions under which abortions are performed. While women who are better off have access to relatively safe and expensive illegal abortions, poorer women get abortions in unsafe and debasing conditions. As a consequence, abortion is the most common cause of maternal death in our country. The high rate of mortality and illness associated with unsafe abortion is a common problem not only in Argentina but also in many other developing countries, where abortions are performed in extremely unsafe conditions. As Nils Daulaire points out, "whatever one's moral views on abortion, this is a public health crisis that health professionals must address."[39]

One way of dealing with these public health issues in our country consists in offering more and better programs for fertility control, including educational campaigns for both sexes and the free provision of a variety of contraceptive methods. Such measures could significantly reduce the number of undesired pregnancies, and, as a consequence, the number of unsafe abortions. However, these measures will not put an end to undesired pregnancies or to abortions. Nor will they put an end to the need for discussion and revision of present laws.

Given that restrictive laws do not appear to reduce the number of abortions but lead to a high level of maternal mortality and morbidity, a consequentialist argument could be made in favor of legalizing abortion. It could be argued that restrictive laws do not prevent abortions but lead to the death, illness, and suffering of women. So, the argument continues, at least some of these evils could be prevented by a change in the laws. However, this argument may not convince those who are opposed to abortion on the grounds that human life has absolute value from the moment of conception. This attitude—that could be called "embryo worship"—tends to be adopted only by some religious people who think that permissive laws on abortion do not show sufficient respect for human life. However, even though embryos and fetuses may have some moral value, a view that grants such priority to embryos and fetuses and neglects the consequences of illegal abortion seriously fails to respect human life: the life of women.[40]

Although some religious people hold that embryos and fetuses have absolute value from the moment of conception, this position has problematic implications. Despite an appeal to scientific knowledge of the reproductive process in recent arguments used by the Catholic Church, this view involves an arbitrary interpretation of a biological process and a decision to assign the highest value to embryos from the moment of conception. Moreover, this view differs from past positions adopted by the Catholic Church, and is not shared by a minority of contemporary Catholic theologians and groups, for example, Catholics for the Right to Choose.[41] The official Catholic view also has the counterintuitive implication that the use of contraceptives that prevent implantation such as IUD is equivalent to an abortion. Against a view that attaches such significance to conception, and taking into account the possibility of cloning, Lee Silver points out "if a human life can begin in the absence of conception, then it is scientifically invalid to say that conception must mark the beginning of each new human life."[42]

In fact, when carefully examined, people's moral intuitions about the value of embryos and fetuses differ in significant respects. Many people assign embryos different values during their development, giving almost no value to early embryos and a high value to late fetuses. Others assume that embryos or fetuses with serious anomalies do not have the same value as healthier embryos or fetuses. Moreover, most people agree that when the life or health of a pregnant woman is at risk, her interests should take priority. Given that women are moral persons and that the status of embryos and fetuses is controversial, an argument could be made in favor of giving pregnant women the authority to decide whether to carry their pregnancy to term. Although we do not deny that some decisions to get an abortion may be mistaken or wrong, we think that the pregnant woman is in the best position to decide how much value she assigns to the (early) fetus she is carrying. Alison Jaggar has provided an argument of this sort. She holds that the consensus that abortion is permissible on some occasions, together with the lack of consensus about which occasions those are, provides a political justification for leaving the decision to individual women.[43] In our view, the law should leave the decision about whether to carry a pregnancy to term to the pregnant woman's judgment, because concern for beings whose status is controversial cannot justify the coercion of actual persons.

6. Concluding Remarks

The first two sections of this chapter developed an argument in defense of a woman's right to make decisions to control her reproductive capacities. This argument relied on the idea of respect for individual autonomy. The ability to control fertility was presented as an significant aspect of a woman's capability to develop a life plan according to her convictions, which increases her chances of attaining a satisfying life. Although respect for women's rights to make reproductive decisions and women's health and well-being are connected, appeals to the notions of health and well-being have not been theoretically useful. This is because the notion of health most commonly employed is too wide and equates it with well-being in all matters related to reproduction. Moreover, even if the notion of health employed is not too wide, it may open the door to paternalistic restrictions on reproductive rights based on the goal of protecting women's health. Given the authoritarian and paternalistic tradition prevalent in Latin American societies, these notions may provide an effective strategy for political debate in the short run, but they are not useful to challenge existing prejudices and lack of respect for women's choices. For this reason, we have emphasized the need to develop a more tolerant culture that accepts that reproductive decisions are personal issues on which women should be free to make up their minds. Rather than identifying respect for personal freedom or autonomy with non-interference, laws and public institutions should be designed to empower women to make effective decisions about their lives, and this includes making decisions about how to control their fecundity.

In the second half of the chapter, recent laws and public policy in Argentina were discussed in order to determine the extent to which they guarantee women's reproductive rights, translated into the more specific rights to access to contraception and abortion. The most influential views opposed to the recognition of these rights were identified. These opposing views stem from a perceived geopolitical need to increase the size of the population, and from religious views about the proper exercise of human sexuality and the absolute value of embryos and fetuses. These views were criticized from a liberal perspective that emphasizes individual rights and tolerance for different life plans and conceptions of the good. Turning to the present practice of contraception, restrictions on women's access to adequate methods and other limitations on informed choice were discussed, stressing the importance of the ideas of respect for autonomy and informed consent for the improvement of present services. Finally, the impact of the restrictive law on abortion was discussed in connection with the ambivalent attitudes and lack of consensus in our society toward this issue. Given a framework of lack of consensus, an argument in favor of granting women the authority to decide to terminate their pregnancies was offered.

The above discussion indicates the direction in which the law and public policy must change if it is to guarantee women's reproductive rights in our society. However, the policies that we have been defending—legalizing abortion and securing access to safe contraceptive methods—are only two ways of promoting women's reproductive rights in our society. Wider social change is required as well. The notion of respect for autonomy is the most promising way to defend reproductive rights, although they receive additional support from other arguments. Respect for autonomy should not be understood as mere non-interference, but rather in more positive terms. Reducing respect for autonomy to mere non-interference would exempt the state from the responsibility to foster the material and cultural conditions that are necessary for developing and exercising the capability for individual decision-making. As the discussion of the situation in Argentina shows, the full exercise of autonomy in reproductive choices is inseparable from a favorable set of material and cultural conditions. We have explored one of these conditions: the existence of a pluralist social environment that acknowledges women's individual right to make personal decisions.[44]

NOTES

1. John A. Robertson, "Noncoital Reproduction and Procreative Liberty," *The Ethics of Reproductive Technology,* ed. Kenneth D. Alpern (New York, Oxford: Oxford University Press, 1992), p. 249.

2. Dan W. Brock, "Reproductive Freedom: Its Nature, Bases, and Limits," *Healthcare Ethics: Critical Issues for Health Professionals,* eds. John Monagle and David Thomasma (Rockville, Md: Aspen, 1994), pp. 43-46.

3. Susan Sherwin, *No Longer Patient: Feminist Ethics and Health Care* (Philadelphia: Temple University Press, 1992), p. 117.

4. Mary Briody Mahowald, *Genes, Women, Equality* (Oxford: Oxford University Press, 2000), pp. 209-224.

5. Rebecca J. Cook, "International Human Rights and Women's Reproductive Health," *Women's Rights, Human Rights*, eds. Julie Peters and Andrea Wolper (New York, London: Routledge, 1995), pp. 256-275.

6. United Nations, *Platform for Action: Fourth World Conference on Women*, Beijing, China (1995), art. 96.

7. See Lucila Scavone, ed., *Género y salud reproductiva en América Latina* (Cartago: Libro Universitario Regional, 1999); Teresa Durand, ed., *Avances en la investigación social en salud reproductiva y sexualidad* (Buenos Aires: AEPA, CEDES, CENEP, 1998); Susana Checa and Martha Rosemberg, *Aborto hospitalizado: un problema de salud pública, una cuestión de derechos reproductivos* (Buenos Aires: El Cielo por Asalto, 1996).

8. See Lucila Scavone, "Anticoncepción, aborto y tecnologías reproductivas: entre la salud, la ética y los derechos," *Género y salud reproductiva en América Latina*, ed. Scavone, pp. 24-36.

9. See Teresa Durand and María Alicia Gutierrez, "Tras las huellas de un porvenir incierto: del aborto a los derechos sexuales y reproductivos," *Avances*, ed. Durand, pp. 296-298.

10. See Arleen L. F. Salles, "Autonomy and Culture: The Case of Latin America," in this volume.

11. María Victoria Costa, "El concepto de autonomía en la ética médica: problemas de fundamentación y aplicación," *Perspectivas bioéticas en las Américas*, 1:2 (1996), pp. 89-116.

12. See Anne Donchin, "Understanding Autonomy Relationally: Toward a Reconfiguration of Bioethical Principles," *Journal of Medicine and Philosophy*, 23:4 (1998); and Susan Sherwin, "A Relational Approach to Autonomy in Health Care," *The Politics of Women's Health: Exploring Agency and Autonomy*, eds. Susan Sherwin et al. (Philadelphia: Temple University Press, 1998), pp. 19-47. Also Salles, this volume.

13. Donald Warwick, "Is There a Population Problem?", *Encyclopedia of Bioethics*, ed. Warren Reich (New York, London: Macmillan, 1995), p. 1959.

14. Amartya Sen, "Fertility and Coercion," *The University of Chicago Law Review*, 63 (1996), pp. 1035-1061.

15. Cristina Zurutuza, "El derecho como garantía de los derechos sexuales y reproductivos: ¿utopía o estrategia?", *Mujeres sanas, ciudadanas libres*, eds. Mabel Bianco, Teresa Durand, et al. (Buenos Aires: FEIM, Foro por los Derechos Reproductivos, CLADEM, FNUAP, 1998), pp. 52-53.

16. Argentina, Decree 659/1974.

17. Argentina, Decree 3938/1977.

18. Quoted in Mónica Gogna and Silvina Ramos, "El acceso a la anticoncepción: Una cuestión de derechos humanos y de salud pública," *Perspectivas bioéticas en las Américas*, 1:2 (1996), p. 135 (our translation).

19. Argentina, Decree 2274/1987.

20. Buenos Aires (City), Law 418/2000.

21. Zurutuza, "El derecho como garantía," pp. 54-62.

22. Hans Martin Sass, "Responsibilities in Human Reproduction and Population Policy," *The Contraceptive Ethos*, eds. Stuart Spicker, William Bondenson, and Tristam Engelhardt (Dordrecht: Reidel, 1987), p. 152.

23. Law 17.132 art. 20 inc. 18 (our translation).

24. Delia Iñigo de Quidiello, "Esterilización de personas incapaces por causa de enfermedad o deficiencia mental. Supuestos y consentimiento válido," *El Derecho* (1990), p. 839.

25. Lee M. Silver, *Remaking Eden: Cloning and Beyond in a Brave New World* (New York: Avon Books, 1997), p. 39.

26. Susana E. Sommer, "Nuevas formas de procreación," *Género y salud reproductiva en América Latina*, pp. 326-328.

27. Rosemarie Tong, *Feminist Approaches to Bioethics* (Boulder, Col.: Westview Press, 1997), p. 111.

28. See Judith Richter, *Vaccination against Pregnancy: Miracle or Menace?* (Melbourne: Spinifex, 1996). See also Aurelio Molina, "Anticoncepción, salud reproductiva y ética," *Género y salud reproductiva en América Latina*, p. 113.

29. Gogna and Ramos, "El acceso a la anticoncepción," pp. 136-140.

30. Robert Hatcher *et al.*, *Contraceptive Technology: 1986-1987* (New York: Irvington Publishers, 1986), p. 232, quoted in Tong, *Feminist Approaches to Bioethics*, pp. 104-105.

31. Helen Bequaert Holmes, "Can Clinical Research Be Both Ethical and Scientific?" *Feminist Perspectives in Medical Ethics*, eds. Helen Bequaert Holmes and Laura Purdy (Bloomington, Ind.: Indiana University Press, 1992), p. 163.

32. Elsa López and Liliana Findling, "La diversidad de discursos y prácticas médicas en la salud reproductiva: ¿qué se dice, a quién y cómo?", *Avances*, ed. Durand, pp. 79-103.

33. Ana Regina Gomes dos Reis, "Norplant in Brazil: Implantation Strategy in the Guise of Scientific Research," *Issues in Reproductive and Genetic Engineering*, 3:2 (1990), pp. 111-118.

34. Zulema Palma, "La anticoncepción de emergencia, un aporte para los derechos sexuales y reproductivos de las mujeres," *Avances*, ed. Durand, pp. 331-342.

35. Molina, "Anticoncepción, salud reproductiva y ética," p. 89.

36. Criminal Code art. 86, inc. 1 and 2 (our translation).

37. World Health Organization: Hereditary Disease Program, *Guidelines on Ethical Issues in Medical Genetics and the Provision of Genetic Services* (Geneva: WHO, 1995), p. 53.

38. Susana E. Sommer, *Genética, clonación y bioética* (Buenos Aires: Biblos, 1998), pp. 100-101.

39. Nils M. Daulaire, "Global Health Population Growth and United States Policy," *Great Issues for Medicine in the Twenty-First Century, Annals of the New York Academy of Sciences*, 882 (1999), p. 195.

40. See Ronald Dworkin, *Life's Dominion* (New York: Knopf, 1993), ch. 2.

41. See Margarita M. Valdés "Abortion and Contraception in Mexico: The Attitudes and the Arguments of the Catholic Church," this volume.

42. Silver, *Remaking Eden*, p. 40.

43. Alison M. Jaggar, "Regendering the U.S. Abortion Debate," *Journal of Social Philosophy*, 28:1 (1997), pp. 127-140.
44. The authors thank María Julia Bertomeu, Joshua Gert, and Arleen L. F. Salles for their comments, and Zulema Palma for her information.

Four

HASTENING DEATH

Martín Diego Farrell

Translated from Spanish by Arleen L.F. Salles

1. Introduction

That people might want to hasten their own death might be initially hard to believe. Life is usually presumed to have a positive value. Accordingly, death is considered to be a misfortune, and an action that would end one's life would be wrong. However, an examination of some cases of suicide shows that under some conditions being alive might not be regarded as good.

There are many reasons why life might not be valuable. For example, life might seem meaningless to people afflicted with a terminal illness, who deteriorate rapidly and whose pain cannot be adequately controlled. By virtue of their medical condition, some human beings may be better off dead.

People approach questions about euthanasia in different ways. In this chapter, questions concerning the permissibility of euthanasia are discussed from different viewpoints. My main purpose is to present a few considerations to show that people call for the prohibition of euthanasia for religious reasons. I then argue that since this is so, euthanasia should be decriminalized.

2. Characterization of Euthanasia

I mean by euthanasia the act of painlessly ending a person's life in his or her best interest when he or she has so requested. But this definition raises issues that need to be clarified. First, to require the person's request might be too extreme. A patient may make a voluntary decision about death by requesting help in dying so that death be less painful, or by giving informed consent to a particular course of non-treatment.

It might be objected that we could never be certain that patients who are acutely suffering or terminally ill are mentally competent to make an informed decision. If these patients were unable to make decisions, euthanasia in those cases would not be voluntary. However, I believe that a patient's competence to make this kind of decision must be presumed. The burden of proof lies with those who deny that patients can competently consent to die. Those who hold that a normal adult patient is unable to consent to, or request to die, must show that this is so. Thus, even if it could be argued that patients under great emotional distress or in severe pain are less than competent to make decisions, this is something that has to be proven; it should not be taken for granted.

In fact, consent seems to be a weaker condition, and I believe that it can be a sufficient condition in most cases. In any case, I want to eliminate "involuntary euthanasia" from consideration because this practice does not have much in common with euthanasia, as I understand it. The moral principles supporting voluntary euthanasia are quite inadequate to justify involuntary euthanasia. The two practices are so different that they might as well have a different name.

Since I believe that the patient's consent is sufficient for euthanasia, my definition must be broadened: by euthanasia I mean the act of painlessly ending a person's life in that person's best interests when the person has requested or, at least, consented to the act.

The demand that the act of ending the other person's life be painless must be reasonably qualified: this depends on different situations. A terminally ill cancer patient who requests a lethal dose of morphine is still euthanized even if the shot itself is painful. But ending the patient's life must be done as painlessly as possible.

Many problems remain with a broader definition of euthanasia: one has to do with incompetent patients unable to request, or even consent to ending their own life. I focus on this elsewhere.[1] Instead, I want to focus on another element in the definition: that the act is beneficial to the patient.

In a seminal article, Philippa Foot has argued that, when we discuss euthanasia, we are talking about a death that is not an evil but a good for the person who dies.[2] One of the reasons why we are reluctant to refer to Hitler's programs as "euthanasia" is because we suspect that the deaths were not for the sake of those who were dying but for the sake of an allegedly superior race.

However, some cases are more complicated. These are the cases in which the death is allegedly a good for the person who dies but the action is performed for some other reason. An example of a clear case involves withholding necessary medical care from children with Down's syndrome not because of the interests of the infant but because of the psychological, social, and economic costs of keeping the infant alive. However, in other cases providing euthanasia to severely impaired infants could be justified insofar as death would be in their best interests. But again, I do not focus on these cases here for they are cases of involuntary euthanasia.

How are the questions raised by euthanasia approached? In what follows I identify four points of view.

3. The Moral Point of View

In order for a behavior to be judged moral or immoral, reasons justifying such judgment must be provided. A good moral theory is one that presents good reasons to justify its judgments. Some theories invoke moral rights. Others appeal to consequences. But all moral theories must provide reasons for the moral principles that they advocate. This is the difference between moral theories and religion.

4. The Religious Point of View

Religion tells us what to do and not to do, yet it does not provide reasons for its commandments. People are supposed to obey because God said so, or because God's name is invoked. Religious people do not follow their religion's precepts because they find them reasonable (even though they might), but because they have faith.

Since morality requires reasons and religion does not, the fact that so many times religion is identified with morality is surprising. Nevertheless, it is possible to see why this might happen: some moral and religious principles have the same content. Thus, if we focus solely on a particular rule or principle we cannot determine whether it is moral or religious. Let us consider the principle "You shall not kill" that grounds opposition to euthanasia. Is this a moral or a religious principle? The answer depends on how we answer the question: Why shouldn't I kill? If the answer is "Because God has so ordered" then the principle is religious. If instead the answer appeals to reasons, such as the importance of "preventing harm to others" or of "promoting a peaceful community" then it is based on a moral principle.

The distinction between moral and religious principles is crucial. Ideally the law should be able to pass successfully the test of morality. However, the law does not need to pass the test of religion. This is precisely what separates a democracy from a theocracy. And this leads us to the legal point of view.

5. The Legal Point of View

Law motivates actions and omissions by punishing opposing behaviors. Many behaviors motivated by the law agree with those that morality advocates, for example, not killing. However, some of the conducts motivated by the law are not correlative to moral or religious principles, for example, driving on the right.

But even when the law is interested in fostering moral behavior by discouraging immoral behaviors, it would be unreasonable to expect that all immoral behaviors become a crime under the law. A society may think that benefits martyrs, unless one has specific beliefs about the after-life. But then, one would not be talking in moral terms but in religious terms. Perfectionism does not focus on the interests of those whose autonomy is restricted or violated. It imposes an ideal of human thriving judged to be good whether or not it benefits the person. It is in this sense that perfectionism is stronger than paternalism, and that it requires different arguments. It is clear that paternalism does not imply perfectionism. But perfectionism seems to imply paternalism in the sense that any restriction of personal autonomy justified on perfectionist grounds would be *a fortiori* justified on paternalistic grounds. By this I mean the following: if restricting the autonomy of a person is justified when the person is not benefited, restricting a person's autonomy would seem to be even more justified if such restriction benefits the person. However, I prefer not to dwell on this implication, for often perfectionism forbids interventions that can be justified on paternalistic grounds. Thus, the claim that perfectionism is stronger than paternalism is intended to underline that, generally, perfectionism is more at odds with respect for autonomy than paternalism.

Those who defend perfectionism ground their opposition to euthanasia on a particular view about the good life. But this is not adequate to ground opposition to voluntary euthanasia, for it is possible to live a good life and still request for that life to be over. Those who appeal to this kind of argument seem to be moving into the domain of moral ideals. Thus, they are moral perfectionists. Moral perfectionism is the view that people have to live a particular kind of life, a life of moral excellence, regardless of whether such a life is actually beneficial to them.

In order to be convincing, perfectionism needs to support the view that its strict moral principles can be objectively demanded. However, perfectionism cannot do this because no proof exists that there are objective values. But there is something else. It seems odd that anybody would defend the existence of moral principles requiring, for example, martyrdom for its own sake and not to promote a particular goal.

The practice of euthanasia is not illegal because people believe that an important scientific discovery will pull dying patients through. It is illegal for another reason. Terminally ill and suffering patients are forced to live, and others expect them to do just that: remain alive. But, what is the moral view that justifies this demand on them? I believe that if opponents of euthanasia appeal to perfectionism, the kind of perfectionism they are appealing to is religious and not moral. But if this is true, then they are vulnerable to the objections mentioned in section 4.

I respect religious principles. In fact, I have religious principles. But I do not believe that public policy on euthanasia and assisted suicide in a pluralist society should be based upon narrow religious principles. Religious principles are necessarily metaphysical, not amenable to proof, dogmatic, authoritarian, and many times immune to critical reasoning. Many Western philosophers have considered that religious feelings cannot be grounded on rational arguments. Others believe that all traditional arguments for religious beliefs are defective or inconclusive. However, laws must be respected by all, believers and non-believers. Laws must be rationally supported and argued for. They do not rest on dogma.

8. Conclusion

I propose that we make a distinction between ethics and religion, and that we allow ethics but not religion to critically examine the law. Furthermore, I suggest that we limit our moral evaluation to those acts that harm others without consent, thus emphasizing the importance of respecting the autonomy of people. This attitude will lead to the decriminalization of voluntary euthanasia and, in turn, will require that we confront the sociological standpoint and develop legal mechanisms to prevent excesses and avoid the possibility of acts that harm others under the guise of euthanasia.

NOTES

1. Martín Diego Farrell, *La ética del aborto y la eutanasia* (Buenos Aires: Abeledo Perrot, 1993).
2. Philippa Foot, "Euthanasia," *Virtues and Vices* (Berkeley: University of California Press, 1978).
3. John Stuart Mill, *On Liberty* (Indianapolis, Ind.: Hackett Publishing Company, 1978).

PART II

JUSTICE AND THE RIGHT TO HEALTH CARE

Five

SOME PHILOSOPHICAL CONSIDERATIONS ON MEXICO'S EDUCATION, HEALTH, AND FOOD PROGRAM

Paulette Dieterlen

Translated from Spanish by Ana Bazdresch and Maurizio Tazzer

1. Introduction

One of the major bioethical issues is the allocation of health care resources. Since money and resources are scarce, it is not possible to satisfy everybody's health needs and preferences. It is necessary to assign priorities and justify them. In this chapter, I focus on the philosophical discussion relevant to a national program in Mexico whose objectives are, among others, to provide health services.

A discussion of this topic is significant in Mexico for two reasons. First, there has not been a public debate about the distribution of goods and medical services in the country. Second, since Mexico has a high poverty rate, many people cannot acquire the necessary goods and health services. At present, an estimated forty million Mexicans live in poverty; of these, twenty-six million are considered extremely poor. Thus, government programs designed to fight extreme poverty deserve attention. Furthermore, article four of the Mexican Constitution guarantees the right to health care goods and services for all citizens.

In general, the health care delivery system in Mexico is constituted by several elements, each covering a different portion of the population. The Instituto Mexicano del Seguro Social (Mexican Institute of Social Security) concentrates on the working sector. The Secretaría de Salud (Ministry of Health) provides medical services to the uninsured. The Instituto de Seguridad Social al Servicio de los Trabajadores (Social Security Institute Serving State Employees) concentrates on citizens who work for the state. Finally, IMSS-Solidaridad (Mexican Institute of Social Security-Solidarity) is a public service institution funded with federal resources and managed by the Mexican Institute of Social Security for the urban and rural population not covered by the aforementioned programs. Originally, potential beneficiaries were meant to help build hospitals and provide some basic medical services. According to official information, in 1997 sixty-five million Mexicans had access to health services.[1]

2. Education, Health, and Food Program: Main Characteristics

The Education, Health, and Food Program (PROGRESA) was decreed by the President in August 1997. Its main objective is to eliminate extreme poverty in rural regions of the country. The program has the following characteristics:

(1) Since extreme poverty is mostly found in rural environments, the program focuses on rural communities, defined as settlements with less than 2,500 inhabitants. The program is implemented by a Coordination (CONPROGRESA) that puts together the activities of the Ministry of Public Education, the Ministry of Health and Social Development, and IMSS-Solidaridad. The cooperation of several public institutions is crucial in fighting poverty in an integral way.

(2) PROGRESA uses targeting methods in two ways:

First, polls are carried out throughout the Mexican Republic to identify extremely poor households. Several poverty indicators exist. One is by determining whether a person has enough income to acquire the Canasta Alimentaria Normativa (Basic Food Basket) established by the Bank of Mexico. Other poverty indicators are the percentage of illiteracy in people over age fourteen; the percentage of houses without running water or sewage; the percentage of houses with no electric power; the average number of people living in one room; percentage of houses with dirt floors; percentage of the population of each sex and age group employed within the primary sector; and above all, availability of health care services.

Second, the program targets women in charge. This aspect is a novelty, for it recognizes that within marginal groups there are subgroups and, among them, women. The relationship between the Coordination and communities is held by a female "community promoter" elected by members of each community.

(3) PROGRESA requires communities to provide basic education and health services. Communities must have a classroom for elementary school, a classroom for secondary school, a dispensary, and a small hospital or mobile clinic.

(4) PROGRESA demands the shared responsibility of beneficiaries. They must make a commitment to send their children to school, attend preventive medicine talks, see doctors regularly, and spend the money they receive on the improvement of their family's living conditions.

(5) PROGRESA has long and short-term objectives. Its first long-term objective is to help members of qualified families to overcome their condition

of extreme poverty. The second is to promote education and health so as to enable beneficiaries to improve their marginal situation. Monetary support is given for three years with the possibility of three-year renewal. At this time, two million Mexican families are PROGRESA beneficiaries.

(6) In order to co-ordinate actions in matters of education, health, and food, PROGRESA provides educational and financial support, and health care services. The educational support is designed to help children and young adults complete their basic education. The program encourages school enrollment, regular attendance, and promotes parental involvement to help children take advantage of their education. Health care services are provided to all members of the family, and they are also intended to promote a new attitude toward health services, generating a more preventive approach. Financial support is to be used for a more adequate supply of foods and nutrients. Special aid is given in cases of malnutrition in extremely poor families.

3. PROGRESA: The Philosophical Issues

The relationship between a philosophical analysis and a government program of distributive justice can be stated as a subject of "practical ethics," which is concerned with showing that philosophical theory can be applied in practice. The relationship between theory and practice is twofold. The practical application of social policies such as PROGRESA allows us to examine the underlying philosophical concepts. Philosophical reflection provides tools to specify the use of distributive concepts and principles, and to clarify the arguments used when distributive policies are chosen.

PROGRESA is part of what Jon Elster calls global justice. Elster makes a distinction between local and global justice. Global distributive policies are centrally designed at a national government level; they try to compensate people for the adverse fortunes that result from the possession of "arbitrary moral properties," and always adopt the form of money transfers. In contrast, principles of local justice are designed by relatively autonomous institutions that, even if following lines suggested by a central government, have some freedom to design and implement the scheme that works best for them. They do not compensate each other, and if they do it is only partially. For example, a health care institution can compensate bad fortune exclusively in terms of curing sicknesses. Finally, local justice is only concerned with the assignation of benefits and burdens that are not expressed in money.[2] As a national program that gives funding to extremely poor household, PROGRESA finds itself in the sphere of global justice.

Recently Max Charlesworth stated,

every health system...is faced with the need to decide (either informally or formally) what proportion of the community's total resources should be spent on health care; how resources are to be apportioned; which human diseases and disabilities and which forms of treatment are to be given priority; which members of the community are to be given special consideration in respect of their health needs; and which forms of treatment are the most cost-effective.[3]

Many of these sensitive issues surround PROGRESA. In this section, I discuss them.

A. Targeting

PROGRESA is a program designed to benefit the poorest families. According to the *Lineamientos Generales para la Operación del Programa de Educación, Salud y Alimentación* (General Operative Guidelines for the Program of Education, Health, and Food),

Targeting attempts not only to achieve efficiency but also to translate it into a principle of fairness. Because resources, abundant as they might be, will always necessarily be scarce in fighting poverty, it is indispensable to make sure that they benefit those who need them the most, not to allocate them to those who receive other supports or don't find themselves in an emergency situation.[4]

Targeting in the allocation of resources has been the subject of controversy, for in most cases it has been used to substitute subsidies that, even if occasionally inefficient, reach a larger group of beneficiaries. However, targeting presupposes the following mechanisms to identify families qualified to receive benefits.

(1) Objectivity refers to the characteristics of the families receiving the benefits. Such characteristics do not depend on each family's self-perception but on the family situation. Examples of elements that can be considered to be objective are housing conditions, number of children, and educational level of parents.

(2) Transparency, as opposed to secretiveness, refers to access to information about the criterion used to allocate resources. It involves the possibility, for those who participate in the distribution process, to review the data about qualified families and the program.

(3) Impartiality refers to the equality of conditions that are relevant when distributing financial aid. The beneficiaries of PROGRESA are families in extreme poverty and marginality conditions, and this has nothing to do with composition, family structure, and place of residence. Neither their religious

beliefs nor political convictions are deemed relevant to determine whether they qualify.

(4) Efficiency is connected with the search for more adequate means of distribution. Since PROGRESA provides basic goods—education, health, and food—it is necessary to search for expeditious measures of assignation.

Yet the use of targeting is controversial. First, some people find good reasons for the application of generalized subsidies to help a larger number of people rather than focus just on vulnerable groups as future resource receivers.

Second, problems inherent to the mechanism itself can be identified. One of them is the possible meddling into the private life of program beneficiaries in order to get the information needed to implement the mechanism.

Another problem has to do with how to understand those receiving the benefits. Do we see them as child-like passive individuals, or as agents who enjoy the capacity to design their own life projects? This leads to discussions on the validity of arguments justifying paternalistic policies.

Third, it is necessary to establish transparent criteria for identifying the beneficiaries, and for applying the mechanisms with which benefits are assigned. As already indicated, objective, public, impartial, and efficient criteria reduce external factors that for political or economical reasons can alter the correct functioning of the program.

Another problem with targeting is the possibility of antagonism in the community between those people who get benefits and those who do not. Although the poll is aimed at carefully identifying qualified recipients, the end result often causes feelings of resentment and envy. Sometimes the difference between the poor and the extremely poor is very small.

Amartya Sen has discussed some of the problems involved in targeting, among them, the invasion of an individual's privacy and the stigmatization of the poor.[5]

B. Beneficiaries

Who are those in need of support from distribution programs? In PROGRESA's case, the extremely poor form the group. Nevertheless, one of PROGRESA's characteristics is that within the extreme poverty group it stresses gender. In that way,

> PROGRESA promotes gender equality and seeks to give women the power to have authentic egalitarian opportunities for their whole personal development, while acknowledging that when women's conditions improve they are in a better position to raise the living conditions of other family members, especially their children.[6]

Thus, one of PROGRESA's main objectives is to improve the situation of women. This is done in two ways. First, program beneficiaries are housewives. Second, school grants are higher for girls than for boys.

Empirically, several studies show that housewives make a more efficient distribution of resources than men do.[7] Philosophically, three reasons exist for a social policy to focus on women. The first is linked to the idea of compensation, and refers to the situation of exclusion that women have confronted in the past. According to this view, it is essential that women be compensated for their systematic cultural and social subordination.

This view has been challenged by some, for example Elster, who states that distributive justice must be "presentist" in the sense that it should not include arguments about possible compensation for injustices committed in the past.[8] Yet authors such as Robert Nozick insist that the principles of justice must include the rectification of past injustices.[9]

The second reason for focusing on women is consequentialist. It refers to the impact that the improvement of the situation of women will have on families and society at large. For example, it has been found that a woman who is better educated is more likely to have fewer children, thus allowing them to receive better care. Schooling gives women the means to exercise their reproductive preferences. However, the difficulty with consequentialist arguments is their weakness in justifying ethical or political decisions, for we have no guarantee that the expected consequences will occur.

The third reason is supported by a deontological approach and, in this case, refers to the 4th article of the Mexican Constitution. That article prescribes, "man and woman are equal before the law. This will protect the organization and development of the family." This leads us to reflect on Ronald Dworkin's concept of equality. Dworkin identifies equality with the idea that the State has the obligation to treat every citizen with equal concern and respect. To treat people with equal concern and respect implies to take rights or guarantees seriously.[10] The right of equality for women is part of the individual guarantees granted by the Mexican Constitution, and for this reason a social program that tries to promote this equality is justified.

C. Patterns of Assignation

One of the most vexing questions in the distribution of health resources refers to patterns of assignation. By "pattern" I understand, following Robert Nozick, that which fills the blank in the sentence "to each according to his or her...."[11] PROGRESA fills the blank by referring to the satisfaction of basic needs and the exercise of preferences.

In philosophy, the discussion of basic needs has become crucial. This is reflected in the application of social policies, especially in multicultural societies.

PROGRESA's introductory document states,

> PROGRESA seeks to remove obstacles that prevent poor families from accessing adequate nutritional levels and health care, and from benefiting from the development and the capabilities that are acquired through adequate basic education. PROGRESA seeks to ensure that families living in extreme poverty have genuine opportunities to satisfy their basic educational, health, and nutritional needs for the development of their members and their families' well-being.[12]

Furthermore,

> PROGRESA's financial support aims to increase the income of those families and to improve their purchasing level as well as to promote that families decide the best way to exercise that supplementary purchasing power.[13]

For this reason, it is convenient to analyze the concepts of "needs," "capabilities," and "preferences."

In many discussions about distributive justice, the use of the concept of needs as a criterion for distributing goods and services is associated with Marx's famous statement in the *Critique of the Gotha Programme*, "from each according to his [or her] ability, to each according to his [or her] needs." Yet egalitarian liberal theorists have also studied the concept of needs, and their discussions are even more interesting.[14] In contrast to the Marxist principle that assumes a background of abundance, egalitarian philosophers incorporate the problem of scarcity.

In what follows, I focus on the concept of basic needs because a wider treatment including instrumental needs would require a distinction between the concepts of "need," "wishes," and "wants."[15]

D. Needs

We can make a distinction between two weak definitions of needs. According to the first, people have a basic need of a good when the lack of it prevents them from reaching a minimal state of welfare. According to the second, people have a basic need of a good when we cannot conceive a future state in which they wouldn't suffer any harm if they do not have such good.

Yet these definitions present some problems by virtue of the relativism of their concepts. Different ways of measuring and conceiving levels of welfare exist. It is not easy to establish the degree of harm that people are willing to accept if they do not have a certain good.

Some authors have pointed out that human needs are not stable throughout history.[16] Needs extend through time, generating changes in character and customs. Furthermore, a society produces needs, altering even those that seem to be "natural."

Amartya Sen, has criticized the concept of needs.[17] He states,

> there is a tendency to define basic needs in the form of needs for commodities (e.g. for food, shelter, clothing, health care), and this may distract attention from the fact that these commodities are no more than *means* to real ends (inputs for valuable functioning and capabilities). This distinction is particularly relevant since the relationship between commodities and capabilities may vary greatly between individuals even in the same society (and between different societies). For example, even for the elementary functioning of being well nourished, the relation between food intake and nutritional achievements varies greatly with metabolic rates, body size, gender, pregnancy, age, climatic conditions, epidemic characteristic, and other factors.[18]

According to Sen, focusing on capabilities can help to understand the real problems that underlie the worry for basic needs, and to avoid the fetishism of primary products.

Other thinkers, like Nozick, state that appealing to needs leads to paternalistic behavior.[19] Paternalism has been defined as "interference of action that is justified by reasons concerning the needs of the coerced person or persons."[20] A policy is paternalistic when it interferes with the freedom of action of a person, it is coercive, and the person has not consented to it.

Sometimes paternalism is justified on the basis of harms and risks. An example may be illustrative. Let us suppose that a social program undertakes a vaccination campaign, and people in the community refuse to be vaccinated. To justify paternalism in this case it is necessary to consider the harm and risks involved, and the goals of the community. The factors to be discussed are the following. First, the possibility of harm, for instance, in case of an epidemic, how likely is it that community members will be infected? Second, the seriousness of the harm compared to the risk of taking the paternalistic action. In some cases the harm inflicted by the disease can be lethal or irreversible, and the application of the vaccine implies no risk at all. Third, the knowledge that the goal of the paternalistic action is important to the community: for example, that people want to be healthy. Finally, another factor to consider is whether the paternalistic action is justified as the best option to reach the proposed goal. For example, is the vaccine the only known method to prevent that illness? When we focus on basic needs, it is possible to find several cases of justified paternalism.[21]

One way to avoid the difficulties that surround a justification of paternalism is to turn needs into rights and claim that independently of theoretical discussions on the subject, Mexicans have the right to education and health as stipulated in the Mexican Constitution. The attribution of a right weakens paternalistic attitudes because every citizen can exercise the right to health and education. Nevertheless, the substitution of rights for basic needs presents two serious problems. One has to do with the concept of rights itself, and the other with the practice of social rights, particularly in Mexico.

Joel Feinberg made a distinction between negative and positive rights.[22] Positive rights are those that require that others aid the rights-bearer in some way. Negative rights imply that others have a duty to refrain from interfering with the rights-bearer. Sometimes, the problem with positive rights is that even if we know who has the obligation to honor them by providing something—the state in the case of social rights—the lack of resources may make it impossible to honor them. In Mexico, citizens have a constitutional right to health care; however, it is not easy to determine the minimum medical services that the state has an obligation to provide. Concerning education, even if the state can make an effort to cover in a quantitative way the demand for education, sometimes it cannot commit to providing high quality education.

Another problem when considering basic needs as rights is that in Mexico in practice, as José Ramón Cossio states, the so called constitutional social rights are more political programmatic norms than rights. Their interpretation and application have been historically more political than judicial.[23] Sara Gordon observes:

> every legislation concerning the access to social rights, framed in a corporate model, privileges organizations above individuals .... This makes it difficult to socially recognize individual and political rights, and tends to socially subordinate individual demands to collective, organized demands against the state.[24]

For these reasons, instead of replacing needs with rights, it is better to elucidate the notion of basic need, for this concept is a good candidate to fill the blank in "to each according to...." Nevertheless, the notion of distribution according to needs must work within a constitutional framework that allows the exercise of individual demands.

E. Wiggins, Nussbaum, and Doyal on Basic Needs

David Wiggins has recently argued that the objectivity of basic needs is compatible with the forms of relativism mentioned above. According to Wiggins, we require a satisfaction threshold of needs that can vary between individuals, societies, and cultures, and can change throughout history. If we accept changes in the threshold, we can weaken Sen's criticisms, for an undernourished individual would have a larger demand threshold than one who is not. Moreover, his criticism refers to a social policy that attempts to equate the distribution of primary products among people who have different biological, cultural, and social antecedents. However, if we focus on extreme poverty we find that it is difficult to keep the difference between basic capabilities and needs. Undernourished people need a special diet so that they can develop their capabilities, and this is equivalent to saying that they need a special diet because the lack of food is harming them.

The characterization of needs made by Wiggins pretends to go further than the recognition of a threshold. According to him, an extended investigation of the notion of need requires that one distinguish different questions. First, the question of the badness of needs: how much harm or suffering will be produced if the person does not have the thing in question? Second, a consequential question of urgency: given that a person might be considerably harmed by not having the good in question, how soon must this good be supplied? Third, the entrenchment of a need: is it flexible to modification, and to what extent? On the basicness of needs, Wiggins states:

> one might stipulate that y's need for x is basic just if what excludes futures in which y remains unharmed despite his not having x are laws of nature, unalterable, and invariable environmental facts, or facts about human constitution.[25]

Finally, Wiggins adds,

> y's need for x is substitutable with respect to x if some slight lowering of the standard by which y's harm is judged permits us to weaken claims of need by disjoining y's having x with his having u or w or whatever.[26]

An urgent need that has to be satisfied, that is entrenched, that is basic, and that is non-substitutable is an objective need that must be attended by a social justice program. An example of basic need is constituted by the amount of calories and proteins that an individual must consume to remain healthy and be able to develop (2,082 calories and 35.1 grams of daily proteins).[27] Consumption of calories and proteins meets the requisites articulated by Wiggins. In every possible world with the same laws of nature, environmental conditions, and a human constitution, human beings will be harmed if they do not get the minimum required calories and proteins.

Following Aristotle, Wiggins affirms,

need is a modal concept of a special kind which implies the linked ideas of a situation and a non-negotiable (or in-the-circumstances-non-negotiable) good that *put together* leave no real alternative....[28]

Another strategy to defend the idea of basic needs and the duty of the state to meet those needs is the one followed by Martha Nussbaum. She starts from an internal essentialist position to claim that people have common traits. According to Nussbaum,

> we always recognize others as human beings in spite of time and place divisions. No matter what differences we find, we seldom doubt about whether we are dealing with humans or not.... [secondly] we have a general consensus, widely shared, about those characters whose absence signifies the end of a human form of life.[29]

By examining them, we can come up with a working list of basic human functional capabilities presupposing the satisfaction of needs that do not depend on historical, cultural, or social circumstances.[30] Her list includes:

> being able to live until the end of a complete human life, as far as possible; not dying prematurely or before one's life is so reduced as to be not worth living; being able to have good health; to be adequately nourished; to have adequate shelter; having opportunities for sexual fulfillment; to move from place to place; being able to avoid unnecessary and damaging pain and to have pleasant experiences; being able to use the five senses, to imagine, to think and to reason; being able to have attachments to things and persons outside ourselves; to love those who love and care for us, to grieve at their absence; in general, to love, grieve, feel longings and gratitude; being able to form a conception of the good and to engage in critical reflection about the planning of one's own life; being able to live with and for others, to recognize and show concern for other human beings, to engage in various forms of familial and social interaction; being able to live with concern for, and in relation with, animals, plants, the world of nature; being able to laugh, to play, to enjoy recreational activities; being able to live one's own life and nobody else's; being able to live one's own life in its very own surroundings and context.[31]

According to Nussbaum, it is reasonable to take these as legitimate concerns when questioning how a public policy can foster the well-being of human beings.[32]

Len Doyal is another thinker who has high expectations of what people should do for the satisfaction of needs.

Attempts to deny the objectivity of need have proved popular and superficially plausible. People do have strong feelings about what they need, and these feelings can vary enormously between cultures.[33]

Nevertheless, he believes that subjective feelings do not constitute a trustworthy source to satisfy demands on needs. This is occasionally due to the fact that we can strongly wish for things that hurt us, and not be aware of what is necessary to avoid such harm. Thus, the idea that basic needs have an objective and universal basis must be accepted. An objective basis is one that, whether empirical or theoretical, is independent from subjective desires and preferences. A universal basis means that the harm caused by the absence of a good is the same for every human being.

Doyal says that the word "need" is used, explicitly or implicitly, to refer to universalizable goals. In this sense, needs are distinguished from other goals that have to do with what people want or wish and that depend on preferences and cultural environment. Human beings have universal goals that correspond to basic needs, and those needs must be satisfied to avoid serious harm. Thus, according to Doyal, basic needs are universalizable preconditions that allow the active participation of women and men in the life-style that they would choose if they had the opportunity to do so.[34] Two such needs are health and personal autonomy. In order to act and be responsible people must be physically and mentally able to do so. They must possess a living body governed by every relevant causal process, and the mental competence to deliberate and choose. Competency and the capability for choice constitute the most basic level of personal autonomy. Physical survival and personal autonomy are preconditions of people's actions, independently of their culture.

Doyal defines physical health in a negative way, as that without which it would be impossible to have a life expectation, and whose absence would cause physical diseases that could be conceptualized in biomedical terms.[35] Doyal argues that three ideas are essential to understand the notion of personal autonomy. The first refers to the way people understand themselves, their culture, and what is expected from them. The second is related to the psychological capability that men and women have to create their own options. The third refers to the objective opportunities that allow a person to act or stop acting. Autonomy is intimately related to formal education. According to Doyal, the existence of even minimal levels of autonomy will entail characteristics such as:

having the intellectual capacity for the formulation of aims and beliefs common to their form of life; having enough confidence to want to act and thus to participate in some form of social life; acting through consistently formulating aims and beliefs and communicating with others about them; perceiving one's actions as having been done by one and not by someone else; understanding the empirical constraints on the success of their actions; being capable of taking moral responsibility for what they do.[36]

Personal autonomy can then be understood in a negative way when one emphasizes the objective harm that could result if the characteristics previously mentioned are absent. Such characteristics are independent of the culture to which men and women belong.

Nussbaum's account is Aristotelian, for it emphasizes the satisfaction of basic needs that are essential to help human beings upgrade their potentiality. In contrast, Doyal supports a Kantian position when he emphasizes the universality of basic needs. But both Nussbaum and Doyal claim that there are essential, universal, and objective basic needs, while at the same time recognizing the importance of the person's culture and society. Perhaps the position of these authors is not much different from Sen's. After all, Nussbaum states that the concept of capability is similar to Aristotle's potentiality, and Doyal's negative definition coincides with capabilities.[37] That is because if we examine the notion of harm, we see that it commits us to the satisfaction of those goods that an individual needs not to be harmed, whether they are a primary product or not. It is also possible to consider harm as an obstacle to exercising a capability and to its adequate functioning.

Doyal's concept of autonomy is related to the capability that people have of choosing, and such capability is closely related to the exercise of preferences. In fact, the concept of preferences plays an significant role in matters of distributive justice.

F. Preferences

A theory of distributive justice according to preferences would state that "to each according to his or her preferences." The notion of preference was historically developed from the concept of self-interest. In 1881, Francis Y. Edgeworth initiated a new and revolutionary school of thought demonstrating that an economic theory could be explained by setting an order of preferences.[38] The concept of preference included the idea that the first principle of economy is agents acting motivated by their own interests. The term "interest" refers to the concept of utility introduced by John Locke and David Hume in the seventeenth and eighteenth centuries and later developed by Jeremy Bentham and John Stuart Mill.

In the nineteenth century, philosophers and economists used the notion of utility as an indicator of the global welfare of people. They took utility to be a numerical measure of a person's happiness, and they thought that people's choices had to do with maximizing utility, that is, happiness.

Problems such as how to measure and determine utility and what role utility should play in different choices made philosophers and economists severe the concept of utility from the notion of happiness. Mill's famous phrase, "it is better to be a human being dissatisfied than a pig satisfied; better to be Socrates dissatisfied than a fool satisfied," created nothing but perplexities. It is not clear why we should assign more value to Socrates's unsatisfied pleasures than to an idiot's satisfied pleasures. As Edgeworth thought, utility, instead of being related to happiness, was linked to the concept of preferences. This move allowed the following psychological supposition: if we observe that people prefer x and reject y, we can state that they prefer x over y. Preferences can be numerically represented by assigning a higher value to the preferred alternative. Given these characteristics, an action can be interpreted in the light of utility maximization. The only thing we need is consistency in the choice.

In a theory of rational choice, preferences are usually required to be complete (some goods can be compared and the individual can choose one of them), reflective (a given good is at least as good as another), and transitive (if an agent thinks that x is as good as y and y is as good as z, then x is as good as z).

The advantage of this kind of approach is that it allows us to express numerically and graphically a series of choices that explain human conduct, and allows for the assignation of numerical value to the utility that people derive from the acquisition of a good.

According to Sen,

the popularity of this view in economics may be due to a mixture of an obsessive concern with observability and a peculiar belief that choice (in particular, market choice) is the only human aspect that can be observed.[39]

An advantage of this point of view is that it concentrates on people and considers the value of resources in virtue of what they do in human life.

The theory of preferences avoids some of the problems found when we talk about distribution according to needs. People choose what is more convenient for them, and paternalism can be avoided. It also eludes the problem of relativism, as this approach allows us to include societal, cultural, and historical changes. Nevertheless, this theory still presents some problems, one of them having to do with the information required for people to exercise their preferences adequately.[40] For example, uneducated people might choose foods with neither sufficient calories nor proteins. Another problem is that preferences are only measured as the result of a choice from an ordinal point of view, in the sense that we can know that people prefer x over y but we don't know how much they prefer it. But its most serious problem is the impossibility of making interpersonal comparisons. This could bring us to maintain that a situation in which a person must choose between a piece of bread or a tortilla is just like one in which the election is between a bottle of French red wine and a bottle of champagne. Thus, Nussbaum writes the following:

> It is the fact, frequently emphasized by Aristotle, that desire is a malleable and unreliable guide to the human good on almost any seriously defensible conception of the good. Desires are formed in relation to habits and ways of life. At one extreme, people who have lived in opulence feel dissatisfied when they are deprived of the goods of opulence. At the other extreme, people who have lived in sever deprivation frequently do not feel desire for a different way or dissatisfaction with their way. Human beings adapt to what they have. In some cases, they come to believe that it is right that things should be so with them; in other cases, they are not even aware of alternatives. Circumstances have confined their imaginations.[41]

Despite the problems of the notion of preference, a social policy will be enriched if it includes some elements of valuation. The preferences of people must be considered not only because we can observe them, but also because preferences allow people to evaluate the possibilities that are presented to them and to be responsible for their choices. Thus, we may lose some precision but we win on application. Furthermore, we can translate the notion of preferences into the concept of autonomy discussed by Doyal so that the possibility of exerting a preference could be considered a basic need, even if it is minimal, as in the case of extremely poor people.

Gerry Cohen and Julian Le Grand have proposed a mixed principle that not only considers preferences but also recognizes that in many occasions the range of possibilities from which people choose is beyond their control.[42] In other words, they consider that while some inequalities are due to people's preferences, other inequalities depend on other factors. That is why it is necessary to stipulate a principle that considers the satisfaction of basic needs when the individual does not have many choices. To the extent that needs are satisfied, we draw closer to a more egalitarian access to opportunities that enables the exercise of preferences.[43] By "access" I mean the opportunity to have a preference and the capability to practice it.

Le Grand states,

> our judgments as to the degree of inequity inherent in a given situation depend on the degree to which we see that situation as the outcome of individual choice. If one individual receives less than another due to his own choice, then the disparity is not considered inequitable; if it arises

for reasons beyond his control, then it is inequitable. This idea can be expressed more formally as follows. The factors beyond an individual's control are to be defined as his constraints. These constraints limit the range of possibilities over which an individual can make his choices. The set of possibilities bounded by the individual's constraints is to be defined as his choice set. Then a situation is equitable if it is the outcome of an individual's choosing over equal choice sets.[44]

This idea has two advantages. It addresses the inequality existing when one has to range options, and it states that injustices are derived not only from the choices and the preferences of agents but also from factors that are beyond their control. If what is beyond people's control is related to the lack of something without which people would be harmed, then that is a basic need. To the extent that needs are satisfied, the possibility of exerting preferences will increase. When we talk about the extremely poor we must recognize that their choices are extremely limited. However, the exercise of a preference must still be a habit or a practice. According to this proposal, the blank that must lay down the pattern for distribution would be filled in the following way: "To each according to his [or her] needs so he [or she] can exercise his [or her] preferences."

By means of monetary support PROGRESA tries to satisfy basic educational, health, and nutritional needs. The aim of the financial aid provided by the government is to allow beneficiaries to determine the best way to spend the money.

4. PROGRESA: Practical Issues

PROGRESA is a program appointed to satisfy basic needs and to enable people to exercise their autonomy and their preferences. Next, I explain how it works.

The educational aid aims at promoting school enrollment, discouraging withdrawal, and ensuring that beneficiaries take advantage of education. The program provides scholarships and school supplies. Thus, after the *Lineamientos,*

> educational grants are assigned to every boy, girl, and person younger than eighteen who is member of a family that benefits from PROGRESA, and who are enrolled and go to school ... from third grade in primary school to third grade in secondary school. Grants are given during the school academic year. The amount of money increases in upper grades. Furthermore, in secondary levels, grants for female students are slightly higher than for males so as to promote attendance of female students, for

more females than males have a tendency to drop out of school, and they do it earlier in extremely poor families.[45]

Now, let us focus on health care services and priority treatments. PROGRESA tries to satisfy health's basic needs by turning to health care delivery, prevention, and attention to mal-nourishment.

> Health care services are provided through the application of the Health Services Basic Package defined by the Mexican Health National Council, composed by thirteen measures characterized by their high effectiveness and their mainly preventive character, without neglecting treatment and control of the main diseases. From the point of view of its impact upon the population's general health condition, it concentrates on preventing diseases and illnesses.[46]

Among these measures we find the following. Basic sanitation at a family level including pest control, in-the-home water disinfecting, and sanitary garbage disposal. Family planning including counseling, provision of, and information on contraception, identification of population at risk, management of infertility, and education on reproductive health. Prenatal and delivery care and attention to newborns, and supervision of nutrition and infant growth, including the identification of children under five, diagnosis and follow up of undernourished children, mother's training, and supply of micro-nourishment. Immunization, consisting of vaccination according to the operative guidelines of the *Cartilla Nacional de Vacunación* (National Vaccination Record). Treatment and prevention of prevalent medical conditions potentially life-threatening and transmissible such as dysentery, parasite infections, and breathing infections. In-home handling of diarrhea cases, which refers to the mother's qualification and training. Prevention and control of arterial hypertension and diabetes. Accident prevention and initial treatment of injuries. Community training for health self-care which includes health promotion, protection of auto-consumption food provisioning sources, general health care, and the use of services. Prevention and detection of cervical-uterine cancer, which implies health promotion for risk groups, and opportune detection through cervical studies.[47] Each measure is complemented with a health education program.

Prevention and treatment of malnutrition is one of the most important aspects in health care services. Charlesworth quotes Hafdan Mahler, former Director-General of the World Health Organization, who notes that health workers seem to believe that providing the best health care entails applying everything known to medicine to each individual.[48] The World Health Organization has rejected this idea, emphasizing the relationship between health and economic development. People should have a more encompassing

NOTES

1. *Mexico's New Social Policy* (Mexico City: Secretaría de Desarrollo Social, 1998) p. 27. Document presented at the Meeting on Social Politics of the Organisation for Economic Co-operation and Development in Paris, June 1998.

2. Jon Elster, *Local Justice* (Cambridge, England: Cambridge University Press, 1944), p. 4.

3. Max Charlesworth, *Bioethics in a Liberal Society* (Cambridge, England: Cambridge University Press, 1993), p. 107.

4. *Ibid.*, p. 9.

5. Amartya Sen, "The Political Economy of Targeting," *Public Spending and the Poor Theory and Evidence*, eds. Dominique van de Wale and Nead Kimberly (Baltimore, London: The World Bank, The Johns Hopkins University Press, 1995), pp. 11-23.

6. CONPROGRESA. *Lineamientos Generales para la Operación del Programa de Educación, Salud y Alimentación* (México, Coordinación Nacional del PROGRESA, 1999), p. 10.

7. I thank Fernando Cortés for this remark.

8. Elster, *Local Justice*, p. 195.

9. Paulette Dieterlen, "Sobre la rectificación de las injusticias cometidas en el pasado," *Dilemas éticos*, ed. Mark Platts (México: UNAM-FCE, 1997), pp. 163-180.

10. Ronald Dworkin, *Taking Rights Seriously* (Cambridge, Mass.: Harvard University Press, 1977), p. 227.

11. Robert Nozick. *Anarchy, State, and Utopia* (Oxford: Basil Blackwell, 1980), p. 159.

12. *PROGRESA. Programa de Educación, Salud y Alimentación. México*, Poder Ejecutivo Federal, s/f, p. 5.

13. *Ibid.*, p. 50.

14. See *e.g.*, Bernard Williams, "The Idea of Equality," *Problems of the Self* (Cambridge, England: Cambridge University Press, 1979), pp. 230-249; Adam Wagstaff, Eddy van Doorslaer, and Frans Rutten, "Introduction," *Equity in the Finance and Delivery of Health Care. An International Perspective*, eds. Adam Wagstaff, Eddy van Doorslaer, and Frans Rutten (Oxford: Oxford Medical Publications, 1993), p. 10.

15. Mark Platts, *Moral Realities: An Essay in Philosophical Psychology* (London: Routledge, 1991), pp. 35-38; and David Wiggins. "Claims of Needs," *Morality and Objectivity*, ed. Ted Honderich (London: Routledge and Kegan Paul, 1985), pp. 159-161.

16. Gerald A. Cohen, *Karl Marx's Theory of History: A Defense* (Princeton: Princeton University Press, 1978), p. 103.

17. Amartya Sen, "Capability and Well-Being," *The Quality of Life*, eds. Martha Nussbaum and Amartya Sen (Oxford: Clarendon Press, 1993), p. 40n.

18. *Ibid.*

19. Robert Nozick, *Anarchy, State, and Utopia*, pp. 155-160.

20. Gerald Dworkin, "Paternalism," *The Monist*, 56:1 (1972), p. 66.

21. Joel Feinberg. *Social Philosophy* (Upper Saddle River, N.J.: Prentice Hall 1979), p. 45.

22. *Ibid.*, p. 59.

23. José Ramón Cossio, "Los derechos sociales como normas programáticas y la comprensión política de la Constitución," *Ochenta años de la vida constitucional en México*, ed. Emilio O. Rabasa (México. Cámara de Diputados. LVII Legislatura, Comité de Biblioteca e Informática, 1998), pp. 295-327.

24. Sara Gordon, "Pobreza, y patrones de exclusión en México," *Pobreza, exclusión y política social*, ed. Menjívar Larín y Kruijt (Universidad de Utrecht, Costa Rica: UNESCO, FLACSO, 1997), p. 431.

25. Wiggins, "Claims of Needs," p. 158.

26. *Ibid.*, pp. 157-159.

27. *Macroeconomía de las necesidades esenciales en México. Situación actual y perspectivas al año 2000* (México: Siglo XXI, 1989), pp. 134-145.

28. Wiggins, "Claims of Needs," p. 167.

29. Martha Nussbaum, "Capacidades Humanas y Justicia Social: Una defensa del esencialismo aristotélico," *Necesitar, desear, vivir. Sobre necesidades, desarrollo humano, crecimiento económico y sustentabilidad*, ed. Jorge Riechmann (Madrid: Los Libros de la Catarata, 1998), p. 61.

30. *Ibid.*, pp. 43-104. See also Martha Nussbaum. "Non-Relative Virtues: An Aristotelian Approach," *The Quality of Life*, eds. Nussbaum and Sen, pp. 243-269.

31. Martha Nussbaum, "Aristotelian Social Democracy," *Necessary Goods. Our Responsibilities to Meet Others' Needs*, ed. Gillian Brock (Oxford, New York: Rowman & Littlefield Publisher, 1998), pp. 150-151.

32. *Ibid.*

33. Len Doyal, "A Theory of Human Need," *Necessary Goods*, ed. Gillian Brock, pp. 157-172.

34. *Ibid.*, p. 158.

35. *Ibid.*, p. 159.

36. *Ibid.*, p. 160.

37. Nussbaum, "Aristotelian Social Democracy," p. 140. See Amartya Sen, "Capabilities and Well-Being," *The Quality of Life*, eds. Nussbaum and Sen, p. 46.

38. Francis Y. Edgeworth, *Mathematical Psychics: An Essay on the Application of Mathematics to the Moral Sciences*, mentioned by Amartya Sen, "Rational Fools," *Philosophy and Economic Theory*, eds. Frank Hahn and Martin Hollis (Oxford: Oxford University Press, 1979), p. 87.

39. Amartya Sen, *The Standard of Living* (Cambridge, England: Cambridge University Press, 1990), p. 12.

40. Dan Brock, "Quality of Life Measures in Health Care and Medical Ethics," *The Quality of Life*, eds. Nussbaum and Sen , p. 96.

41. Nussbaum, "Aristotelian Social Democracy," p. 143.

42. Gerry Cohen, "On the Currency of Egalitarian Justice," *Ethics*, 99:4 (1989), pp. 906-943; Julian Le Grand, "Equity as an Economic Objective," *Applied Philosophy: Morals and Metaphysics in Contemporary Debate*, eds. Brenda Almond and Donald Hill (London: Routledge, 1991).

43. Cohen, "On the Currency of Egalitarian Justice," p. 916, and "Equality of What? On Welfare, Goods, and Capabilities," *The Quality of Life*, eds. Nussbaum and Sen, p. 39.

44. Le Grand, "Equity as an Economic Objective," pp. 190-191.

45. CONPROGRESA, *Lineamientos*, p. 31.

46. *Ibid.*, p. 32.

47. *Ibid.*, pp. 33-36.

48. Charlesworth, *Bioethics in a Liberal Society*, p. 117.

49. *Ibid.*, p. 118.

50. Michael Walzer, "Pluralism: a Political Perspective," *The Rights of Minority Cultures*, ed. Will Kymlicka (Oxford: Oxford University Press, 1996), p. 149.

51. Jon Elster, *Local Justice*, p. 155.

52. I would like to thank: José Gómez de León (National Coordinator of PROGRESA) for allowing me to spend my sabbatical year—from May 1998 to April 1999—at the National Coordination of PROGRESA; Arleen L. F. Salles and María Julia Bertomeu for their valuable suggestions and comments; and Arleen L. F. Salles for revising the translation.

Six

MORAL PERSON AND THE RIGHT TO HEALTH CARE

María Julia Bertomeu and Graciela Vidiella

Translated from Spanish by María Teresa Lavalle

1. Introduction

Over the past few years, a paradoxical situation has emerged in Argentina regarding the right to health care. From an economic perspective, a profound shift from a state-centered and planned economy to a free-market model has had an impact on the provision of health care. Yet the right to health care has been included in the 1994 amendment to the Constitution, both in general and in particular as a protected right.[1] This is a paradox because during the 1990s the Argentine government implemented a number of measures to stop inflation that had an impact on social services. Those measures included the decentralization of state functions and services, the opening to world markets for greater efficiency and competitiveness, the cutting down of public expenditure, the increase of taxes to secure a surplus, and the sale of state-owned assets.

Regarding social services, the government also recommended decentralization, focalization according to the urgency and needs of selected groups of people, and privatization. The government embraced a neo-liberal economic model that promotes the dismantling and privatization of state-held social services. On this model, laws of offer and demand define priorities in health and the kind of health care one enjoys, and the market replaces a state politically committed to redistribution of resources. In practice, this means that, as in other periods in Argentine history, the public sector with noticeably lower resources has to confront growing demands caused by changes in the production sector and a deep crisis in social security.

As to health services, the new economic model also recommends decentralization, focalization, and privatization. The aim of decentralization is to increase the efficiency and effectiveness of public expenditure. The objective of the focalization of programs and actions is to satisfy the crucial basic needs of less protected groups. Finally, privatization aims at minimizing the fiscal crisis by diverting the production of public goods and services to the profit-making private sector.[2]

The shift to a free-market model in policy decisions about resource allocation implies a shift from a universalistic tradition, where the rights of citizens to education, health, housing, and social care are mainly guaranteed by the state as provider, to principles of selection that target poor segments of the population. The free-market model also entails breaking away from all commitment to free access, and leads to privatization of services aimed at the poor.[3] In health care, all these measures may easily turn into some kind of governmental neo-beneficence, without the recognition of equal and universal rights.

The notion of a competitive market in health care illustrates to what extent health is no longer considered a social good monitored by the state, but a consumer item. The market is increasingly regarded as the sole guarantee that resources are not wasted, that the system is efficient, and that the quality of services improves.

Those advocating the use of market forces provide several arguments to support their view. First, they argue that under the free-market model consumers of health services are more directly involved in decision-making, which increases offers and enhances the quality of care. A wider range of options trains consumers who then learn how to choose the best service. Second, they hold that the market acts as a barrier against corporations because it fosters competition among providers. Third, they claim that laws of offer and demand curtail over-pricing, reduce costs, and have a democratic effect because more people have access to services. Fourth, they argue that markets foster creativity and minimize state intervention, thus stimulating personal initiative and freedom.[4]

Unfortunately, in practice the market in medical services does not work that way. It is often dominated by a monopoly in offer and demand. Demand can be created artificially and deliberately, and needs can be manipulated accordingly.

Moreover, variations in risks lead medical insurance companies to deny coverage to people with the most critical need of medical care. Financial incentives may prompt some health care providers to recommend unnecessary treatments, spawning a great deal of overuse of medical services. Patients are not true consumers; they are not in a position to distinguish between different products, to compare, and to test their quality. They cannot be equated to rational agents aware of their preferences, which is the basic assumption underlying the market mechanism.

Viewing medical practice as a business may bias the choice physicians make and the advice they provide, thus making conflicts of interests more frequent. For example, physicians may refer their patients to medical care facilities in which they have financial interests. Finally, that markets reduce costs remains to be shown. In fact, they seem to promote the development of high technology as opposed to preventive medicine.

2. Structure of the Health Care System in Argentina

Three segments compose the Argentine health care system: state or public care, social security, and private care. The public sector covers a network of national, provincial, and municipal hospitals. It has a 94,800-bed capacity and low-complexity health centers aimed at coping with simple problems in local communities. Currently, public hospitals and health centers are practically the only alternative for the lower- or medium-income populations not protected by social security, and for those with limited access to it. At the federal level, the administration of this sector is in charge of Public Health, under the jurisdiction of the Ministry of Health Care and Social Work.

The social security sector accounts for over half of the medical care in the country. It is a complex and extremely heterogeneous segment, constituted by union, state, provincial, and managerial social security organizations, and combinations of these. Approximately 85 percent of social security services are coordinated by the National Administration, the rest depend on provincial and municipal organisms. This segment provides fairly limited medical care. Private companies ultimately provide most services, with the social security organization operating chiefly as a financing organism. Its largest income comes from mandatory deposits from employers and workers.

In 1993, the government took the first steps toward de-regulation of social security services. Its most significant ordinance was allowing members from any social security service to join any other of their choice. This policy was founded on the belief that free choice of goods and services would have a disciplining effect on the market, thus ensuring better quality and a more equitable distributive effect.

Lastly, the private sector comprises private hospitals, clinics, and diagnosis centers owned by individuals or stock companies. It provides care to private patients and to those covered by social security services and pre-paid medical groups. Insurance companies, financial groups, and professional or non-medical organizations originally set up pre-paid medical groups that have increased notoriously over the past years. Although they cover the whole country, they are localized mostly in the wealthiest provinces: Buenos Aires, Córdoba, Santa Fe, and in the city of Buenos Aires.

The health budget in Argentina is comparable to that of some developed countries: 8.9 percent of the GDP, similar to that of the Netherlands and Canada. Nevertheless, its expense *per* inhabitant is markedly lower. Argentina has a high infant-mortality rate. The main causes of death are nutritional and perinatal problems, and the occurrence of infectious diseases; this is similar to what happens in under-developed countries. Over half of those deaths could be avoided with adequate prevention and medical care.[5]

The process of state reform initiated in Argentina, compounded by a crisis in the economy and the steps taken to overcome it, has produced a stratification of society in hierarchical levels. In this chapter, we defend models of distributive and universal coverage for health, education, housing, and those social goods that cause incapacity and vulnerability in people when unavailable. We believe that direct action that focuses on poverty, although essential in a state of need, is compatible with a society with an absolutely unfair or non-existent pattern of distribution. Underlying social policies that focus on poverty is a conception of the state as a mechanism that makes up for market deficiencies by transferring money to people below the poverty line. We are in the antipodes of such a notion. We favor a state with a distributive model of social policy, which should satisfy the basic needs of all its citizens in terms of universal rights.[6]

3. The Right to Health Care

The right to health care is one in a group of second-generation rights (economic, social, and cultural) that supplement the traditional listing of civil and political rights such as the right to life, liberty, and the security of the person. The right to health care was mentioned in several documents of international law during the era of a flourishing economy after the end of World War II. It was the climax of the welfare state, whose main trait was the reallocation of a few basic goods with the purpose of mitigating the distribution of power and wealth. Resources were allocated to institutions that addressed the basic needs of citizens: health, education, social security, housing, and food. Through these institutions, the state took over the planning and administration of social policies aimed at the entire population.

The right to health care illustrates some of the difficulties involved with the actual recognition of rights. It is widely held that, like economic and social rights and unlike civil and political rights, the right to health care is a positive right. Negative rights require that something not be done to us, that others refrain from interfering with our exercise of those rights. For example, we have the right not to be damaged in our integrity and not to have our freedom of speech restricted. Positive rights require a third party to do something and not just to refrain from interfering. Every right entails a correlative obligation. In the case of negative rights, the obligation is clearly defined: my right to freedom of speech entails that others have an obligation to refrain from interfering with my right. This is not the case with positive rights. What is the obligation implied by the right to work or by the right to an adequate standard of living? Unlike negative rights, meeting obligations implied by positive rights involves availability of resources and willingness to bring them about.

This is something that many states cannot guarantee, as is evident when we focus on health care.

Progress in medical technology has increased costs and made them virtually unlimited. Even in the wealthiest countries, health care costs have a significant impact on the economy. If the state had to guarantee the highest level of health for all its citizens, according to the principles set out by the World Health Organization, its economy might collapse.

This has led some authors to argue that there is no right to health care, and others to defend just a right to a "decent minimum."[7] Recently, there have been talks about essential clinical services in the context of developing countries.[8] The recommendation is that the governments of developing countries fund a limited set of public health measures and essential clinical services. Once a minimum has been guaranteed, those governments might decide to define their own set of national measures in wider terms. However, this proposal is based on the notion that providing an adequate health level will allow a "tolerable life." But health is not divisible; no distinction between basic and superior health is possible; health needs are usually urgent and do not admit of levels.

The satisfaction of some basic needs is crucial for autonomous functioning. We believe that meeting those needs belongs in the sphere of justice. Thus, to give up all discussion on rights before examining them is inappropriate. Upon close examination, the strict distinction between negative and positive rights, on which most arguments about their status is based, is not totally adequate. Virtually all rights have positive and negative aspects. The right to life, for example, is not exercised merely by being free from actions that may cause death or harm by third parties; it also requires respectable housing, health care, adequate working conditions, and a healthy environment. Likewise, the right to freedom of speech is only formal if people cannot enjoy access to the media, an acceptable level of education, and the like.[9] In what follows, we explain an alternative approach to rights.

4. Moral Person and Basic Capabilities

We referred to the intrinsic connection between basic rights and the notion of an autonomous moral person. Immanuel Kant's description of the autonomous subject is the most profound so far: the irreducible core of morals is the notion of subjects capable of self-determination based exclusively on their practical reason. Any democracy that recognizes rights has the notion of an autonomous subject, conceived as someone who can think about his or her own ends from the point of view of everybody else, as a normative core.

The normative notion of a person enjoying inalienable rights has two characteristics.

(1) It implies an end in itself, and it is the concept of full autonomy based on the self-determination of the person's reason. The term "person" entails not only freedom—implying maturity and the capability to formulate and set one's own ends as goods—but also competence to attain those ends, and the moral capability to take responsibility for one's actions.

(2) The notion of person has a teleological structure. It involves the idea of an interest understood in a practical sense. This is the interest of individuals to develop their intellectual, emotional, and creative capacities, consonant with the development of similar capabilities by other members of the social and political community. As a member of a rational community every person has this interest.

The notion of moral person is crucial in John Rawls's concept of justice as fairness.[10] The principles of justice defended by Rawls are justified on the basis of a notion of moral person that tries to make use of key features of the Kantian moral subject, albeit with no metaphysical tenets. Rawls maintains that Kant's greatest legacy to moral philosophy is not the principle of universality, but the concept of autonomy of the will.[11]

Yet, unlike Kant, Rawls's main concern is social. Therefore, the ideal of an autonomous subject is shifted from the solitude of moral consciousness to the full life of the citizen in a well-ordered society. Principles regulating such society focus on bringing about the necessary conditions for citizens to develop as fully autonomous moral persons. Rawls proposes the notion of full autonomy to account for two defining aspects of the moral personality: the capability to set its own ends and the capability to have a sense of justice. Fully autonomous moral agents carry out their projects under the sole restriction imposed by their reasonable capability to follow public rules of justice. Like Kant's moral subject, citizens in the well-ordered society are autonomous for two reasons. They choose and carry out their projects under no external pressure, and they are capable of limiting their own interests to principles willed by all citizens.

Although we have underscored autonomy, Rawls also refers to the person as an end in itself. Kant uses this notion to develop the idea of equality among subjects based on dignity. Rawls holds that his two principles of justice offer a social interpretation of the norm in the second formulation of the categorical imperative.[12] Both principles constitute criteria for an equitable distribution of the primary social goods essential for citizens to carry out their personal projects. Those goods are not ends in themselves; yet they are necessary means to carry out any notion of the good that is compatible with the restrictions set by both basic norms. By distancing himself from any substantial idea of the good, Rawls backs a deontological model that can warrant the autonomy of the person.

Rawls's aim is to explain how citizens in advanced democracies understand themselves. His explanation is not intended to apply to citizens in other communities. But Rawls's achievement is his bringing out and elaborating the basic characteristics of Kant's moral subject from the point of view of a theory of justice. Admittedly, in this case its normative force is limited to some societies. In what follows, we examine this notion in order to work out patterns of distribution that may be applied to societies that do not comply with the conditions presumed by Rawls.

Amartya Sen's proposal represents a step forward in this direction. Sen's aim is to find grounds for parameters of distribution to overcome the flaws he finds in Rawls's theory and in the utilitarian approach. Unlike Rawls, and following utilitarianism, for Sen individual well-being is an essential notion that should not be overlooked by any moral theory. Yet Sen agrees with one important Rawlsian objection to utilitarian ethics: by reducing the human being to a passive receptacle of desires whose demands must be satisfied, such view ignores the autonomous character of moral agents. The utilitarian usually equates well-being with the satisfaction of individual preferences regarded as minimum units that can be turned into figures; this allows for maximization without having to compare between incommensurable items or preference-holding subjects. According to Sen, since utility maximization is all-important, its distribution and its beneficiaries are irrelevant. Thus, distribution according to the utilitarian principle cannot prevent people with extravagant tastes from getting more satisfaction than those with simpler preferences. Insofar as utilitarians deem preference satisfaction as the only important point, they are unable to distinguish among different kinds of preferences. This can lead to large inequities in the distribution of social goods. In the case of health issues, Sen notes that the following consequence cannot be avoided: sick people should be allotted fewer resources because they would derive less utility than healthy people, whose chances to make use of such resources are less limited.[13]

Sen also rejects the identification of well-being with subjective mental states difficult to measure when making the interpersonal comparisons needed to determine distribution criteria and to correct inequalities caused by the natural or social lotteries. In fact, the same quota of "utilities" can help some and harm others. In other words, some needs (for example, those related to health and education) cannot be mathematically determined: they are "relative to ourselves." Since the notion of utility is a quantifiable and abstract unit, which may be distributed with no regard for personal characteristics, it cannot account for those kinds of needs. In Sen's view, not even Rawls's primary social goods manage to solve this particular problem satisfactorily. The egalitarian distribution of Rawls's index could also cause profound inequalities in people's actual freedom.[14] For example, disabled people may be unable to accomplish their projects, even though they may have the same index of primary goods as others. Not only are primary goods unable to account for these situations, but they cannot justify differences between persons labeled "normal." People have widely differing needs related to region, sex, and culture, among others, and this makes judging comparative advantages from the point of view of basic goods a difficult task. If the only issue were how to distribute available goods and services in a community, using a primary goods index as the sole parameter for determining distribution might not be a major problem. But this is not the only issue. The other is how distribution meets people's needs. And this is where we find a wide range of differences that depend on personal assets and characteristics.

Sen uses the case of nutrition to make this point. Good nutrition depends not only on the availability of food, but also on age, sex, metabolism, medical conditions, climate, social relationships, education in general, and nutritional and sanitary education in particular, access to services, and the capability to use them.[15]

Sen distinguishes two ethically relevant aspects in the concept of person: well-being and agency. Focusing exclusively on well-being, as utilitarians do, leads to ignoring the autonomy of the moral agent; concentrating solely on agency, as some liberals do, implies justifying criteria of justice which favor acute inequalities. Rather than as a state, Sen sees well-being as an activity related to people's functioning: the way in which people cope with their social environment. The notion of functioning involves states (being able to read and write, being well-fed, being free from malaria) and actions (eating, reading, taking part in social life, having fun). People's well-being is shown by their functioning vector: set of different functionings that they achieve in the various walks of life. Knowing people's functioning vector means being aware of their capabilities regarding some aims in particular. Well-being is not measured exclusively by the functioning vector people actually attain, but also by their capability to choose any other vector at their disposal.

The connection between functionings and capabilities is related to the second relevant trait in well-being: freedom to choose among different functioning vectors. Let us take the case of two people who are starving. One has made a choice on religious grounds. The other is hungry because he or she is poor. If we compare them in terms of needs or goods, the only difference between them is in terms of freedom. The first could make a choice; the second could not.[16] Insofar as the notions of functioning and capabilities focus on people, they allow for interpersonal comparisons that may serve as guidelines for working on distribution criteria. Unlike utilities and primary goods, these notions might lead to a more accurate assessment of people's needs. A person with an income similar to another's but unable to develop a basic capability would be entitled to a higher income or to a special good to help him or her develop that capability—for example, an automatic vehicle for an invalid, or a guide for a blind person. Sen suggests that minimum demands on the state are justified. They are connected to basic functioning vectors—for example, being healthy, not being hungry—and to freedom seen from the point of view of well-being—such as having the necessary means to feed oneself and to get an education.

But well-being does not exhaust the ethically relevant concept of a person discussed by Sen. Human beings are also responsible beings. The agency aspect—what the person is free to do and achieve—is as related to the Kantian notion of autonomy of the will as Rawls's rational faculties characterizing the moral personality are. When connected to well-being, freedom refers to people's capability to have several functioning vectors at their disposal. When connected to agency, freedom presumes that agents are free to carry out their life plans and to face them responsibly.

One of Sen's merits is that he emphasizes the importance of well-being for the individual without giving up autonomy. This is what makes his proposal more adequate than Rawls's when it comes to working out a theory of justice that will be more appropriate to our Latin American situation. Cultural diversity notwithstanding, unacceptable differences among individuals and nations exist. Functionings and capabilities criteria may be useful for evaluating those differences, and for showing the needs of those who cannot attain a given social threshold. Yet the notion of moral person resulting from this standpoint must not be necessarily understood in terms of the conception that people living in developed societies have of themselves. It may also be taken as a normative category, which allows for a critical assessment of current conditions in the world as a whole.

Nevertheless, Sen's proposal raises some problems. How are we to define minimum capabilities and functionings leading to legitimate demands? What criterion may be appealed to, for example, when rejecting the capability to develop expensive tastes? It is not clear how we are to solve these difficulties when we must determine a partial index of capabilities to be developed by everybody. Sen suggests that we should combine some uniform general preferences with a set of established conventions in each society. But this turns his proposal into a culturally dependent one.

However, even if Sen's theory of justice is not totally appropriate, it is promising because it may promote reflection on the indispensable capabilities needed by individuals to fully exercise their autonomy. Those capabilities might entitle people to demand that society satisfy their needs, creating rights with their corresponding obligation on the part of the state.

Drawing on a notion suggested by Martha Nussbaum, we provide a list of functioning capabilities connected to the concept of moral person.[17] When related to Rawlsian type universal principles of justice, they might ground basic rights to determine evaluative criteria in various contexts.

The list is:

(1) Capability to be free from avoidable illnesses.

(2) Capability to be well fed.

(3) Capability to enjoy respectable housing.

(4) Capability to use all five senses or to compensate their lack.

(5) Capability to imagine, think, reason, have feelings, and show them.

(6) Capability to interact with others and establish affective links.

(7) Capability to have a personal concept of the good life, to follow it, and to act it out.

(8) Capability to acknowledge inter-subjective norms.

(9) Capability to receive an education and proper information in one's own environment.

The list is wide and, consequently, vague. Yet it is inevitably so, for its purpose is to identify in general terms capabilities corresponding to the minimum functioning required by the concept of moral person. It can be further specified when applied to each context so as to determine how to efficiently help individuals develop their capabilities. For example, the capability to be free from avoidable illness varies from one individual to the other, and it is also influenced by environmental conditions. In a rural area it may be closely connected to the capability not to be infected by Chagas disease or Junín disease (viral haemorrhage); in an urban area, it may mean the capability to be free from heart disease, stress, or some infectious disease in particular. Similarly, schooling may vary enormously from one society to another, so adequate policies to educate people within one context may not be appropriate in others.

The capabilities listed above are mutually dependent, albeit in different degrees. The capability to acknowledge inter-subjective norms is linked to the capability to imagine and to think, to have a concept of the good, and to receive appropriate schooling. The capability to be free from avoidable illness is closely connected to that of being nourished, to enjoy adequate housing, and to receive the necessary information and education. One of the conditions for enjoying good health is to know how to avoid illness.

5. Moral Person and the Right to Health Care

As part of their effort to defend an egalitarian right to health care, some authors have tried to show that health is a special good. Ronald Green suggests that it should be equated to political freedom.[18] Norman Daniels implies the peculiar relevance of health care by relating the effects of disease to the lack of equal opportunity that should be enjoyed by all people in a just society.[19]

The trouble with this kind of strategy is that it cannot account for a trait common to health needs. Health care needs are closely linked to other goods not encompassed by health care services. We refer to a non-excessively polluted environment, adequate work conditions, housing, and the like. We believe that although health is an important good, it is not more so than other goods that may also be deemed basic in light of the list of capabilities mentioned above.

In order to defend this standpoint, we begin by comparing three well-known rival conceptions of health. The first, the biologicist or uni-causal concept of health, underscores somatic components among causes of disease. According to this view, disease is a failure of the body in its fight against internal or external forces. The uni-causal concept shows a marked tendency to specialization, based on the introduction of state-of-the-art technology, and it requires a medicine-oriented society.

The exclusively somatic notion of health is at odds with a second conception of health. This is the one stated in the Argentine Constitution: "Health is the state of complete physical, mental, and social well-being, and not only the absence of sickness or disease."[20] In its time, this view constituted a crucial step forward and contributed to displace the uni-causal view. Yet it is open to criticism. Inspired by utilitarian thought, it equates health with well-being. Thus, it brings to the notion of health the difficulties found in the notion of well-being. Moreover, it is too ambitious a notion of health whereby all those people who have not achieved "complete well-being" would qualify as sick.

We find the multi-causal view more appropriate. This third view sees health-illness as a process resulting from the combination of four components:

> population with its biological elements, the environment in all its aspects —intra-uterine, physical, chemical, socioeconomic, etc—individual and social human behavior, and health services.[21]

Despite their differences, the uni-causal and the multi-causal definitions stress the effect of social and psychological factors, besides somatic ones, on a person's sanitary conditions. Health is not independent from education, the environment, socioeconomic and work situations, habits, and nutrition. Poor populations in Latin America are very vulnerable to infectious, bronchopulmonary, digestive, and parasitic diseases. Many of these diseases are related to an unhealthy environment, inadequate access to drinkable water, no treatment of sewage water, inefficient or non-existent garbage disposal, overcrowded households, and deficient nutrition and education.

Approaching health as a special good clearly differentiated from others perpetuates the idea that therapeutic efficiency is the main goal of health care. Yet several experts on the subject have shown the inadequacy of the medical model that embraces this view.

The multi-causal view supports our view that health should be understood in terms of basic functioning capabilities, and promotes a full consideration of needs connected to the development of those capabilities. Health must be secured, but so must education, nutrition, and access to information. These are necessary conditions to ensure the development of autonomy, and they justify rights.

Finally, based on the normative framework we have defended, what kind of health care system should the state offer? Our notion of person is intrinsically connected to four universal principles of justice: universality, equality, equity, and solidarity. These principles warrant the defense of an equal and universal right to health care, which implies duties of the state toward all its members.

On account of its universal character, all the members of society should benefit from such a right. If health is one of the rights connected to the basic capabilities needed to develop a moral personality, then everybody is entitled to it. This view is opposed to the notion of a welfare state seen as an instrument to provide help for the poor.

Universal access to health care must be viewed from a double perspective. First, a demand for non-discrimination, in the sense that nobody must be excluded on account of economic status, sex, age, and type of illness. Persons are entitled to satisfy their legitimate demands within the possibilities and means of their society. Inevitable rationing produced by shortage of resources, and increasing costs should be carried out according to egalitarian criteria publicly discussed.

Second, the system must not be exclusively oriented to the poor. This is the difference between seeing health care as a right, and seeing it as beneficence from some privileged groups toward the poorest members of society. In a democratic society, health is a collective and individual good; therefore, only a system based on universal grounds can favor citizens' commitment to the public sphere.

The principle of equality must be considered from the point of view of removing any hurdles that may hinder the capability to be free from avoidable illness, even if that means allotting many more resources to some individuals in particular. That is the reason why health care should not be limited to basic needs. Health is not a divisible good, thus, it is not possible to plausibly defend the idea of an acceptable minimum. There is no such thing as basic and superior quality health care, such as is the case with lodging. A modest home is not incapacitating, but insufficient health care is.

The notion of solidarity includes concern for our neighbors' well-being because we acknowledge them as fellow human beings in an inter-subjective life. Solidarity favors social cohesion and cooperation. It is an active element of justice that promotes the development of morally autonomous persons and contributes to equality of opportunities. Each person's autonomy can only be exercised and carried out through the enjoyment of goods produced socially.

The health system must also be guided by the principle of equity. One of the traits that characterize a just society is the egalitarian distribution of benefits and social costs. Persons who have been benefited by natural fortune or social circumstance do not have absolute rights on such advantages. They must contribute to benefit those in a less favorable position.

If the health care system is to be a reflection of the principles of solidarity and equity, its costs and benefits must be shared by all concerned. In order to ensure a fair distribution of costs, the criterion will rule that those who have more will contribute more generously through income taxes, assets, value-added taxes, or employers' contributions to social security. This means that the most fortunate will participate in solving the problems of the least fortunate, and everybody will receive according to their needs, and contribute according to their possibilities.

6. Concluding Remarks

According to some authors, one of the differences between a social policy and mere social assistance is that the social policy has a universal reach, targeting the whole population, while social assistance focuses on the poorest and most marginal segments, namely, those left out by market forces.[22] Neo-liberalism backs this stance. In this chapter, we outlined a proposal that is incompatible with that view. Social policies whose primary and only aim is to focus on the poor are discriminating. The main idea of the focus-paradigm is that social policies must concentrate exclusively on those segments classified as vulnerable or in high risk. This entails segmenting the set of goods and services aimed at social areas.[23]

A universal theory of distributive justice must advance arguments supporting social policies that ensure that every citizen has access to a set of goods that become rights and duties. It favors national systems of health care, and education programs aimed at ensuring access instead of limiting it. This kind of theory targets the causes and not only the effects of poverty. It also intends to find ways to ensure cohesion in democratic societies by identifying general needs, instead of merely addressing individual interests by focusing on social policies. Here we defend a tradition in philosophy, inherited from Kant, concerned with providing normative grounds for an authentically democratic institutional framework that will guarantee a set of basic rights for individuals that acknowledges their dignity as persons. The right to health care is one of them.[24]

NOTES

1. Guillermo Guevara Lynch, ed., *Constitución de la Nación Argentina* (including the 1994 amendment) (Buenos Aires, EDIGRAF, 1994), article 42.

2. Aldo Neri, *Sur, penuria y después* (Buenos Aires: Emecé, 1995).

3. María Julia Bertomeu and Graciela Vidiella, "Asistir o capacitar. En defensa de un derecho a la salud," *Perspectivas bioéticas de las Américas,* 1:1 (1996).

4. See E. Haavi Morreim, *Balancing Act: The New Medical Ethics of Medicines New Economics* (Dordrecht, Boston, London: Kluwer Academic Publishers, 1992).

5. Organización Panamericana de la Salud, "Las condiciones de salud en las Americas, 1994" (Washington: PAHO, 1994); Hugo Arce, *El territorio de las decisiones sanitarias* (Buenos Aires: Macchi, 1993).

6. See Robert Erikson, "Descriptions of Inequality: The Swedish Approach to Welfare Research," *The Quality of Life*, eds. Martha Nussbaum and Amartya Sen (Oxford: Oxford University Press, 1993); Horacio Fernández Fingold and José Busquets, "Políticas públicas sociales: un examen no exhaustivo de algunas opciones en el debate," *Cuadernos del Claeh*, 62:17 (1992)

7. See Tristram Engelhardt, *The Foundations of Bioethics* (New York: Oxford University Press, 1986); Allen E. Buchanan, "The Right to a Decent Minimum in Health Care," *Philosophy and Public Affairs*, 13 (1984).

8. *Securing Access to Health Care* (Washington: US Government Printing Office, 1983); *Informe sobre el desarrollo mundial 1993* (Washington: World Bank, 1993).

9. See Eduardo Rabossi, "El fenómeno de los derechos humanos y la posibilidad de un nuevo paradigma teórico," *El derecho, la política y la ética*, ed. David Sobrevilla (México: Siglo XXI, 1991); and Carlos Santiago Nino, *Ética y derechos humanos* (Buenos Aires: Paidós, 1984).

10. John Rawls, *A Theory of Justice* (Oxford: Oxford University Press, 1972); John Rawls, "Kantian Constructivism in Moral Theory," *Journal of Philosophy*, 77: 9 (1980).

11. Rawls, *A Theory of Justice*, p. 287.

12. Rawls, "Distributive Justice," *Philosophy, Politics, and Society*, eds. Peter Laslett and W. G. Runciman (Oxford: Blackwell, 1967), p. 74.

13. Amartya Sen, *On Economic Inequality* (New York: W. W. Norton, 1973), p. 16.

14. Amartya Sen, "Justice: Means versus Freedoms," *Philosophy and Public Affairs*, 19 (1990), p. 112.

15. Amartya Sen, *Resources, Values, and Development* (Cambridge: Harvard University Press, 1984), p. 510.

16. Amartya Sen, "Well-Being, Agency, and Freedom," *Journal of Philosophy*, 82 (1985), p. 199.

17. Martha Nussbaum, "Human Functioning and Social Justice," *Political Theory*, 20:2 (1992).

18. Ronald Green, "Health Care and Justice in Contract Theory Perspective," *Ethics and Health Policy*, eds. Robert Veatch and Roy Branson (Cambridge, England: Cambridge University Press, 1985).

19. Norman Daniels, *Just Health Care* (Cambridge, England: Cambridge University Press, 1985).

20. *Constitución de la Nación Argentina* (Santa Fé, Paraná, 1994).

21. Emilio Quevedo and Mario Hernández, *La salud en Colombia. Análisis socio-histórico* (Bogotá: Ministerio de Salud, 1990).

22. Susana Lumi, Laura Goldbert, and Emilio Tenti, *La mano izquierda del estado* (Buenos Aires: CIEPP, Miño Dávila, 1992).

23. Alberto Barbeito and Rubén Lo Vuolo, *La modernización excluyente. Transformación económica del estado de bienestar en la Argentina* (Buenos Aires: Unicef, Ciepp, Losada, 1992).
24. Our thanks to Arleen L. F. Salles for her helpful comments on earlier versions of this chapter and for revising the translation.

PART III

EXPERIMENTATION ON HUMAN SUBJECTS

Seven

RESEARCH IN DEVELOPING COUNTRIES: THE ETHICAL ISSUES

Florencia Luna

1. Introduction

At present, international multi-centric research is carried out in several developing countries. These studies pose not only the ethical problems generally associated with research, but also the more specific one of whether research designs thought in industrialized countries can be carried out in developing ones. In this chapter, I focus on these issues. Some of the questions that will guide my discussion are: when is it unethical to conduct a trial in a developing country? What is the minimum care that should be offered? Can we alter standards of protection honored in industrialized countries for the sake of a scientific goal? Do standards of care in research vary among countries, depending on their infrastructure?

In the first part of this chapter, I concentrate on the controversy surrounding the AZT trials in Sub-Saharan Africa. I take this as a starting point because some of the problems raised by these trials are similar to those that international researchers may face in Latin American countries. I identify the key arguments in favor and against these trials to point out some of the difficulties generally found in research in developing countries.

In the second part of the chapter, I characterize additional factors that in my experience in a Latin American developing country, Argentina, are relevant for the continuing protection of research subjects. I take up the usually neglected notion of structural corruption. I argue that the existence of corruption in several countries, and its possible incidence on research, should be taken into account. Only once we recognize practices and problems that hinder research may we be able to design and implement better trials.

2. The Arguments

A. A Case Study

The current controversy over the moral permissibility of clinical trials in developing countries was prompted by AZT trials conducted in Sub-Saharan

Africa, Thailand, and the Dominican Republic.[1] They were carried out to establish the minimum dose of AZT necessary to prevent vertical transmission of HIV from infected mothers to their fetuses. The main goal was to identify the cheapest, most effective, most feasible, and most affordable treatment to prevent transmission in these countries. To achieve this objective, female subjects were randomly assigned to several dosage and placebo arms.[2] But AZT has been proven effective in blocking approximately two thirds of transmission of HIV to the fetus (ACTG 076).[3] Thus, within two months of the announcement of the results, the United States Public Health Service concluded that the ACTG 076 regimen must be recommended for all HIV-positive pregnant women without substantial prior exposure to zidovudine.

The United States Public Citizen's Health Research Group—a private non-governmental health watchdog organization—stated that the trials conducted in those countries violated one provision of the Helsinki Declaration: that every patient enrolled in a clinical trial receive the "best proven treatment." Peter Lurie and Sidney Wolfe, members of this group, exposed the problems of these trials in an article in the *New England Journal of Medicine*. The article was accompanied by a very strong editorial by Marcia Angell, and followed by another editorial in *The Lancet* criticizing the trials.[4] Researchers from developed and developing countries got involved in the controversy. Harold Varmus, Director of the National Institutes of Health, and David Satcher, Director of the Center for Disease Control and Prevention, justified the trials by distinguishing them from merely exploitive experiments. They noted the extensive in-country participation, and pointed out the economic and socioeconomic differences between developed and developing countries.[5] The Medical Research Council Joint Ethical Committee of the Gambia Government, and Eduard Mbidde from Uganda contended that the *New England Journal of Medicine*'s articles and editorials on the AZT case revealed ethical imperialism, ignorance of socioeconomic heterogeneity of societies, and lack of respect for African ethical considerations.[6]

Even if hotly debated, the arguments for one side or the other are not definite. There is general consensus on the aim of the treatment: the identification of a less expensive, similarly effective treatment that might prove beneficial given the limited resources for medical care in most developing countries. However, some of the arguments given in favor of the research are problematic, and serious new criticisms question whether this kind of research can effectively comply with its goals.[7]

Yet, leaving aside this criticism, one of the main controversies in the initial debate involved the use of placebo in the control group. Lurie and Wolfe claimed,

> The sole point of disagreement is the best comparison group to use in assessing the effectiveness of less expensive interventions once an

effective intervention has been identified. The researchers conducting the placebo-controlled trials assert that such trials represent the only appropriate research design, implying that they answer the question, "Is the shorter regime better than nothing?"[8]

B. The "Time Saves Lives" Argument

Research on human subjects is often justified on utilitarian grounds: successful research will bring benefits and progress to society. Obstacles to it produce long term harm. Several versions of this line of reasoning exist. One states that since a placebo controlled trial can be completed in a much shorter time than an equivalent alternative study, obtaining information through a new design would take much longer.

However, those who argue against the trials do not question the value of research. Instead, they question the evaluation of harm if protections to research subjects are kept, or the original design is altered to achieve this goal. The issue can be formulated thus: we can obtain results less quickly but protect those involved in the research, or we can decide that good ends justify the quickest mean. This leads us to one of the central controversial issues in the debate although not explicitly presented: the idea that time saves human lives.

The argument says that since placebo controlled trials will most probably offer faster results, in the end those trials will save more lives than research carried out without placebo. Placebo research will surely require sacrificing the lives of those in the placebo control group, but in the long run it will save more lives because it will achieve the desired results and it will be immediately implemented. Research without placebo, on the other hand, will take more time for the same results, and will let children who will not profit from faster results die. It will effectively protect only those on the research protocols, just a sample compared to the thousands who might be saved before the implementation of the newly tested therapy.

Two approaches against this kind of utilitarian reasoning can be identified. The first is grounded on deontological considerations: it stresses the importance of respecting moral rules or principles. On this view, conducting placebo-controlled trials would violate one of the rules designed to protect research subjects, for these trials do not offer the best proven therapy. Some notion related to the principle of respect for persons is introduced in the discussion. Research subjects deserve protection and should not be treated as mere means to an end. However, even if this is a good response, utilitarians are unlikely to accept this an adequate justification because of its deontological nature.

The second approach to the "time saves human lives" argument rejects the argument on the basis of three utilitarian considerations.

First, human deliberation is uncertain and fallible. This becomes relevant in this case because of the nature of research itself. When more than minimal risks are imposed on people, the uncertainty of the results should raise concerns. Even when a procedure being tested can eventually be proven effective, its effectiveness is not known when the research is designed.[9] Moreover, the "time saves lives" argument assumes the immediate availability of the tested drug. Either the argument presupposes the good faith of governments when they say they will provide the cheaper regimen, or it assumes the possibility of private access by HIV-infected women. But in Sub-Saharan Africa not even the proposed reduced prices of the drugs make them available to people.[10] And if those drugs are not immediately available, the calculus does not work. In short, two assumptions underlie the "time saves human lives" argument: first, good clinical results will be obtained through research; second, there is effective access to the needed drug. But these depend not only on human deliberation but also on economic and political variables that are quite difficult to control.[11] If one or any of these factors is missing, the expected benefits will not be achieved and research subjects and their offspring will be harmed.

In the second place, the implications of relaxing the rules that protect research subjects are troublesome. Nearly all research is expected to benefit humanity, and if time in achieving the desired results is the main concern, we might as well allow experimentation with selected groups of people and avoid moral standards altogether. After all, it is quicker and more effective to expose subjects not only to minimum risks but also to greater ones in the hope of achieving faster results. Consider the case of possible HIV vaccine trials. It might be easier to carry them out without any counseling on risks and preventive behavior. High rates of risky activity would then quickly and conclusively illuminate whether or not a trial vaccine might be effective. The point is that if we prefer the quickest and most effective results over the safety of research subjects, it becomes difficult to determine what kind of subject protections to sustain.

Finally, relaxing the protection of research subjects will result in negative consequences for research itself. People might end up distrusting research and this, in turn, might make finding volunteers difficult. That this is a possible consequence is suggested by the comments and lack of confidence in research of young African-Americans with little education, as signaled by the United States Advisory Committee on Human Radiation Experiments.[12] African-Americans were one of the traditional targets of abusive research in the past, and their current reaction to research is one of mistrust and rejection. Breaking rules that protect research subjects may bring negative consequences because research subjects will fear that other rules will also be broken.

Hence, even if breaking the rules sometimes is beneficial in the sense that good results will be accomplished and that therapy will be readily available to the population of the countries where the research is conducted, respecting rules that protect research subjects might still be good to avoid the negative consequences of doing otherwise.

C. The "Gold Standard" Argument

This argument defends the design of the AZT trials by pointing out the scientific criteria they comply with. Placebo control is considered to be the best research design because it provides a quick response with few subjects involved. Varmus and Satcher find this argument compelling because it offers definitive answers to questions about safety in the setting in which the study is performed. They state,

> A placebo-controlled trial is not the only way to study a new intervention, but as compared with other approaches, it offers more definitive answers and a clearer view of side effects.[13]

It is true that randomized-controlled trials are considered the "gold standard" of clinical research, and that they must be used whenever possible. However, sometimes a more flexible approach must be adopted. Different designs, comparisons between populations, equivalency studies, and other end points must be considered and made available. Rigid adherence to given scientific standards may be an obstacle to alternatives that may deal more adequately with the problem and still be effective.

Those who favor AZT controlled trials do not propose randomized trials without control but without placebo control. This is a proposal accepted by international codes regulating research. Even strong defenders of placebo controlled trials recognize that it would be possible to obtain statistically significant results or make causal inferences without placebo-controls.[14] In addition, the continuation of research based on ethically dubious grounds without the attempt to modify questionable aspects of it may lead to an unfavorable international reaction (by non-governmental organizations and agencies funding research) and, thus, to the termination of such research.

Comparison of different dosages has been thought to be a legitimate option, because it does not deprive any of the arms of the trial of treatment. When Lurie and Wolfe criticize those trials, they refer to one of the trials as being a model of an ethically conducted study.

In 1994, Marc Lallemant, a researcher at the Harvard School of Public Health, applied for NIH funding for an equivalency study in Thailand in which three shorter zidovudine regimens were to be compared with a regimen similar to that used in the ACTG 076 study. The NIH study section repeatedly put pressure on Lallemant and the Harvard School of

Public Health to conduct a placebo-controlled trial instead, prompting
the director of Harvard's human subjects committee to reply that "the
conduct of a placebo-controlled trial for [zidovudine] in pregnant women
in Thailand would be unethical and unacceptable, since an active-
controlled trial is feasible." The NIH eventually relented, and the study is
now under way.[15]

This kind of design was criticized because it could not meet the goals of the
research.[16] If this is so, and comparison between different dosages does not
work, other possibilities should be explored.

In short, randomized-controlled trials with placebo control are the gold
standard and should be implemented wherever possible.[17] But if there are
serious ethical objections to a placebo design, a different one should be sought
and a strong effort should be made to solve the ethical problem within a
different scientific design.

D. The Financial Argument

This argument shifts the focus to the economic aspect, concentrating on
financial blocks to possible research as carried out in developed countries. For
instance, Mbidde states,

Policies regarding health management differ within and between
industrialized and developing countries because of their different
economic capabilities. Whereas it is established policy that all HIV
positive pregnant women in the United States and other developed
countries are offered AZT, this is not achievable in many developing
countries because the costs of the drug and logistical support are
prohibitive.[18]

Mbidde is right on the issue of costs. Scarce resources raise several problems
in ordinary health care in developing countries. However, Mbidde does not
differentiate between the research context and the policy context or the present
situation. A distinction must be made between what happens in health care
settings and what must happen in a research context. Even if as a society we
have an obligation to eradicate poverty, this obligation is weaker than the
obligation that researchers have toward research subjects. In a research
situation, the interests of the persons involved must be considered. They
deserve protection and the best standard of care for their participation, and
researchers and sponsoring agencies must take the necessary steps to make
sure that this is so.

Researchers have access to AZT and other interventions needed in
research. They have the obligation to care for and monitor patients, and to

meet standards in order to conduct a trial. The sponsoring agency should help achieve those standards.

Now, there might be exceptions, for example "a standard of care that required an exorbitant expenditure, such as the cost of building several coronary care units." However, "since zidovudine is usually made available free of charge by the manufacturer for use in clinical trials, excessive cost is not even a factor in this case."[19] In short, if minimal standards are not met, research should not be approved. This is not a "high standard requirement."

E. The Socioeconomic Argument

This is the most compelling argument presented for placebo-trials. The emphasis is not so much on the possible costs of providing AZT but on socio-economic factors that hamper research.

Socioeconomic problems are difficult to solve. They depend not only on economic resources but also on entrenched population practices and habits. Mbidde and the Ethics Committee of Gambia offered this argument as well. They noted that lack of prenatal care, rural deliveries, few deliveries in health facilities, and risk of infections if the newborn is not breast-fed make it difficult to carry out research. Referring to the standard treatment, Varmus and Satcher state,

> Although this regime has been proven effective, it requires that women undergo HIV testing and receive counseling about their HIV status early in pregnancy, comply with lengthy oral regimen and with intravenous administration of the relatively expensive, antiretroviral drug zidovudine, and refrain from breast-feeding. In addition, newborn infants must receive six weeks of oral zidovudine, and both mothers and infants must be carefully monitored for adverse effects of the drug.[20]

These problems make it difficult to transplant research designs initially carried out in developed countries to developing ones. But the question is, is it absolutely necessary to conduct these trials in extremely poor countries without a minimal sanitary infrastructure? Is it not preferable to perform them in other developing countries with a minimal infrastructure, and then implement the results in countries with fewer resources?

F. The Standard Practice Argument

The so-called "standard practice argument" is not explicitly formulated by researchers but it can be inferred in its most extreme version from Angell's criticism.[21] One version of the argument states that in developing countries placebo controlled trials are morally acceptable because the majority of women do not have access to any treatment.

One response to this argument is that risky and miserable living conditions are not exclusive to developing countries. Marginalized and poor populations exist in many developed countries as well. To say that populations living in misery or vulnerable conditions should be exposed to major risks puts us very close to justifying disturbing chapters in human research history, such as Tuskegee, and it is unlikely that researchers would want to do that.

A milder version of the argument states that since no treatment is generally available for women in many of the countries in which the trials are being carried out, any treatment is better than no treatment. The idea is that even if not beneficial, such treatments are not harmful, for they do not cause any damage that would not "naturally" occur. Deborah Zion points out the disturbing implications of this argument. It would mean, she says,

> that it is ethically acceptable to exploit the suffering of vulnerable populations even though the means to alleviate it are known, because if no trial at all were offered the women in question would have passed on the infection to their children anyway.[22]

The standard-practice argument confuses the research context and the "real life situation" context, and fails to take into account the moral obligations involved in research. While policies or health finances of a country cannot be easily altered, researchers do have obligations toward the people involved in clinical trials.

Furthermore, when other aspects are taken into account, the previous vision of the situation of the women participating in these trials can be challenged. Consider women who have to take days off from work or leave their children with others in order to go to the hospital. It is very likely that they will have to travel to get there. Their pregnancy will be medicalized— quite unusual in a population that is not accustomed to it. The effort of these women deserves both respect and praise. Instead of treating them as if they were receiving typical health treatment or the share their society is able to afford, researchers should evaluate what these women's "extraordinary" efforts merit. Receiving treatment that will prevent the transmission of the infection is the least they deserve.

3. Devalued Particularities in Developing Countries

A. Protections and Developing Countries: The Case of Argentina

Are there additional reasons, peculiar to developing countries, for sustaining protections to research subjects? To analyze this, I turn to my country.

Argentina might be considered to be in a better economic situation than most African countries. There is a large middle class and relatively good public education. Yet it is a developing country with problems common to many other developing countries. Hence, even if developing countries differ and Argentina is in a better situation than other countries, some endemic issues it faces suggest the need to be cautious. If this is true of Argentina, those issues could be even more problematic in other developing countries facing those and other financial and social problems.

The first problem concerns the role that the financial interests of physicians and researchers do and should play. In Argentina, physicians and researchers in public institutions are not well paid. Physicians generally supplement their income by going into private practice, or by holding simultaneous positions in different hospitals to earn a decent salary. It is informally known that in many cases the "industry" pays extra money to researchers and physicians working in research. They may even get paid *per* research subject enrolled in a study, and this may raise doubts as to the adequate selection of research subjects. In these cases, money is not transparently allocated, nor is it delivered to the institution: it goes directly to the researchers' pocket. It is true that not all researchers in Argentina are tempted by these incentives. Serious and conscientious researchers exist. But financial inducements have an impact on some researchers eager to participate in almost any research project without a critical perspective.

Second, in Argentina most research is done in public hospitals. The population available is typically the most vulnerable: illiterate, with scarce resources, and with no other access to health care. In general, beneficiaries are grateful for the services received and do not dare to question anything. How could they? Behavior toward them is paternalistic.[23] Many times these patients are desperate, in a bad socioeconomic situation, and willing to accept almost anything. If a physician is conducting a clinical research, and a person is in a vulnerable position with nearly no other options for treatment, it is really quite difficult to refuse participation.

It could be objected that the lengthy regimen as a control could be considered an "undue inducement," for those who have nothing are very likely to participate in those trials just to get some kind of treatment. But even if medical supervision, monitoring, and the "best proven treatment" could be characterized as an inducement to enter trials, they are also the only way to minimize the vulnerability of trials participants.

In the case of the AZT trials there is an extra element: the pressure felt by women to undergo treatments or trials "for the sake of the baby." This is reinforced by the power exerted by some religious views. In Catholic countries, such as Argentina and most countries in Latin America, research to benefit the fetus must be accepted, because of the importance given to fetuses and to the reproductive role of women.

In addition, a general lack of respect for persons is evident in many developing countries. In countries where death is common, where there is a long history of dictatorships, murders, and violations of human rights, there is a tendency not to respect persons. This happens not only in research but also in many other medical and non-medical situations. The patient-physician relationship remains a paternalistic one, and with illiterate and poor patients such paternalism is easily tainted by authoritarianism. The possibility of real choice is remote. Consider the practice of informed consent. In Argentina, for instance, the tendency is to identify informed consent with a legal instrument in favor of the physician or the institution, and against the patient himself.

It is quite possible that some of these problems exist in developed countries as well. Nonetheless, in the case of developing countries these exist in addition to other problems such as poor mechanisms to control or punish wrongdoing and corruption. Hence, the cumulative effect of all these elements together should be carefully considered when deciding whether to keep safeguards for research subjects.

B. Corruption? What Corruption?

In the discussion of incentives, I introduced the notion of corruption. The possibility of corruption should be acknowledged when designing international multi-centric research to be conducted in developing countries. In what follows, I analyze the possible relations between "structural corruption" and research.

Let us start with some facts about corruption in a few countries. Transparency International, an international non-governmental organization, has done a scale of corruption perception. In a rank ordering of countries from 1 to 85, Denmark and Finland are among the countries with highest transparency perception. In contrast, countries like Argentina, Yugoslavia, and Thailand rank 61, Bolivia 69, Uganda 73, Kenya 74, Russia 76, Venezuela and Ecuador 77, Colombia 79, Nigeria and Tanzania 81, Honduras 83, Paraguay 84, and Cameroon 85.[24] The calculus is based upon the results of surveys to businessmen, risk analysts, journalists, and the general public who were asked about the dishonest practices of public officials and politicians. The scale included not only developing countries, but also Eastern and Central European countries.[25]

A different scale of measurement also provided by Transparency International gives 10 points to countries where practices are very transparent and 0 to countries where corruption is rampant. On this scale, Denmark got 10 points, Argentina 3, and countries with a lower position in the first scale mentioned such as Mexico (56) got 3.5. In Latin America, Chile seems to be the exception to the average corruption perception: it ranks twentieth, which can be translated into a 6.8 in the scale from 10 to 0.

Even though the survey covered only 85 countries, it shows that many Latin American and African countries are in a similar situation concerning the perception of corruption. According to Transparency International, some of the reasons for the prevalence of corruption in a country are institutional weakness, poor democratic history, no tradition in freedom of expression, and no operative access to information (denial of information access to journalists, lack of transparency). Corruption is also related to poor participation of civil society. This does not necessarily mean that there is no corruption in developed countries with longer democratic traditions, consider some cases in Italy and Spain.

> But what is corruption? It has been pointed out that corruption is not merely an act in contradiction with the law. It is a phenomenon both allowed and stimulated by other systems of formal and informal rules, public and private which coexists with the prohibited norms.... Exclusively focusing on criminal law disregards the fundamental fact that it is under a manifold of complex rules that we live and act.[26]

In this vein, Michael Reisman explains that every normative system is a combination of the formal rules enacted by an official and probably legitimate authority, known as mythical rules or codes, and of another set of rules, co-existing with the mythical rules, called operational code. These rules define how and when a formal rule can be broken and punishment avoided, and who can do it. This is not a mere problem of absence of rules. On the contrary, we find two perfectly identified normative systems acting simultaneously.[27]

Robert Klitgaard proposes a formula for determining corruption based on monopoly, discretion, and the lack of transparency. Corruption (C) is equal to monopoly (M) plus discretion (D) minus transparency (T): $C= M+D-T$.[28] For Klitgaard, when an individual has the monopoly of a decision in any given organization—whether public or private—he or she exercises this decision at will. When there are no limits of rules or control systems, and the proceedings used do not allow for open scrutiny, we face a situation in which corruption is potentially present.

C. Possible Influence of Corruption in Clinical Trials

Research involves not only scientific values but also money and power. Fast research and favorable cost-benefit ratio could bring enormous benefits to the pharmaceutical industry. Moreover, science and research are changing dramatically from altruistic and transparent ideals where knowledge was to be shared by all, to a more profit-oriented business where patenting first and millionaire benefits might change the rules. This can transform international multi-centric research in a fertile soil for the development of corruption.

At first glance, no problem may appear with research. If we follow Klitgaard's proposal, it seems that research will satisfy transparency objectives because it has to be approved by an ethical committee in the sponsor and host country. However, once we consider the possible interconnections of mythical and operational codes and the level of structural corruption in some countries, things do not appear so clear.

In Argentina there are ethics committees, but they lack an adequate education in ethics.[29] They meet *ad hoc* to approve a protocol. Generally, their members are other "colleagues" (physicians and researchers). Furthermore, there is strong pressure to approve international protocols. It is customary for an outraged investigator to ask, "Why was this protocol good enough for Harvard but not good enough for this institution?"[30] In addition, no adequate control mechanisms exist, and nearly all local institutional review boards are merely formal entities. Furthermore, research could be cheaper in developing countries where there is no sharing of patents, and meeting the requirements for approving research is easier.

In addition, consider the point made before about physicians and researchers in public institutions not being well paid, and the "incentives" provided by the "industry." I am not saying that corruption in research is necessarily present in developing countries. But it might be a possibility, even more so when there is systemic corruption. If this is the case, it has to be prevented. In the case of international multi-centric research, there should be an awareness and acknowledgement of the different formal and informal rules and operative codes at work. Generally, corruption is not seen as a problematic factor, and "partly to escape being labeled imperialists, many present-day scholars have simply avoided sensitive topics like corruption."[31]

Once the possibility of corruption is acknowledged we can identify different ways to avoid it. One strategy is to avoid incentives. This strategy is based on the idea of corruption as an operational problem in turn based on the idea of multi-standard system of rules. Other approaches may view corruption as an educational or legal problem. These strategies are not incompatible, they can complement each other. Nonetheless, the operational approach helps to develop more flexible and efficacious ways of preventing corruption.[32] Avoiding incentives may require not paying money to the researcher *per* subject enrolled, and searching for transparent ways of allocating that money, for instance, to the institution or the department where the trial is carried out. It must exhibit more transparency and accountability. It might be published in different media, posted on the Internet, in order to allow patients, research subjects, researchers, and the general public to know how the money is allocated.

Another possibility is to implement international review bodies or surveillance (including inspectors) to carefully monitor some research. Trials to be monitored could be those that use placebo when there is a standard treatment in industrialized countries, when there is no demand of individual voluntary consent—specially when it poses more than minimal risk—or when it proposes a research not acceptable for developed countries. Namely, carefully international monitoring of research that goes beyond international ethical codes such as Helsinki, or when there are contradicting positions among the different international ethical codes, or when the kind of research is sensitive and controversial (that is, the development of AIDS vaccine trials).

Several sensitive issues surround corruption. Nonetheless, we do not have to be paralyzed by its possibility nor remain blind to it by denying its pervasive influence in society in general and in bioethics in particular. We should realize the potential pitfalls of international multi-centric research and work through these issues by providing new tools to avoid its occurrence.

D. The Need for Research in Developing Countries

From the previous considerations, someone might conclude that trials should not be conducted in developing countries. This is a mistake. Research in developing countries is fundamental. However, safeguards must be maintained, the risk-benefit ratio must be evaluated, and vulnerable populations must be protected. In short, I am endorsing the relevance of ethical standards previously set, and I am showing why they should be specially respected in developing countries. But in designing and implementing research, there should be an awareness of the concrete problems each country poses, including the incidence of corruption and its possible influence on research.

In this chapter, I do not endorse a rigid view of research. AIDS, AIDS activists, and public debate in this arena showed how research has been transformed in several ways over the years. The debate brought to light the need for research on populations formerly neglected, such as adolescents and women, and considered safeguards and benefits for them. The challenge to research standard practices produced changes, among them, the introduction of alternative design trials, such as different end points as the consideration of the viral load instead of death. In the United States, this challenge resulted in modifications to FDA regulations. The consideration of the interests and claims of people with AIDS, in turn, made for a more efficient agency. These changes have benefited both research and subjects.

Socioeconomic factors also are to be taken into account. Developing countries are in need of research, not only for humanitarian but also for scientific reasons. For instance, AIDS vaccine trials have to address different kinds of viruses in different parts of the world. Large populations suffer from this devastating disease, and the reasons for carrying out research are valid. But the rights of the poor and uneducated should not take back seat to the fastest and easiest way to implement research. The alternative is to search for better and less rigid designs. This might prove more difficult but more compassionate.

4. Conclusion

Research in developing countries poses peculiar problems. A world turning into globalization and fostering international research should pay more attention to the challenges these countries present.

In this chapter, I showed some of the problems in the arguments presented in the discussion of the AZT case. This case exemplifies not only African challenges but also several problems developing countries face regarding the ethical use of placebos and the interpretation of adequate care. I also examined other variables that show the significance of maintaining safeguards and respecting ethical codes in developing countries. Patients-subjects of research deserve protection, and they can be protected if researchers follow ethical rules such as the one presented in Helsinki, "In any medical study, every patient—including those of a control group, if any—should be assured the best proven diagnostic and therapeutic method."[33] We must be cautious in eliminating some of these safeguards or in dubiously reinterpreting them. Finally, I tried to show the impact that "structural corruption" may have on international multi-centric research and suggested possible ways of avoiding it. I propose that we carefully consider the situation of the country where the research is to be implemented.

The real challenge lies in new methodological designs for ethically problematic research that offer protection to research subjects and, at the same time, allow for positive scientific work.[34]

NOTES

1. Peter Lurie and Sidney Wolfe, "Unethical Trials of Interventions to Reduce Perinatal Transmission of the Human Immunodeficiency Virus in Developing Countries," *New England Journal of Medicine*, 337:12 (1997), pp. 853-856, at p. 853.

2. *Ibid.*

3. Edward M. Connor, Rhoda S. Sperling, *et al.*, "Reduction of Maternal-Infant Transmission of Human Immunodeficiency Virus Type 1 with Zidovudine Treatment," *New England Journal of Medicine*, 331:18 (1994), pp. 1173-1180.

4. Lurie and Wolfe, "Unethical Trials," and Marcia Angell, "The Ethics of Clinical Research in the Third World," *New England Journal of Medicine*, 337:12 (1997), pp. 847-849.

5. Harold Varmus and David Satcher, "Ethical Complexities for Conducting Research in Developing Countries," *New England Journal of Medicine*, 337:14 (1997), pp. 1003-1005.

6. Gambia Government: Medical Research Council Joint Ethical Committee

"Ethical Issues Facing Medical Research in Developing Countries," *The Lancet*, 351 (1998), p. 286; and Edward Mbidde, "Bioethics and Local Circumstances," *Science*, 279 (1998), p. 155.

7. Udo Schüklenk, "Unethical Perinatal HIV Transmission Trials Establish Bad Precedent ," *Bioethics*, 12:4 (1998), pp. 312-319.

8. Lurie and Wolfe, "Unethical Trials," p. 854.

9. Michael Balter, "Impending AIDS Vaccine Trials Opens Old Wounds," *Science*, 279 (1998), p. 650; Elliot Marshall, "Controversial Trial Offers Hopeful Result," *Science*, 279 (1998), p. 1299.

10. Schüklenk, "Unethical Perinatal," p. 317.

11. Carlos Del Rio, "Is Ethical Research Feasible in Developed and Developing Countries?", *Bioethics*, 12:4 (1998), p. 330; Joe Tomas, "Ethical Challenges of HIV Clinical Trials in Developing Countries," *Bioethics*, 12:4 (1998), pp. 325-326; and Schüklenk, "Unethical Perinatal," pp. 316-319.

12. Nancy Kass and Jeremy Sugarman, "Are Research Subjects Adequately Protected? A Review and Discussion of Studies Conducted by the Advisory Committee on Human Radiation Experiments," *Kennedy Institute of Ethics Journal*, 6:3 (1996), p. 275.

13. Varmus and Satcher, "Ethical Complexities."

14. David Resnik, "The Ethics of HIV in Developing Countries," *Bioethics*, 12:4 (1998), pp. 297-298.

15. Lurie and Wolfe, "Unethical Trials," pp. 853-854.

16. Resnick, "The Ethics of HIV in Developing Countries."

17. Benjamin Freedman, "Equipoise and the Ethics of Clinical Research," *New England Journal of Medicine*, 314 (1987), pp. 141-145.

18. Edward Mbidde, p. 155.

19. Wolfe and Lurie, "Unethical Trials," p. 855.

20. Varmus and Satcher, "Ethical Complexities," p. 1004.

21. Marcia Angell, "The Ethics of Clinical Research in the Third World."

22. Deborah Zion, "Ethical Considerations of Clinical Trials to Prevent Vertical Transmission of HIV in Developing Countries," *Nature Medicine*, 4:1 (1988), p. 11.

23. Florencia Luna, "Paternalism and the Argument from Illiteracy," *Bioethics*, 9: 3-4 (1995), pp. 283-290.

24. Transparency International: 1998 IPdC *Comunicado de Prensa*, pp. 4-9.

25. *Ibid*.

26. Luis Moreno Ocampo, "Normative Systems." Paper presented at the Woodrow Wilson Center, Washington, 1996.

27. Michael Reisman, *Mentiras encubiertas, ¿un remedio para la corrupción?* (México: Fondo de Cultura Económica, 1975).

28. Robert Klitgaard, *Controlling Corruption* (Berkeley: University of California Press, 1991).

29. Ruth Macklin and Florencia Luna, "Bioethics in Argentina: An Overview," *Bioethics*, 10:2 (1996), p. 150.

30. Charles Mc Carthy, "Challenges to IRBs in the Coming Decades," *The Ethics of Research involving Human Subjects*, ed. Harold Y. Vanderpool (Hagerstown, Md.: University Publishing Group, 1996), p. 135.

31. Klitgaard, *Controlling Corruption*, p. 9.

32. Florencia Luna "Corruption and Research," *Bioethics*, 13:3-4 (1999), pp. 262-271.

33. *Declaration of Helsinki*, 1989, II, 3.

34. I would like to thank Ruth Macklin, Eduardo Rivera Lopez, and Arleen L.F. Salles for their discussion and detailed comments to previous versions of this chapter. I am also indebted to Arleen L. F. Salles for improving its style.

Eight

BIOETHICS AND RESEARCH IN BRAZIL

José Roberto Goldim

My objective in this chapter is to provide an outline of the evolution of the relationship between research with human beings and bioethics in Brazil, and to highlight some of the important contributions made by ethics to biomedical research in Brazil in the twentieth century. This is a first step toward systematizing the accomplishments resulting from this interaction.

Biomedical research has been carried out in Brazil since the nineteenth century. Initially, it focused on several issues involving infectious and contagious diseases, such as yellow fever and smallpox. More recently, biomedical research has broadened its field of action to include almost all branches of specialization in medicine and related healthcare professions.

In 1902 in the city of São Paulo, Emilio Ribas, a physician, replicated experiments originally carried out by the American researchers Walter Reed and Jesse Leazar in Cuba in 1900 to investigate the transmission of yellow fever. As in the earlier experiment, the group of Brazilian researchers performed autoinoculation, and three researchers were contaminated. At a later stage, the research also included Italian immigrants who had recently arrived in São Paulo.[1]

Brazilian scientific research continued to be carried out in systematic fashion, especially at new universities and research institutes. Countless partnerships with North American and European institutions, especially after the 1940s, helped to promote the exchange of ideas and techniques among existing researchers and to train new researchers. The resulting scientific output was recognized and published internationally. However, no guidelines or norms for conducting research involving human subjects can be found dating to the 1970s.

In 1974, the Hospital de Clínicas de Porto Alegre of the Federal University of Rio Grande do Sul established an ethics committee to assess and follow up on all research being carried out within the institution. This was possibly the first council body overseeing biomedical research projects at a Brazilian teaching hospital. The committee was created following a suggestion by researchers from the hospital who had just returned from an internship at the National Institutes of Health in Washington, where the first institutional review boards were being implemented.

In 1975, the Brazilian Federal Council of Medicine (Conselho Federal de Medicina), organization responsible for overseeing medical accreditation and

Beings). This publication had a great academic impact, triggering a fierce debate about the limits of research.

The National Council of Health was created in 1988 to establish national health policies in Brazil. In its first deliberation, it proposed the first set of guidelines for health research in Brazil.[9] The guidelines stemmed from the discussions started in 1982, and entered the national debate initiated during the 8th National Conference on Health.

The guidelines made internal ethics committees compulsory in all Brazilian institutions carrying out biomedical research. They were to be set up as bodies formed by researchers from different areas of professional expertise, and their responsibility would be to assess and follow up on research proposals being carried out in each institution. It proposed something similar to the Internal Review Boards already underway in the United States. Furthermore, the guidelines made informed consent mandatory. The document described in detail the steps involved in obtaining informed consent, which was officially dubbed "post-informed consent."

The guidelines followed the ethical tradition of protection of research subjects seen in all documents of this kind since the Code of Nuremberg. Yet it also included new concepts such as the protection of researchers, staff at research institutions, and the environment. The addition of these new concerns was a result of the extensive participation of representative segments of Brazilian society in National Health Board meetings. The resolution was long and detailed, and it presented a view that was comprehensive and current for its day. Its theoretical framework recognized the autonomy of individuals, and preserved the perspective of justice. It categorized research proposals according to associated risk, in opposition to the Declaration of Helsinki, which recommends that proposals be categorized according to probable benefit to individuals. Three levels of research risk were established: less than minimal risk, minimal risk, and more than minimal risk. Informed consent became mandatory for minimal risk or more than minimal risk research.

However, the implementation of the new Brazilian *Guidelines for Health Research* was not as effective as expected. The use of informed consent was not incorporated to research practice, and most institutions did not adequately promote the guidelines among researchers, nor did they set up internal ethics committees. The creation and implementation of such committees was hindered in large measure by the excessively bureaucratic procedures instituted by the National Council of Health. Moreover, the Council did not have the necessary means to enforce and oversee the activities taking place at all the research institutions applying for accreditation.

In 1992, the Brazilian government passed a new federal law regulating the utilization of unclaimed cadavers in research and teaching activities.[10] According to this law, cadavers unclaimed by relatives for thirty days following repeated warnings published in the local press would become available for research. This, however, was nothing more than a regulation establishing legal procedures for the ritual liberation of a cadaver for research and teaching.

Following a request by the Federal Council of Medicine, a study was carried out in 1994 to assess the state of affairs in the reviewing of health research proposals at Brazilian University hospitals.[11] The data obtained at twenty-six teaching hospitals in the country were extremely worrisome. Within this highly representative sample of the health research network, only two institutions were found to have working committees in accordance with the legal requirements in effect. They were Hospital São Lucas of the Catholic University of Rio Grande do Sul, and Hospital de Clínicas de Porto Alegre of the Federal University of Rio Grande do Sul, both located in the southern Brazilian city of Porto Alegre.

The creation and implementation of these two committees in Porto Alegre had different histories. At Hospital de Clínicas, a newly created Health Research and Ethics Committee was added to an existing Scientific Research Board in order to take charge of the attributions mandated by the guidelines of 1988. At Hospital São Lucas, Joaquim Clotet was teaching the first graduate course in bioethics in Brazil long before the new regulations were drafted and publicized. Furthermore, researchers at this hospital needed approval by a biomedical research ethics committee to publish their work abroad. This resulted in the establishment of a Committee for Health and Research Ethics at that university hospital. Though via different routes, the institutional culture at these teaching hospitals had already developed a sensibility to the new proposals for bioethics so that they were able to comply with the new regulations immediately.

In 1995, the National Foundation of Brazilian Indians (Fundação Nacional do Índio), a federal agency responsible for policies protecting native Brazilian peoples, created the regulations for conducting research in indigenous reservations.[12] Its aim was to protect these populations against culture shock and contamination by diseases infrequent among them. The directive established several requirements to be met before any Brazilian or foreign researcher would be granted legal access to any area occupied by indigenous populations.

At the same time, a new federal law was passed to regulate the use of genetic engineering techniques and the release into the environment of genetically modified organisms.[13] This law prohibited the production of human embryos for research purposes and the genetic manipulation of human germ cells.

In addition, the National Technical Committee for Bio-Safety (Comissão Técnica Nacional de Biossegurança) was created to establish national policies on bio-safety and to oversee research in this field.

In 1995, the National Council of Health attempted to set up a national database to store the Brazilian health research output. However, Brazilian laws did not mandate that research institutes and university teaching hospitals submit all their research projects for registration and assessment by the Council. The health research regulation in effect at the time entitled the Council to act as an appeals forum which could request the auditing of proposals, but it did not entitle the Council to conduct the assessment proper.[14] The institutions, however, were legally liable for the confidentiality of information provided by their researchers.

In late 1995, the National Council of Health proposed a taskforce to discuss biomedical research in Brazil and to review biomedical research regulations. The taskforce, chaired by William Saad Hossne, one of the representatives of the scientific community, included a wide range of professionals from different areas and representatives of society. A preliminary document was drafted and distributed to all institutions that could have some interface with research with human subjects. In October 1996, the National Council of Health passed a new set of guidelines regulating research involving human beings, after a national debate on the topic involving more than thirty thousand people.[15] The most important innovation of the new resolution was its scope: it was extended to all research involving human beings, not just biomedical research, as in the case of preceding ones. The new resolution included areas in the applied human sciences, where the discussion on the ethical aspects of research had not yet begun. Informed consent was renamed "free and knowledgeable consent" (Consentimento Livre e Esclarecido), but the rules for obtaining consent remained the same. Local research boards began to be called Research Ethics Committees. The administrative procedures for the creation of these new committees were streamlined. The National Commission for Ethics in Research (Comissão Nacional de Etica em Pesquisa) was created. The aim of this agency was to review proposals in special theme areas, and to update and clarify national guidelines.[16] Special theme areas were those at the forefront of research and development, such as research in genetics and reproduction, and those involving research with at-risk groups or populations, such as indigenous peoples.

The new guidelines were simplified and widely publicized. As a result, many institutions were reached, and research ethics committees were established everywhere. Today more than 270 institutions have ethics committees. Two reasons may be at the root of this significant increase in the number of ethics committees in such a short period of time. First, institutions may have created committees simply in order to abide by the law. Second, the committees may have been created to meet the need for approval of research proposals by internal review boards.

With the rapid increase in the number of ethics committees, the qualifications of committee members and the adequate functioning of these committees became an important issue. The National Commission of Ethics in Research has been carrying out regional meetings to assess the weaknesses of local committees and to address their needs. Due to the great demand on the part of individual committee members and research institutions for expert consultation on biomedical research ethics, in 1997 Hospital de Clínicas de Porto Alegre created a distance learning course on the Internet to train those wishing to act as members of ethics committees.[17] By 1999, more than eighty people nationwide, most of them healthcare professionals had graduated from the program.

In 1997, the National Technical Commission of Bio-safety issued a directive that prohibited carrying out any experiments involving genetic manipulation and the cloning of human beings in Brazil.[18] This regulation, issued by a technical biosafety agency, was similar to the ones previously established in different countries as a direct consequence of the controversy following the cloning of Dolly.

In turn, the National Commission of Ethics in Research issued additional directives to complement the 1996 Guidelines, in order to specify regulations concerning research with pharmaceuticals[19] and research with foreign participation.[20] A new resolution regarding human genetics research is being drafted at the present time.

At present, many groups of researchers and research institutions in Brazil produce world-class science. Several research projects are being carried out in association with foreign institutions, especially from Europe, North America, and Japan. Consequently, research projects in Brazil have been following international guidelines on research ethics and methodology, thus consolidating the principles of good clinical practice in Brazil.

International rules and guidelines have brought about several modifications in the process of carrying out health research in Brazil. The Bioethics Research Group at Hospital de Clínicas de Porto Alegre has been investigating these issues since 1986. Our local research has gathered data comparable to those obtained in other countries in terms of the criteria for approval of proposals by Research Ethics Committees and the criteria for obtaining informed consent.

A survey of over 1,200 research proposals submitted to the Hospital de Clínicas Research Ethics Committee indicates that, by 1996, the most frequent ethical problem was adequacy of the informed consent form.[21] The study was then extended to include 1,348 research proposals reviewed at the same teaching hospital between 1986 and 1997. The objective of the study was to examine the process of obtaining informed consent from the patient. Only 18 percent of the proposals had adequate informed consent forms that could be approved without any amendments. Prior to 1994, the most frequent problem was the lack of a consent form; after 1994 the most frequent problem was the lack of adequate information in the consent form, and the inappropriate wording of the document.[22] It was not until May 1993 that the Research Ethics Committee at Hospital de Clínicas de Porto Alegre began to function regularly as an educational body within the institution. Only then did researchers begin to draft consent forms following the reviews of their proposals. The educational role of the committee was of great importance for consolidating an ethical and legal perspective regarding the reviewing of proposals.

After overcoming the initial resistance against the use of informed consent forms in research, it became important to start assessing the adequacy of the instruments used and of the process for obtaining informed consent. In 1998, a qualitative study was carried out with six Hospital de Clínicas patients who participated in research projects in oncology. The study assessed the patients' experiences as participants in the project. Results indicated that all six patients had decided to participate before reading the informed consent form. Their decisions were based on previous information given to them verbally. In the study, all six patients emphasized the importance of receiving the necessary information and of clarifying doubts regarding the research projects they would participate in.[23]

The study created an additional concern for the ethics committee, whose members realized that the informed consent form was being regarded only as a written document and that it did not take into consideration the means by which the patient was invited to participate. Furthermore, the study led committee members to the conclusion that since the information given verbally to patients had been more decisive in patient decision-making than the written informed consent form itself, lower levels of formal education should not be considered a limiting factor for patient participation in research procedures. Evaluating the procedure used for obtaining patient consent *per se* and the ability of patients in giving an informed consent was more important.

Yet another sets of studies concluded in 1999 were carried out with the objective of evaluating the adequacy of informed consent through an integrated assessment of its "information" and "consent" components. The project was divided into three different studies. The first two studies were preliminary, and they assessed patients' ability to consent and the way information was given to them. The first study validated a proposal to be used with large numbers of patients for evaluating their ability to consent. The second study successfully validated a Brazilian Portuguese version of the Flesch reading ease and of the Flesch-Kincaid readability scales. The third and final study included a sample of fifty-nine patients from six different research projects. Data were analyzed using parametric and non-parametric tests, and correspondence analysis. The evaluation of the informational component included assessment of the difficulty in reading informed consent forms using the readability index. All informed consent forms used required a level of formal education greater than or equal to twelve years, which meant that it was a difficult document to understand. Using Kohlberg's scale of moral development and Loevinger's sentence completion test, all fifty-nine patients were considered capable of deciding whether to participate in the research projects. Most patients reported that they had received previous verbal explanations regarding the protocols in which they were taking part (52.8 percent); that they had understood the information imparted verbally (55.9 percent); that their doubts had not been clarified (76.3 percent); and that the informed consent form was difficult to understand (74.6 percent). These data were in agreement with those from the qualitative study previously carried out. Patients were also asked whether they could remember the information they had received. Results indicated that 47.5 percent of subjects remembered the procedures and benefits presented to them, and only 22 percent remembered the risks.

The study reached the following conclusions. First, the readability of informed consent forms was more compatible with a higher level of education than that of most patients. Second, the majority of patients did not remember the risks related to their studies. Third, 44.1 percent of the patients gave their consent to participate in a study without fully understanding procedures, risks and benefits.[24] Such studies underscore the importance of the ethical education of researchers.

The issue of ethics in research with human beings has developed significantly in Brazil. However, laws, guidelines, rules, research ethics committees, and informed consent forms are not enough. All professionals involved in research activities must recognize the importance of grounding research on ethical principles. In addition to complying with the law, research proposals must also be justifiable in terms of their contribution to the production of new knowledge, their relevance, and their feasibility. Researchers must conduct their studies for the welfare of society as a whole and of each and every person as well.[25]

NOTES

1. Sonia Vieira and William Saad Hossne, *Experimentação com seres humanos* (São Paulo: Pioneira, 1987), p. 23.

2. Brasil, Conselho Federal de Medicina, *Resolução* 671/75. URL: http://www.cfm.org.br/ResolNormat/Alfabetica/Pesquisas_medicasOuClinicas.htm (25 March 1999).

3. Brasil, Conselho Federal de Medicina, *Resolução* 1098/83.

4. DIMED, Brazilian National Department of Health, *Portaria* 16/81.

5. *Ibid.*, and DOU (14 December 1981), pp. 23745-23746.

6. José Roberto Goldim and Carlos Fernando Francisconi, "Os Comitês de Ética Hospitalar," *Revista de Medicina* ATM, 15:1 (1995), pp. 327-334.

7. Conselho de Organizações Internacionais de Clínicas Médicas, *Diretrizes Internacionais propostas para a Pesquisa em Seres Humanos* (Brasilia: Ministério da Saúde, 1985).

8. "Code of Community Health Rights," *Revista Instituto Medicina Tropical,* 28:278 (1986).

9. Brasil, Conselho Nacional de Saúde, *Resolução* 01/88; *Diário Oficial da União* (14 June 1988).

10. Brazilian Federal Law 8051/92.

11. Carlos Fernando Francisconi, Délio José Kipper, Gabriel Oselka, Joaquim Clotet, and José Roberto Goldim "Comitês de Ética em Pesquisa: levantamento de 26 hospitais brasileiros," *Bioética,* 3:1 (1995), pp. 61-67.

12. *Normas para Ingresso em Terras Indígenas para Fins de Pesquisa,* Instrução Normativa 01/95/PRESI– FUNAI/Brasil.

13. Brazilian Federal Law, 8974/95.

14. Brasil, Conselho Nacional de Saúde, *Resolução* 01/88.

15. Conselho Nacional de Saúde-Brasil. "Resolução 196/96 sobre pesquisas envolvendo seres humanos," *Diário Oficial da União,* (16 October 1996), pp. 21082-21085.

16. Corina B.D. Freitas, "Os comitês de Ética em pesquisa: evolução e regulamentação," *Bioética* 6:2 (1998), pp.189-196.

17. Conselho Nacional de Saúde-Brasil. "Resolução 196/96 sobre pesquisas envolvendo seres humanos," *Diário Oficial da União* (16 October 1996), pp. 21085-21082.

18. The National Technical Commission on Biosafety, *Instrução Normativa* 08/97.

19. National Council of Ethics in Research, *Resolução* 251/97.

20. National Council of Ethics in Research, *Resolução* 292/99.

21. Ursula Matte and José Roberto Goldim, "Pesquisa em saúde: aspectos éticos e metodológicos envolvidos na avaliação de projetos de pesquisa," *Revista HCPA,* 15:2 (1995), p. 135.

22. Márcia Mocellin Raymundo, Ursula Matte, and José Roberto Goldim, "Consentimento Informado e Avaliação de Projetos de Pesquisa no Período de 1996 a 1997," *Revista HCPA,* 18 (supplement) (1998), pp. 30-31.

23. María Alice Vargas Viegas, *O processo de consentimento informado em estudos clínicos em Oncologia: percepções dos pacientes* (Porto Alegre: Curso de Pós-Graduação em Psicologia/Pontificia Universidade Católica do Rio Grande do Sul, 1998). Master's Thesis.

24. José Roberto Goldim, *O Consentimento Informado e a Adequação de seu Uso na Pesquisa em Seres Humanos* (Porto Alegre: Programa de Pós-Graduação em Medicina: Clínica Médica/Universidade Federal do Rio Grande do Sul, 1999). Doctoral Dissertation.

25. I am indebted to Arleen L. F. Salles for improving the style of this chapter.

PART IV

ETHICAL ISSUES IN THE PROCUREMENT AND ALLOCATION OF ORGANS

Nine

WHAT IS (EXACTLY) WRONG WITH SELLING YOUR BODY PARTS?

Eduardo Rivera López

Translated from Spanish by Laura Pakter

1. Introduction

Medical and scientific advances raise a multitude of ethical problems previously nonexistent. Some are related to the possibility of using one person's body parts to treat another. This introduces a new element into the traditional approach to medical treatment wherein everything necessary to curing or attempting to cure a patient belongs to the domain of "things" (instruments, drugs), of work (actions, time), of persons (physicians, nurses), or, at most, of a person's regenerative elements (blood). At this time, a growing and significant, though not generalized, number of cases may require an organ, a tissue, or more recently the limb of another, in addition to all of the above.

In most cases, transplants are carried out utilizing cadaver organs or tissue. In these cases, the moral questions are both multiple and complex, and partly touch on the subject of this chapter. If we believe that the decedent's organs or tissues belonged to the deceased or presently belong to the living heirs, and furthermore we believe that since the person is dead, these organs are "things," the problem is who can rightfully dispose of these organs, and under what conditions. This is normally treated as a problem involving the kind of consent necessary to proceed with organ removal. However, the possibility of considering these "things" goods to be bought and sold, and subject to the rules of the market should not be dismissed. Indeed, at the theoretical level, diverse forms of incorporating market elements into the system of procuring cadaver organs have been proposed.[1]

Yet transplants are possible not only from cadavers, but also from living persons. Sometimes, the extraction of the organ or tissue does not result in the sure death of the donor, as would happen in the case of the removal of the heart or the entire liver of a living person, or in a serious disability. Such is the case of the kidney or part of the liver, or bone marrow in the case of tissues. It is conceivable that organs for transplantation can now be sold not only *post mortem* but also *ad vitam*.

There are differences between the commercialization of organs *post mortem* and *ad vitam*. Here, I focus only on the commercialization of organs *ad vitam* because it exists, while there does not seem to be a market for cadaver organs. One of the reasons for this is that the existence of a *post mortem* market would require a far more complex institutional structure, one that is unsustainable under illegal conditions, whereas in some countries, *ad vitam* sales prove to be a relatively uncomplicated transaction.

My aim in this chapter is to discuss whether the commercialization of organs or body parts of living persons is ethically objectionable, and if it is so, exactly why. This discussion has two aspects: first, the question of whether the action of selling a person's organs is morally objectionable; second, whether the legalization of the sale is morally permissible. Both aspects are related but must be carefully differentiated, as we will see below.

2. Organ Sales in Context

Before turning to the arguments in favor of and against the commercialization of organs, it is important to describe more precisely the issue as it exists today.

The medical costs of transplantation are extremely high. A kidney transplant, on which I focus to make my case, oscillates between US $40,000 and US $60,000 with a post-operative expense of about US $10,000 including controls and immunosuppressive drugs. Heart and liver transplants are substantially more expensive. A heart transplant averages US $100,000 while a liver transplant can amount to US $150,000.[2]

Nonetheless, the case of the kidney is peculiar. Patients suffering from terminal renal failure who are candidates for kidney transplantation have an alternative therapy over a prolonged period of time: hemodialysis. This is not the case with those patients facing a liver or heart transplant whose sole alternative is death within a relatively short span. If the costs of kidney transplantation and dialysis are compared, transplantation turns out to be the more inexpensive option.[3] In the United States, this has led the state to finance kidney transplants through public health care—Medicare and Medicaid—but not always liver or heart transplants. From an economic viewpoint, this is rational if we assume that all patients with renal failure receive dialysis independently of their financial capacities.

However, in many of the so-called developing countries, the state does not finance either remedy, and the burden of the treatment's cost falls on the patient. Furthermore, many of those countries do not even come close to having the technical know-how to carry out transplantation. In several African countries, the few who can afford a transplant or dialysis do so abroad or, in the case of dialysis, in the few private clinics offering the treatment. The rest go untreated. Nevertheless, in other developing countries, although the state finances neither transplants nor dialysis and poverty levels and the lack of health care are overwhelming, such infrastructure exists, at least to some extent. These are countries with striking levels of inequality where extreme poverty prevails together with state-of-the-art technology. The clearest case is India, but other countries fit the description as well. Journalists have reported cases involving citizens in Estonia, Romania, Moldavia, and Russia selling kidneys to Israeli patients.[4] Others refer to transplants in Israel itself with paid "donors" from Arab territories.[5] In the case of Latin America, I have no knowledge of reliable reports denouncing the existence of a black market.[6] However, many of the countries in the region fit the above description (existence of infrastructure and great inequality) to such a point that the conditions favoring such a market exist even if, in reality, it does not.

In the Indian case, it is easy to explain the emergence of a flourishing organ market. Given the shortage of organs in developed countries, where the sale of organs is banned and where the prohibition is effectively enforced, a fixed demand of patients from those countries is guaranteed. And given the lack of cadaver organs in those countries, there also exists a fixed demand of wealthy patients, native or from neighboring countries. It is estimated that in 1988 one thousand kidneys were sold in India. Fifty-six percent of the buyers came from foreign countries (the Far East, the Near East, Europe, and the United States).[7] While India and the majority of countries have passed laws explicitly proscribing the sale of organs, journalistic reports confirm the illegal persistence of such practices.[8]

An overview of additional characteristics of the practice completes a somewhat realistic picture of the situation. First, it seems that in most cases, and as far as the situation permits, sellers are consenting adults. This means that sellers have not been kidnapped or physically coerced into carrying out the extraction.[9] Thus, this practice must be distinguished from another described in reports that have appeared insistently in the media since 1987 about child organ-trafficking. Some reports describe the existence of a criminal organization that kidnaps and murders children for their organs; other reports describe the extraction and selling of adult organs without consent. Unlike the sale of organs of adult donors, the illegality of this practice requires no special legal prohibition, its illegality lies in the kidnapping, murder, or injury of a person. It is difficult to affirm that this practice does not exist. The most reliable reports to which I have had access are skeptical of its existence.[10] But this is not the subject of this chapter.

Second, it is evident that the main cause behind the sale of kidneys in the vast majority of the cases is extreme poverty. Nonetheless, nuances exist in the evaluation of this motivation. Some defenders of the sale of organs are not so categorical. They argue that although poverty in India is an influential factor, it is not the only one. Other reasons are: (1) payment of the dowry of a daughter or sister, (2) maintenance of a disabled relative, and (3) improvement in a person's own financial situation or that of the children.[11]

Third, since organ sales are illegal, there is no control over whether deals are respected. Therefore, it is logical to assume that nonpayment of the fixed price and other swindles are relatively common.[12]

Fourth, a relationship exists between the existence of an illegal organ market and the absence of an effective policy on cadaver organ-donation. Even though India has had a transplantation law forbiding transplant commerce and regulating organ donation since 1994, the number of transplants carried out with organs from cadaver donors is minimal.[13] Several hypotheses have been put forth to explain the reasons for such a low increase in donors. The clearest one is economic. An effective donation policy requires a large pool of donors, otherwise it is difficult to find immune compatibility with potential recipients. This is why it is essential that all or most hospitals possess sufficient infrastructure to diagnose and "maintain" brain-dead patients. Instruments like respirators are virtually nonexistent in countries like India. The results of this failure can be seen in the fact that it was only in January 1999 that India's first successful liver transplant was reported.[14]

Finally, the follow-up of sellers after a renal extraction is either poor or nonexistent. The reason for this is that once the business is over, there is no reason to continue spending money on attention to the seller.

3. Arguments in Favor of Organ Commercialization

In general and in varying degrees, the usual arguments for the legalization of buying and selling organs for transplantation follow one of these two lines.

The first is consequentialist. It is based on the scarcity of existing organs for transplantation and infers, from a series of empirical premises, that the legalization of sales would significantly ameliorate this situation.[15] The empirical premises are those commonly used when favoring an efficient market: the market creates an incentive system that allows us to hope that the demand be satisfied.

The second is deontological. Here we can distinguish two interrelated arguments. The first, not defended very often, falls back on the idea of property rights of persons over themselves. If we are owners of ourselves and have the right to do what we choose with ourselves, then what is to prevent us from selling our body parts?[16]

The second appeals to the value of autonomy. If people were to find themselves in a critical situation, wherein the best option would be to sell an organ, the prohibition of doing so would represent a further restriction on their autonomy. In the words of one of the defenders of this argument,

If our ground for concern is that the range of choice is too small, we cannot improve matters by removing the best option that poverty has left, and making the range smaller still.[17]

These are the principal arguments in favor of organ commercialization. To a large extent, defenders of organ sales are concerned with debating the numerous arguments against it, which we will see below.

4. Arguments against Organ Commercialization

Arguments against the sale of organs are diverse for many reasons. In the first place, there are many kinds of existing or hypothetical practices that can be encompassed within the commercial framework, from a totally unregulated market to strongly controlled forms called "rewarded gifting."[18] In the second place, some arguments are general; they discuss the market model—be it regulated or not—in abstract terms, while other arguments criticize the existence of commercialization under real conditions. Third, some arguments focus on the morality of the individual act of disposing of a body part for money, while others are concerned with the morality of a legal permission to carry out this act. Finally, different reasonings are based on different moral conceptions: some are deontological and others consequentialist. The conjunction of all these variables results in many different combinations and possible arguments.

The following review of arguments does not attempt to be exhaustive. Hopefully, it is clear to which kind of combination each argument belongs.

A. The Kantian Argument

This is an argument that (1) tends to reject any kind of commercialization, (2) is of a completely general character, (3) refers principally to the morality of the act of selling organs, and (4) is purely deontological.

The Kantian perspective operates at two levels. First, it declares that the self-flagellation involved in selling one's organs is immoral. Persons, no matter what their situations may be, must not do so. In the second place, and as a natural consequence of the first step, it justifies the legal prohibition of selling organs. This prohibition could be subject to restrictions that are the product of the existence of such tenable defenses as necessity. How does Kant support his view?

His first point is whether, in general, it makes sense to have obligations toward oneself. Kant himself concedes that, in principle, the notion seems contradictory: if *A* has an obligation to *B*, *B* can always rescind that obligation. Therefore, if *A* has an obligation to *A* herself, *A* can lift that obligation, which is to say that *A* has no obligation.[19] However, and beyond Kant's solution to this problem (through the dualism between person—*homo noumenon*—and human being—*homo phaenomenon*),[20] this is only an apparent contradiction. *A* might very well have an obligation, specially a moral obligation, toward *B* that *B* may not rescind. For example, *A* may be obligated to help *B* even though *B* does not desire it or wish to be helped; or *A* may be obligated not to hurt *B*, even though *B* may be a masochist and wishes to be hurt.

Consequently, whether there are justifiable duties to oneself is not a conceptual question but a normative question that must be dealt with according to each case. What are, then, Kant's arguments in support of the existence of these duties in the case we are concerned with?

First, Kant focuses on suicide, arguing that people have no right to take their own life.

> Disposing of oneself as a mere means to some discretionary end is debasing humanity in one's person (*homo noumenon*), to which (*homo phaenomenon*) was nevertheless entrusted for preservation.[21]

Thus, according to Kant, the case of selling body parts functions as a partial suicide.

> To deprive oneself of an integral part or organ (to maim oneself)—for example, to give away or sell a tooth to be transplanted into another's mouth, or to have oneself castrated in order to get an easier livelihood as a singer, and so forth—are ways of partially murdering oneself. But to have a dead or diseased organ amputated when it endangers one's life, or to have something cut off that is a part but not an organ of the body, for example, one's hair, cannot be counted as a crime against one's own person—although cutting one's hair in order to sell it is not altogether free from blame.[22]

It is difficult to critically evaluate Kant's position without going deeply into the philosophical technicalities of his theory, such as the distinction between *homo noumenon* and *homo phaenomenon*. But for my purposes it suffices to show some of the weaknesses not only of Kant's arguments but also of the views of those who use them to prove the immorality of selling organs.

Perhaps the main problem with accepting the Kantian argument lies in that he understands the disposal of an organ as a partial suicide. Yet the differences between committing suicide and removing a body part are as vast as the difference between selling yourself as a slave and out to hire for a day's work. In the case of suicide, the person is annulled; we can only exist within a living body (I accept here the Kantian dualism between person and human being). In contrast, although removing a body part may represent a risk of death, like so many other permissible human activities, it does not imply the loss of the person. At least, not in the same sense as suicide.

Let us now turn more specifically to the arguments against disposal. If we follow Kant's text we have to conclude that not only is selling a body part morally prohibited, but so is donation (see the example of the tooth). However, and with restrictions, donating an organ is not only legally permitted but also considered a highly altruistic act.

Second, Kant accepts the extraction of an organ that endangers a person's life, most likely in reference to the case of a gangrenous leg or arm. The extraction is the only means to save the individual's life. But what would Kant say if people found themselves in a situation in which selling their organs is the only way for them and probably their family to survive? It is true that in Kant's time the threat of death from a dead limb was greater than the threat of death from not being able to sell an organ. Yet this is relative. What would Kant say if the amputation of the limb, say the leg, were not to save a life but to alleviate unremitting pain? If he accepted this amputation, why would people not be morally justified in selling an organ if this would ameliorate their own misery or that of their family?

We must keep in mind that what we are discussing is not whether it should be legally permitted to sell organs, but whether this decision should be morally objectionable from the viewpoint of the individual who makes this decision.

That Kant himself recognizes the existence of problematic cases is an interesting fact. Following the texts I have cited, Kant states a series of "casuistic questions," such as: Is it right to commit suicide to save your country? Is it right to commit suicide prior to the execution of an unjust death sentence as Nero imposed on Seneca? Is it legitimate to commit suicide when you are suffering from hydrophobia, knowing death is certain, in order not to contaminate others? The question of whether you could legitimately sell an organ to save the entire family from poverty could be counted among these queries.

B. The Paternalistic Argument

We might think that an argument against the commercialization of organs should not focus on the individual act of the seller whose circumstances may, after all, justify or excuse the act. Instead, a solid argument must address the question of whether the legal permission to sell organs is morally acceptable. An argument frequently used for banning behaviors that are not intrinsically immoral is the paternalistic argument. Let us begin with the more general paternalistic arguments, those less dependent on context.

There is an enormous diversity of norms that tend to be justified along paternalistic lines, and this makes it difficult to provide one sole definition of paternalism. Here, I follow Gerald Dworkin's definition: "interference with a person's liberty of action justified by reasons referring exclusively to the welfare, good, happiness, needs, interests, or values of the person being coerced."[23] Common examples are the obligation of motorcycle drivers to wear helmets or to fasten seatbelts in cars. The prohibition to sell oneself into slavery can also be justified on paternalistic grounds. Applying the same criterion, prohibiting people from selling their body parts could be considered justified.

The most common justification for imposing a coercive obligation or prohibition in a paternalistic way is that while the obligation limits the immediate choices of people, it ultimately promotes their autonomy or prevents its diminishment. For example, by being obligated to wear a seatbelt, we lose some freedom or autonomy; we can no longer drive without wearing a seatbelt. Yet doing so minimizes our risk of suffering far more serious harm, which in the end would impinge on our autonomy in a much more obvious way than the obligation to wear the seatbelt.[24] This is John Stuart Mill's argument for not allowing people to sell themselves into slavery. Although signing the contract might be considered an expression of our freedom, the act of doing so precludes any future exercise of freedom.[25]

An extensive debate exists on the limits and acceptability of the paternalistic justification of legal norms. But my concern is to show that the typical case of organ sale does not fulfill the necessary requirements of the argument. So, even if in the above-mentioned cases paternalistic measures could be justified, this is not so in the case of organ sales.

There are two situations in which the paternalistic argument would justify the prohibition of selling organs. First, if the loss of autonomy or harm from the paternalistic prohibition were much less considerable than the benefit gained through this measure (or the harm it intends to prevent), as in the already mentioned case of seatbelts. Second, if even when the loss of autonomy resulting from the coercive imposition of the prohibition were consequential, its sanction led to a complete annulment of the autonomy of the individual, as in the case of the slavery contract.

The case of organ sales for transplantation does not reflect either of those situations. For the person living under conditions of extreme poverty, the inability to obtain resources from the sale of a kidney is not analogous to the prohibition to drive without seatbelts. The loss in this case can be quite significant and even vital to the person or family. On the other hand, the loss of a kidney does not result in the total loss of autonomy, as happens with the lifetime contract of slavery.

To be sure, if the extraction were so risky as to be likened to suicidal conduct, then a paternalistic action could begin to make sense. But under normal conditions, this is not the case. If this were so, altruistic donations would not be permissible, either.[26]

The issue is whether any general moral reason exists to forbid such a sale. An argument is general when it leads to the prohibition independently of the context. I want to show that there is no general moral reason based on paternalism to prohibit organ sales. If paternalism is justifiable, at most what can be shown is that organ sales should be more or less strictly regulated to prevent some cases—for example, the sale of an organ for the purpose of traveling—or that they should be prohibited in some contexts—when sanitary conditions are so poor that the risks of the operation outweigh its benefits.

Let us now evaluate the paternalistic argument within a given context, and not in general terms. The question is, if we consider the context in which kidneys are offered for sale, would the prohibition be justified on paternalistic grounds? Are the conditions in which the operation is effected so risky to the seller that no rational person (in the position of the potential seller) would accept it?

The answer to these questions is difficult. On the one hand, as mentioned before, it is true that organ markets exist under circumstances of extreme poverty, and that the lack of informed consent and abuse of persons is quite feasible. Yet it is also true that this is partly due either to the illegality of the situation itself or, beyond illegality, to the total lack of control. If the only argument against the commercialization of organs rests on the possible harmful consequences to buyers and sellers—poor follow-up of the seller, little control over transplanted organs, the possibility that the seller will be swindled—then the most logical course of action would be to control organ sales, not to prohibit them. Illegality simply worsens the situation.

To see this argument more clearly, let us consider a similar case: drug consumption. If the only argument in favor of the prohibition of drug consumption were the paternalistic concern that dealers might abuse consumers, that quality control is absent, and that swindles are possible, then the prohibition would turn out to be the worst solution. The best solution would be to allow controlled authorization for consumption and commercialization. A defense of the prohibition of drug consumption cannot be based only on the paternalistic argument. The same holds for organ sales.

C. The "Slippery Slope" Argument

If we accept that some norms can be justified on paternalistic grounds, for example not allowing a person to sell herself into slavery, we can develop another argument indirectly based on paternalism.

The argument states that even if it is true that in some contexts the decision to sell an organ may be rational—as in the case of a person living in extreme poverty—acceptance of the practice would lead to accepting practices whose rationality is in question. This, in turn, would lead to accepting other clearly irrational and abominable acts. For example, if we accept that an individual's desperate or critical situation justifies the sale of a kidney, nothing can prevent us from imagining cases that justify more serious self-mutilations, even the desperate situation of consenting to one's death to benefit loved ones.

This argument follows the general structure of "slippery slope" arguments: I accept A (A is, in itself, acceptable), but A leads to B (and B no longer is). As is well known, the "leads to" is ambiguous, which results in two kinds of general slippery slope arguments: one logical and the other causal.[27] That A "leads to" B may mean that, conceptually, if one accepts A, there will be no good reasons to reject B. And it might mean that socially or legally accepting A will lead, in fact, to socially and legally accepting B. In both cases, the argument does not go from something that is morally bad to something that is morally worse, but from something that is, *prima facie,* morally unobjectionable to something that is morally bad. In other words, A is not intrinsically objectionable but only insofar as we cannot avoid moving on to B, which is intrinsically objectionable.

The logical version of the slippery slope argument is nothing more than an argument of universalization. If A is not relevantly different from B, and B is morally impermissible, then A must also be morally impermissible.[28] It is not strictly a question of a slippery slope argument, since it makes no sense to say we "start" by accepting A to "go on" to B. But the question is: if we accept that you can sell an organ, what reason can exist for not accepting the legality of selling yourself into slavery or taking your life to save your children? The point is, as tends to occur in universalization arguments, whether there is any relevant difference between the two situations.

There is, in this case. The difference is that one case produces the disposal of the person as such (that is, of the disposition of the person in the future), while the other produces a disposal of a nonessential part of the person. While individuals do not stop disposing of themselves by selling a non-vital organ, they do stop disposing of themselves if they sell themselves as slaves or take their own life selling vital organs.

The causal version seems to be more promising. A relevant conceptual difference exists between A and B, but the social or legal acceptance of A may well lead to the future social or legal acceptance of B. Selling a kidney is not intrinsically objectionable, but permitting it may lead causally to the future sale of complete human beings, and this is objectionable.

This is the version frequently used to criticize practices such as euthanasia and abortion. If it is socially or legally acceptable to kill a terminal patient who consents, in the future it may be socially or legally acceptable to kill the patient who does not.

This line of argumentation must be analyzed quite carefully since any acceptable practice could lead causally to another that is not. Defense of the argument must then prove with sufficient reasonableness that the causal connection holds.

Furthermore, it is often possible to turn around slippery slope arguments. If the slippery slope really happens, and the sale of organs leads causally to the sale of persons or the sale of oneself into slavery, then why should one think that the slope "began" with the sale of kidneys? The slope could begin with the donation *ad vitam* among family members, which happens in all countries. Indeed, if this practice did not exist, no one would have thought of the possibility of commercialization. Thus, if one accepts the validity of the slippery slope argument, any transplant would have to be prohibited to avoid the risk of causally leading to abominable practices. If we do not want such a counter-intuitive outcome, then we have to admit that we are always at some intermediate point along the "slope." The question is how to find rational criteria to determine the point beyond which a practice is considered morally illegitimate.

D. The Unjust Distribution Argument

Another plausible argument against the sale of organs focuses not on the seller but on the potential buyer. A market system can lead to unjust situations from the point of view of the demand and not only the supply of any good. The current argument refers precisely to this aspect: who has access to organs in the market.

This argument must be treated at two different levels: an abstract level (how would the organ market function under somewhat ideal conditions), and a more concrete level (how would the organ market function in real situations like those described above).

At the abstract level, the argument holds that an organ market would privilege those who have the resources to purchase organs over those who do not. In contrast, a donation system guarantees equal access to available organs.

Yet a serious donation system is only compatible with the state's commitment to finance transplants for all recipients. A state that promotes donations and then allocates these organs only to those who can afford the costly operation would come under sharp criticism. If solidarity is asked of all, there must also be solidarity toward all.

The connection between donation and state funding is not so clear in a society where the sale of organs is allowed. As with any other good, including many necessary for survival like food, nothing prevents the state from not regulating and letting market forces operate up to a certain point. This could lead to what might be considered unjust distribution: a wealthy recipient could obtain an organ before another who lacks the necessary funds, even if the first patient is preceded by the other on the waiting list (or surpassed by the other in such established criteria as urgency and compatibility). Here lies the crux of the argument.

However, what works in the case of any transplant material could work in the case of organs. If we believe that the state must finance transplants for all, then just as with other therapies like dialysis, the state could subsidize the cost of organs for those who cannot afford them. In practice, the state does subsidize transplants in all developed countries through payment of fees, drugs, and surgery. So it would seem that nothing prevents the state from including the cost of an organ—currently cost-free—in the expenses. Assuming the state finances dialysis treatment, since transplants are substantially less expensive than dialysis from an economic point of view, the increase in kidney supply through an economic incentive would likely produce savings or at least no additional expenses. In the United States, the following hypothesis for savings for the case of economic incentives for cadaver kidneys holds: if kidney transplants were to increase by 1,000 *per* year, the medical care system would save thirty million dollars. It is fair to suppose that a similar calculation could be made in case of an increase in the supply of kidneys from living persons.[29]

Thus, from the abstract viewpoint, there does not appear to be a specific reason for prohibiting the sale as long as equal access to treatment is guaranteed to all. The same argument should be valid for any other necessary element such as material and medical fees that nobody questions.

Let us now analyze the issue within the context in which, in fact, an organ sale takes place or it is likely to take place. In this context, the state finances no part of the transplant. Therefore, under those circumstances the injustice in access to transplants already exists, even if there is no commercialization. Only the wealthy have access to organs, bought or donated. The sale of organs does not seem to produce a more unjust situation. It is true that only persons living in extreme poverty are potential sellers, while only wealthy persons are potential buyers. Yet the argument we are discussing here does not refer to this fact or group of facts. It focuses solely on how organs are distributed once procured. It criticizes the method of procuring (purchasing) only insofar as it impacts their later distribution. And in this sense, that an organ was purchased does not constitute a special problem. The problem already exists given that, in the context under discussion, the poor have no access to transplantation, regardless of how the organ is obtained. That the potential sellers are extremely poor has more to do with the argument that follows.

E. The Exploitation Argument

The situation of those who must sell a kidney to prevent their family or themselves from starvation or from suffering extreme deprivations can be qualified as an exploitive situation, at least in the broad sense.

In this context, the term "exploitation" should not be understood in the technical sense that Marxists embrace—the capitalist appropriation of capital surplus—since neither a production process nor a capital surplus exists here. Still, the word is suitable in a broad sense.

In the first place, the act of the seller is "quasi-coerced." A behavior is quasi-coerced when:

(1) The person is not literally coerced. Neither the legal obligation to follow that conduct (legal coercion) nor physical or mental coercion (through threats or direct physical force) exists.

(2) All the alternative courses of action predictably produce serious harm to the subject.

In this sense, we can say that a person who must choose between work and starvation is quasi-coerced to do so.

However, quasi-coercion is not sufficient for exploitation. After all, the large majority of persons must work to avoid starvation. For a situation to be exploitive, the behavior in question must be oppressive or significantly constrain the autonomy of people. In this sense, we can say that people are exploited if they are quasi-coerced into working an eighteen-hour day. Perhaps, the harm implied in having to work eighteen hours a day can somehow be compared to having to sell a body part.

An evaluation of this argument leads me to advance some features of my position on the issue. Even if we accept the reality of exploitation and that it is morally objectionable, blame does not fall on the seller but on the scheme of relationships that quasi-obligates a person to accept the circumstances. Unlike the Kantian and the paternalistic arguments, according to this argument the person who sells a kidney is not doing anything objectionable or irrational. Even more, doing this to survive is as justifiable as working eighteen hours *per* day to survive.

Instead, the issue is whether a legal prohibition on selling organs should be implemented despite the permissibility of the act. And from this perspective the solution to the problem cannot be the mere prohibition, just as solely restricting the work-day cannot resolve the situation of the exploited worker. If the argument says that the subject must act under conditions that present extremely limited viable alternatives, then as we have seen, the argument in favor of the legalization of organ sales is strengthened. The prohibition alone would further restrain the alternatives. While everything else remains the same, an alternative that is viable with permission comes to be nonviable under prohibition.

However, there is something of importance in the exploitation argument that I focus on below.

5. What Is Wrong with Selling Organs?

The above list of arguments is far from exhaustive, but it correctly represents the principal strategies adopted to reject the selling of organs from an ethical point of view.

My analysis shows that the best arguments do not allow for a straightforward justification for prohibiting the sale of organs from living persons, but at most, for strict state control. However, this conclusion might prove unsatisfactory. Something seems to be wrong with permitting individuals to self-mutilate out of need, even when this is their best option. In this section, I explain what it is exactly that is wrong.

We can assume that in a general social context that is somewhat ideal without poverty levels and solid social networks such as the Scandinavian countries, permission to sell organs *ad vitam* would not generate a flourishing market. At most, this would be an exceptional practice.

The moral distress elicited by organ sales arises only because the engine of success behind this market is poverty. It is not necessarily extreme poverty. We can imagine an organ market in countries with moderate levels of poverty such as the United States. But as in any situation of exploitation, distress results not when people sell their organs to travel abroad but when they sell a kidney out of need; when the best option or one of the reasonable options for an individual is selling a kidney.

Consequently, what is distressing is not the sale itself but only the situation that leads to the sale. In this sense, the criticism of exploitation is correct insofar as it focuses on the situation of persons who sell their organs or would do so were it legal. But this situation persists even if organ sales are prohibited and this prohibition is efficiently enforced. So, the mere prohibition to sell organs does not overcome this criticism. Furthermore, I would say that the person who sells a kidney to prevent his or her children from starving is doing the right thing. The individual decision is perfectly rational and morally correct. The mere prohibition supposes, instead, that this decision is morally objectionable in the same way that the prohibition to kill supposes that doing so is morally wrong. For this reason, when we carefully examine the issues we see that simply prohibiting organ sales is a sign of hypocrisy. We do not allow a person to perform an action that in itself is not objectionable, but we do nothing to prevent the situation that forces the individual to perform that action.

By way of illustration, let us take an example of labor exploitation again: persons who must work in subhuman conditions eighteen hours *per* day to survive. Should this kind of exploitation be prevented? The answer is yes. However, simply prohibiting an eighteen-hour workday will not do. Indeed, (as in the case of the sale of a kidney for travelling), we are not morally annoyed at an executive working eighteen hours. What labor laws seek is rather to prohibit employers from forcing workers to work eighteen hours, and to guarantee decent wages for a reasonable day's work, let us say eight hours. In the case of organ sales the simple prohibition will not do. What must be prevented are the conditions that tempt people to sell their organs.

This position must be distinguished from the position of those who positively defend the legal permission to sell organs. This differentiation is of consequence, as arguments are often similar. The philosopher J. Radcliff-Richards and colleagues state that in reality what is objectionable is not the sale of organs itself, but that persons are willing to sell because they find no better alternative to the prevailing situation. If this situation did not exist, the prohibition would be superfluous.[30] However, at the same time, the authors, like the majority of the defenders of commercialization, highlight that the basic concern that leads them to this defense is the continuous scarcity of organs and the failure of current policies based on altruistic donation to overcome it.

Something does not seem to be working well here. If the goal is to increase the supply of organs for transplantation, then what people want is not for quasi-coerced persons to stop selling their organs, but for them to continue doing so, otherwise, the shortage will persist. In other words, if the prohibition were to turn superfluous because no one was impoverished enough to have to resort to the sale, then the number of organs would not rise. What one wants is to take advantage of the situation in which "unfortunately" these persons find themselves, to achieve this increase.

It could be objected that in reality these are two separate things. On the one hand, a highly unfortunate *de facto* situation, poverty, exists. On the other hand, organs for transplantation are scarce. It is not that we wish to maintain poverty to obtain organs. The elimination of poverty would be preferable even if this meant that persons would no longer be willing to sell their organs and, therefore, that scarcity would rise once again. An analogy with cadaver organs could be made. Unfortunately, traffic accidents happen. Yet the fact that this is regrettable, and that we would like to avoid them, does not stop us from taking advantage of the situation of procuring organs for transplants. A significant percentage of brain-dead individuals, possible cadaver donors, originate from these kinds of accidents.

However, this argument does not hold up. A relevant difference exists between the two terms of the analogy, between poverty and traffic accidents. To an extent, the existence of traffic accidents is a situation we all tolerate. We believe that measures should be taken to minimize them, but we know that by living in a modern society we assume risks such as dying in an accident. However, we do not accept poverty as naturally inevitable. We believe it should be completely eradicated.

In order to see why this difference is relevant, suppose that accidents could be completely or almost completely prevented and that the state would be seriously responsible for not implementing policies that would achieve this goal. Also imagine that the organs of victims from accidents (brain dead) for some reason were never utilized for transplantation. In this situation, which now would be analogous to that of poverty, proposing the use of brain-dead individuals, victims of accidents, to resolve the problem of organ shortage would be inadequate since priority should be given to advocating an accident-prevention policy.

Extreme poverty is the main promoter of the possible success of an organ market. If we reject the idea that poverty is simply a state of affairs for which no one is responsible or over which the state has only limited responsibility—as in the case of traffic accidents—and instead hold that society in general or the state in particular is directly responsible for its existence, then for the state to take advantage of this situation to resolve the problem of shortage of organs is morally problematic.

But for the same reason, it is hypocritical on the state's part to prohibit for so-called "moral reasons" behaviors that do not harm others and that are the natural consequence of this state of affairs.

From this, it can be seen that my argument does not seek the legalization of organ sales as a remedy to their shortage. Legalization is no worse than the mere legal prohibition. Strictly speaking, perhaps a legally controlled system would be better than a black market. We are talking about two highly undesirable situations. But the unwanted one does not result from the commercialization of organs, the instrumental use of human beings, the transformation of persons into goods, or any of the arguments discussed so far. It originates uniquely and exclusively from the situation in which individuals willing to sell their organs find themselves. Organ sales reveal this situation but do not in themselves exacerbate it.

6. Conclusion

What is the moral of my argument? It is that the legal status of organ sales is less significant than many people think. The existence of organ markets should scandalize us much less than it does, and we should be scandalized far more by the forms of exploitation and inequality that generate this practice.

If we were to ask what exactly is wrong with organ sales we should respond, precisely, that it is not the sale itself or its mere legalization but the conditions that give rise to it. As long as these conditions persist, its simple prohibition by no means implies a significant moral improvement in society.[31]

NOTES

1. See Lloyd R. Cohen, "Increasing the Supply of Transplant Organs: The Virtues of Futures Market," *George Washington Law Review*, 58: 1 (1989); Henry Hansmann, "The Economics and Ethics of Markets for Human Organs," *Journal of Health Politics, Policy and Law*, 14: 1 (1989); James F. Blumstein, "The Case for Commerce in Organ Transplantation," *Transplantation Proceedings*, 24: 5 (1992), esp. pp. 2195-2196; David Jefferies, "The Body as commodity: The Use of Markets to Cure the Organ Deficit," *Indiana Journal of Global Studies*, 5: 2 (1998).

2. Leonhard Männer, "Zur Versicherbarkeit von transplantationsmedizinischen Leistungen," *Transplantationsmedizin: Ökonomische, Ethische, Rechtliche und Medizinische Aspekte*, ed. Peter Oberender (Baden Baden: Nomos, 1995), p. 75. See Eckhard Nagel, *et al.*, "Ökonomische Aspekte der Transplantationschirurgie," *Effektivität und Ökonomie Chirugischen Handelns*, eds. Edmund Neugebauer, Hans Troidl, and Rolf Lefering (Stuttgart: Thieme, 1994), pp. 136-137; Hans Krueger, "Economic Analysis of Solid Organ Transplantation: A Review for Policy Makers," *Health Policy*, 13 (1989).

3. See *ibid.*, esp. p. 7; and G. Dixaut, *et al.*, "Economic Evaluation of Renal Transplantation: France as an Example," *Organ Transplantation and Tissue Grafting*, eds. P. Hervé, *et al.* (Sydney/London: John Libbey & Company, 1996), pp. 703, 706-707.

4. Andrei Ivanov, "Israeli Link in Estonian 'Human Kidneys For Sale' Scam," *World News* (3 February 1998).

5. Rachelle Fishman, "Status of Living Organ Donors in Israel Questioned," *The Lancet*, 348: 9021 (1996).

6. See E. Santiago Delpín, "Allegations of Organ Commerce in Middle America," *Transplantation Proceedings*, 28:6 (1996).

7. See G. Abouna, *et al.*, "The Negative Impact of Paid Organ Donation," *Organ Replacement Therapy: Ethics, Justice, and Commerce*, eds. W. Land and J. Dossetor (Springer-Verlag: Berlin/Heidelberg, 1991), p. 164.

8. See, for example, *The Indian Express* (13 May, 1998).

9. *Die Zeit* 43 (22 October 1993), p. 23; *Die Zeit* 30 (22 July 1994), p. 25.

10. See Todd Leventhal, *The Child Organ Trafficking Rumor: A Modern 'Urban Legend.' A Report Submitted to the United Nations Special Rapporteur on the Sale of Children, Child Prostitution, and Child Pornography by the United States Information Agency* (Washington, DC: United States Information Agency, 1994); Economic and Social Council, United Nations, *Report of the Special Rapporteur on the Sale of Children, Child Prostitution and Child Pornography*, (Commission on Human Rights, 17 January, 1996), item 7; Economic and Social Council, United Nations, *Report of the Working Group on Contemporary Forms of Slavery*, (Commission on Human Rights, 11 July, 1997), item 44.

11. See K. C. Reddy, "Organ Donation for Consideration: An Indian View Point," *Organ Replacement Therapy*, eds. Land and Dossetor, p. 176.

12. See Abouna, "The Negative Impact", p. 166.

13. See *India Today* (December 1997).

14. See *The Times of India* (24 January 1999).

15. See Blumstein, "The Case for Commerce in Organ Transplantation," p. 2193; J. Radcliff-Richards, A. S. Daar, *et al.*, "The Case for Allowing Kidney Sales," *The Lancet*, 352: 9120 (1998), p. 1950; Jefferies, "The Body as Commodity."

16. See G. V. Tadd, "The Market for Body Parts: A Response to Ruth Chadwick" *Journal of Applied Ethics*, 8: 1 (1991), p. 99.

17. Radcliff-Richards, *et al.*, "The Case for Allowing Kidney Sales," p. 1951.

18. See A. S. Daar, "Rewarded Gifting and Rampant Commercialism in Perspective: Is There a Difference?", in Land and Dossetor, *Organ Replacement Therapy*.

19. Immanuel Kant, *Die Metaphysik der Sitten*, p. 417, (cited following original pagination).

20. *Ibid.*, p. 418.

21. *Ibid.*, p. 423. I follow the translation of I. Kant, *The Metaphysic of Morals* (Cambridge, England: Cambridge University Press, 1996).

22. *Ibid.*, p. 423.

23. See Gerald Dworkin in "Paternalism," *The Monist*, 56 (1972), p. 65.

24. *Ibid.*

25. John Stuart Mill, *On Liberty* (Toronto: Norton, 1975), p. 95. *Cf.* Gerald Dworkin *The Theory and Practice of Autonomy* (Cambridge, England: Cambridge University Press, 1989), p. 129.

26. See Dario Alfani, Paolo Bruzzone, *et al.*, "Issues in Organ Donation: Living Unrelated Kidney Transplantation," *Transplantation Proceedings*, 30 (1998).

27. See Wibren van der Burg, "The Slippery Slope Argument," *Ethics*, 102: 1 (1991).

28. *Ibid.*, p. 56.

29. See "Financial Incentives for Organ Donation. A Report of the UNOS Ethics Committee," (1993) (on Internet: www.concentric.net/~Holloway/financial.txt), p. 4.

30. Radcliff-Richards, *et al.*, "The Case for Allowing Kidney Sales," p. 1951.

31. I thank Arleen L. F. Salles for her comments and suggestions on earlier versions of this chapter.

Ten

INTERDISCIPLINARY ETHICS COMMITTEES FOR DETERMINING CRITERIA OF ORGAN DISTRIBUTION

María Graciela de Ortúzar

Translated from Spanish by María Teresa Lavalle

1. Introduction

At present, organ transplantation is a life alternative for thousands of people. However, unlike most regular therapies, its use depends on the availability of a resource that is scarce: organs. Because the demand for organs far outstrips supply, the development of ethical and legal norms to regulate organ donation and transplantation and to determine fair criteria for distributing organs from dead donors is critical.

In this chapter, I focus on this issue. I am not concerned with the distribution of scarce material and human resources in the health care system, or with the larger problem of guaranteeing equal access to organ transplant. I center on kidney transplants because they are less expensive and better than their alternative treatment, dialysis. Since they are widely accepted in all health care systems, including those with severe financial restrictions such as the Oregon Plan, I do not examine economic restrictions in access to transplantation.

Two stages in the distribution of scarce organs can be identified. First, a patient is admitted to a waiting list for transplants. Second, the organ is allocated. Ethical debate is involved at both stages. Drug addicts, alcoholic, hypertensive, the poor, and mentally or physically handicapped patients have been denied organ transplants.

The criterion physicians apply when deciding admittance to a waiting list is based on "social utilitarianism." Decisions supposedly made on strictly medical grounds and described as objective generally respond to psychosocial and financial values that are morally and medically irrelevant.

The most widely used principle in the final distribution of organs is normally that of "medical utility." The goal is to maximize the results of a given transplant through selection of patients who will benefit most from it. Benefit is explained in terms of longer survival and higher quality of life after the transplant. Medical utility favors efficiency over fairness in the distribution of scarce organs. This means that patients are discriminated because of highly questionable values and medical ratings, such as medical compatibility, and that a large number of additional factors affecting a patient's survival are not considered. In practice, no clear distinction between social and medical utility exists. However, the distinction is theoretically useful, for it shows that many times social utility values are masked behind medical values. This is particularly the case in Argentina, where many medical experts who neither recognize nor respect the autonomy and rights of patients make decisions on organ transplantation.

In this chapter, I take the Rawls-Daniels theoretical framework as a starting point. According to this framework, the distribution of goods should not depend on the acknowledgement of unacceptable patterns of unfair situations in people's health and salaries. As an alternative to "medical utility" as a guiding principle, I defend the use of Rawls's principles in the process of patient-selection.[1] When applied to the distribution of scarce organs for transplantation, the difference principle allows us to favor fairness and impartiality within some limits. Yet the difference principle cannot be strictly applied, because it would only favor those who are medically or socially worse off. It is necessary to strike a balance between favoring the worst off and guaranteeing fairness, efficiency, and patients' welfare.

Ultimately, I propose the creation of Interdisciplinary Ethics Committees to formulate and assess regulations for a fair distribution of scarce organs. These committees should operate within the framework of a deliberative democracy: citizens, professionals, and the state must justify any demand connected to the distribution of public goods, giving reasons acceptable to all those concerned.[2] The system must guarantee equal access to health care in order to secure fair social opportunities.

2. International and National Kidney Distribution Protocols: Critical Analysis and Proposed Alternatives

After carrying out several critical studies on previous schemes of distribution, European countries introduced a new criterion on kidney distribution in March 1996.[3] The 1988 scheme was based exclusively on the compatibility factor and underscored the principle of regionalization. These criteria were replaced because they were deemed responsible for a high percentage of long standing patients on the waiting list.[4]

The plan launched in 1996 aimed at cutting down on the average number of years that patients remain on the waiting list.[5] It was expected to increase the chances of receiving a transplant for patients with uncommon compatibility, and to maintain a balance in the level of national kidney exchanges. According to the new criterion, compatibility is not an exclusive priority. Instead, the new criterion attempts to balance medical compatibility and seniority on the waiting list. Distribution is carried out through a score system geared around the patient and based on the following factors: number of compatible antigens, chances of good compatibility, seniority on the waiting list, distance between donor and transplant programs, and balance in the national network.

One year after the introduction of the new criterion, the percentage of patients who had remained on the waiting list for more than five years and who received a transplant rose from 9 percent to 19 percent. The number of those receiving a transplant during their first year on the waiting list was cut down by 14 percent, and the number of low compatibility patients receiving transplants also rose by 10 percent. Exchange of kidneys between countries was also balanced; there was a slight rise in Austria, Luxembourg, The Netherlands, and particularly Belgium. Numbers decreased, though not significantly, in Germany, the country with the highest percentage exchange transplants.

Most of the patients receiving a transplant after the new kidney distribution criteria went into effect in European countries did not meet the old compatibility criteria. More and more patients with low compatibility are receiving transplants. These patients have remained on waiting lists for an excessive number of years. So there is a greater balance between compatibility, which focuses on efficiency, and seniority on the waiting list, which aims at fairness.

Following the same guidelines, the corresponding agency for reception and implant in the United States put forward a new criterion in 1996.[6] It endeavored to strike a balance between providing more opportunities to patients who spend several years on the waiting list, and promoting regional implants specially aimed at patients living in communities far away from reception centers.[7]

Through a multi-factorial algorithm system, the new criterion grants a greater percentage of points to the number of years on the waiting list. Admittance to the waiting list counts from the time of registration in dialysis. The waiting list criterion is also used as a tiebreaker. The criterion underscores fairness in kidney distribution by granting special attention to children—whose development is threatened—and people already suffering from lack of opportunities in general. The new plan also limits the medical emergency category. It is applied to patients who can only receive peritoneal or vascular dialysis.

In this plan, regionalization, the promotion of local implants, becomes a priority for medical, social, and practical reasons. Medically, regionalization is connected to the minimum time required for preserving organs before an implant. Socially, regionalization is related to the greater possibility of access to renal transplantation among patients in local transplant centers. Practically, regionalization is connected to backing local efforts to ensure donation. To guarantee equality of opportunity, the plan suggests that patients living at a greater distance from the donor facility be allotted additional points. The principle of regionalization is balanced by the time spent on the waiting list. For example, in region one of UNOS, New England, the percentage of kidneys distributed among minority groups (African-Americans and Hispanic) rose from 17 percent to 22 percent after the change in points *per* medical compatibility, and the emphasis on regionalization.

However, racial discrimination in organ transplant is still a reality. This is due to the uneven effect of distribution based on the quality of "compatibility." Compatibility-based distribution does not favor inter-racial transplant. In general, arguments for the compatibility criterion are grounded on the strong connection between compatibility and transplant outcome. This connection has been proven in live, related—genetically similar—donors. However, in cadaver transplant—where donor and recipient have different genetic characteristics—the advantages of compatibility have not been identified, and evidence of its efficiency is unavailable.

Furthermore, in the age of immunosuppressive agents, compatibility should not operate as a restrictive factor for black recipients. A patient's survival curve does not result solely from one factor, as the compatibility criterion suggests. While results may be influenced by a few percentage points with HLA matching, ultimately the outcome is determined by the combination of patient, quality of the donor kidney, surgical skill, improvements in immunosuppressive protocol, reduction of morbidity, and ongoing medical care. Although immunologists and clinicians acknowledge that kidney-graft survival outcomes are multifactorial, the debate continues.[8]

A deeper analysis into the reasons for discriminating minority groups shows that the medical profession tends to exclude patients on racial grounds. That black patients suffer a higher rate of chronic renal impairment and a lower rate of post-transplant survival than white patients has led some authors to suggest that, even if compatibility-based criteria or socioeconomic mechanisms were altered to ensure access to transplantation for black people, results would not change due to racial differences.[9] Since black persons suffer a higher rate of survival in dialysis, peritoneal dialysis is recommended as their best option in the final stages of renal illness. A study of preferences also shows that black patients are less likely to want a transplant.[10] However, in general, patients who have undergone transplant show a higher rate of survival than those on the waiting list do.[11]

We should not underestimate the power and influence of physicians in the determination of patients' preferences and in the selection of transplant-admission criteria. Physicians should give full information to their patients about the advantages and alternative treatments available so patients can make informed decisions. Furthermore, physicians should avoid backing up statements that foster discrimination or exclusion of patients from transplantation based on race. Black patients in dialysis might show a higher survival rate than white patients, and they might have a lower rate of post-transplant survival. However, transplants also enhance the life expectancy of black patients. Estimates indicate that the rise in life expectancy among transplant-patients amounts to six years in black patients and ten years in white patients.

Despite differences in results and because of them, physicians must inform patients on alternative treatments, on their advantages and disadvantages, and on their rights. They must also guarantee non-exclusive criteria in order to avoid discrimination based on race.

In Argentina, the law on kidney distribution for transplantation has undergone two changes.[12] In 1995, the criterion for organ allocation was the final score obtained after taking into account the amount and quality of antigens shared by the donor, length of registration on the waiting list, and age of the recipients.[13] Since the central variable was compatibility, serologic methods were replaced with techniques from molecular biology.[14]

Emergency cases, hypersensitive recipients, and pediatric patients (under 14 years of age) were given priority. Compatibility, blood groups, longer period on the waiting list (in years, months, and days)—also shown as longer period in dialysis—and young age (in years, months, and days) in that order were considered tie breakers. The principle of regionalization also played a significant role in distribution policies. Organs were distributed locally.

Yet, although the criterion included non-medical variables—age and length of time on the waiting list—these did not balance off the high score attributed to compatibility.

The National Transplant Agency of Argentina (INCUCAI) revised the criterion for kidney distribution in 1998.[15] Organ allocation was to be determined by blood group, by the score obtained from the quality and quantity of shared antigens, by the score resulting from the recipient's age (establishing only an under-age category), and by the immunology status of the hypersensitive recipient.

The regionalization principle still holds, but the new criterion for kidney distribution rules out the emergency category. It gives priority to pediatric patients (up to eighteen years of age at the date of distribution) because of growth and developmental problems suffered by children with renal deficiencies.

That compatibility is not the sole determining factor in the revised criterion is shown by the points allotted to quality and quantity of antigens. However, compatibility still plays a central role. The current criterion considers years on the waiting list exclusively as a tiebreaker, and this has great social value for it favors fairness, giving more opportunities to those who have waited longer. The examination of kidney-distribution criteria in

Argentina shows that no criterion balances efficiency-focused factors with fairness-focused ones. Compatibility takes precedence over social factors such as position on the waiting list and regionalization, which favor fairness.

A remarkable difference between changes in distribution criteria in Argentina, Europe, and North America exists. The primary aim of the protocols presented in 1998 in Europe and North America is to reverse the inequalities resulting from the application of distribution criteria exclusively focused on medical compatibility between organ donor and organ recipient. The emphasis on compatibility leads to a high percentage of patients on waiting lists for long periods. It leads to a good number of patients not receiving organs for regional reasons—low input or distance from implant programs in the region. Regarding patient survival, commonly taken into account by physicians when selecting recipients, qualitative and quantitative studies carried out in Argentina show that in living-donor transplantation, the probability of survival is significantly higher than in dead-donor transplantation. Cumulative survival probability in cadaveric transplant diminishes by slightly over 40 percent after five years. In the case of living donors, probability goes down almost thirteen points.[16] Although many people argue for enhancing compatibility in patient-selection based on survival, studies do not show how the compatibility factor operates in patients with cadaveric transplants. There are not enough studies and statistics on cadaveric transplant.

Outstanding transplantation and immunology experts have argued against the compatibility criterion. Thomas E. Starzl and John Fung, from the University of Pittsburgh, and Ronald Guttmann, from McGill University Center for Clinical Immunobiology and Transplantation in Canada, question the absolute weight granted to medical compatibility. They state,

> The emphasis on tissue matching that wrecked the US point-system was the product of lobbying contests between the advocates of tissue matching (who for the most part managed or supplied the histocompatibility laboratories) and the transplant surgeons, who realized that tissue matching did not accurately predict outcome but lacked the passion for debate.[17]

> If there are no new genetic or medical arguments to decide who shall get the next kidney, why is it that rules of rationing are still determined by the medical profession?[18]

In Argentina, compatibility and the decision of medical experts are still the determining factors in selecting potential recipients. Because the focus is on transplant results and the efficiency of the system, an analysis of the factors involved when deciding admission or rejection of patients to the waiting list and organ allocation is crucial. This analysis should also focus on the role played by physicians—seen as experts—in the process of selecting recipients. Let us focus on the "medical" process of admission to the waiting list. This process is a major filter, a step with the highest chances of exclusion. Physicians do not set out clearly the criteria and rules involved in deciding admission. Psychosocial considerations, such as the patient's behavior towards authorities, past record on irresponsible behavior, citizenship, medical insurance, intelligence quotient, marital status, level of education, and employment play an important role in the process. Yet these considerations are not considered relevant to the potential donor status of people.

These criteria make up the so-called "medical criteria of social utility." Allegedly, physicians objectively apply these to select patients who will have access to transplantation. Yet, if the criteria were subject to public debate, physicians would barely be able to find scientific grounds for turning down some patients. This is so because physicians' decision to turn down patients is often based upon notions about the social worth of the patient and the value his life has for society at large.

In Argentina, the decision of the medical expert strongly influences access to the waiting list. Yet, the physician bases his decision on whether to admit the patient on his personal values. Some years ago, for example, the ethics committee in a general hospital discussed the following two cases.[19] The first concerned a deaf and mentally retarded eleven-year-old, poverty-stricken girl. The patient was taken to the hospital because of domestic violence, and was diagnosed with renal deficiency. The standard treatment called for dialysis and admission to the waiting list for renal transplantation, but physicians refused both. The decision was based on two considerations: her disability and her social status. When the ethics committee discussed the case, the consensus was that there were no medical, ethical, or social grounds for denying the girl her right to be admitted to the waiting list, since she needed transplant treatment. Through and because of the ethics committee's intervention, the girl received dialysis and was admitted to the waiting list; later, she had transplant surgery.

A second case discussed by the ethics committee involved a Jehovah's Witness. Because of the religious-based refusal of blood transfusions by members of this group, the surgeon refused to perform a transplant. Jehova Witnesses are usually donors and, with the exception of transfusions, they fully cooperate with physicians. Several Jehovah's Witnesses have received transplants. While it is true that a surgeon should not be forced to perform the transplant and refrain from giving the patient blood transfusions if necessary, he might refer the patient to another surgeon ready to do so. This would not deny access to transplant programs on religious grounds.

These examples show that the values presumed in selection criteria for admitting patients to a waiting list are often non-medical. Social utility parameters are disguised under "medical utility" understood in terms of efficiency and best results.

In Argentina, the reasons that physicians present for not allowing patients to be on the waiting list are supposedly medical, for example, cardiovascular illness, liver diseases, neoplasia, and frequent vascular attacks.[20] These are restrictive conditions when considering organ survival and years of life of the patient. Nevertheless, these allegedly medical causes mask social criteria. Consider, for example, age. The presumption is that being older spells higher chances of cardiovascular illness; thus, older patients are deemed, *a priori*, unacceptable on a waiting list, regardless of their condition.

However, considered within a multifactorial predictive model, results cannot be justified from the standpoint of efficiency. There is no moral justification for basing organ rationing on uncertain outcomes of a narrow range of genetic and medical variables.[21]

Some patients do not have enough information on their right to be admitted to a waiting list; others lack financial resources to travel and apply for state-subsidized transplantation. These people are often kept out of the waiting list because physicians do not fully inform them about their rights and do not inform transplantation centers about the patient's need for a transplant. Physicians do not consider patients to be autonomous agents capable of making decisions. The expert handles the information and decides the variables to be taken into account when allocating resources.[22]

In short, in Argentina, the medical expert determines criteria and decisions on who has access to organ transplantation on the basis of utilitarian considerations. However, those considerations lack an empirical basis. Utilitarian arguments and medical values disguise psychosocial and racial reasons that are morally irrelevant for denying access to transplantation. Patients are helpless because they are not aware of their rights and of the possibility of choosing alternative treatments or refusing treatment.

3. Ethical Arguments Applied to the Distribution of Organs: Utilitarian vs. Rawlsian

At a theoretical level, the ethical conflict in organ distribution is set in the opposition between utilitarians (concerned with efficiency) and Rawlsians (mainly concerned with equality). A third stance, the libertarian view, would limit access to transplantation to those who can pay for it, thus fostering organ-trade. I do not consider this position because it raises issues of rationing material resources and financial restrictions to transplants that are beyond the scope of this chapter. This position challenges the role of the state in providing subsidies for transplants, and implies a radical change in present policies.

Utilitarianism is the most commonly used criterion, widely accepted by the medical community. It calls for choosing recipients according to the best foreseeable outcome. Its basic aim is efficiency. Ethical conflicts inherent to medical education are frequent when physicians must decide whether to choose efficiency or urgency in selecting recipients. In this case, the notion at stake is that of medical need, as opposed to efficiency. Nevertheless, medical utilitarianism is not the only utilitarian criterion for organ distribution.

The second stance, the Rawlsian position, aims at fostering fairness without undermining the criterion of medical efficiency. This calls for a balance between fairness and efficiency in organ-distribution, guaranteeing equality of access above all.

A. Utilitarian Arguments: Medical or Social Utilitarianism?

According to James Childress, "medical utility" is not necessarily opposed to fairness. A fair use of the medical utility criterion would call for selecting patients according to the best predictions on transplant results.[23] In Childress's opinion, this is "unfortunate but not necessarily unfair;" patients who ignore their own medical condition would choose the principle of medical utility.[24] To maximize survival indexes and additional years of life utilitarians would say that organs should go to those who can most benefit from them.[25]

Utilitarian arguments are common in the process of admission to waiting lists. Medical utilitarianism, however, is not the only utilitarian criterion for the distribution of scarce resources. In the case of alcoholics, drug addicts, Down-Syndrome patients, prisoners, the poor, blacks, and women, ethical arguments that appeal to individual responsibility underlie medical arguments, with no empirical data to ground them. In practice, social utilitarianism usually works as the criterion determining admission of patients to the waiting list.

To illustrate this, let us focus on alcoholic patients and on the arguments provided for rejecting them as organ recipients. One argument has to do with the notion of individual responsibility. Alcoholic patients and drug addicts are usually considered responsible for their condition. Thus, their case nicely illustrates the use of "individual responsibility" as a criterion for leaving them out of the health care system. In England, for example, patients who only have themselves to blame for their illness are denied treatment. "Moral risk" is assessed in the allocation of medical resources: smokers, alcoholics, drug addicts, the hypertensive, and the obese would be denied access to transplantation.

A variation of the argument connects it with the notion of deterrence. Allegedly, denying transplants to alcoholics and drug addicts would deter others from such behavior.

Some authors try to soften this stance by arguing that alcoholics should receive transplants but should not have top priority on the waiting list. They argue further that alcoholics should not receive the treatment that patients who are not responsible for their own illness receive.

A different argument used to deny access to alcoholics and drug addicts is that, given the shortage of organs and the high cost of transplantation, public opinion would not agree to such transplants. Allowing alcoholics or drug addicts to receive an organ would be detrimental to organ donation.

Finally, it is argued that alcoholic patients receiving transplantation have low survival rates after transplant and high chances of a recurrence of their condition.

These arguments do not make a clear reference to the social values used to deny treatment to these patients. However, ultimately the values that underlie the selection process are not based on medical utility, medical assessment of transplantation prediction, and survival index. They are actually based on social utility.

Let us examine the arguments, starting with the one that focuses on the notion of personal responsibility. First, the extent to which people are responsible for their condition is questionable. Many people contend that alcoholics have either a genetic disposition or little will power, compounded in many cases by an unfavorable social environment. Alcoholics are ill, just like the other patients on the waiting list. Turning them down because of natural and social differences does not result in fairness in organ distribution for transplantation.

The appeal to the notion of deterrence is not adequate either. It is a fact that people do not stop drinking or taking drugs because they know that they will not receive a transplant if they need one. A tax on alcohol or drugs might be more useful for that end.

Now let us turn to the argument that focuses on organ shortage and public opinion. The fact is that, although statistically the rate of donations is under 50 percent in most countries, this is not connected to the characteristics of the recipients. It has to do with the public not fully understanding basic points about organ donation and transplantation. People do not know much about the organ reception process, do not know what whole brain death is, do not have the necessary information on the process of ablation, and do not trust procurement agencies.[26] Therefore, the argument that says that providing alcoholic patients with transplants would cause a fall in organ donation lacks empirical grounding. It is based on social prejudice and, as such, it is inadequate. Insofar as arguments about approval or disapproval by the public are not based on facts, they are vague and ambiguous.

The argument that concentrates exclusively on medical reasons to reject alcoholics is not adequate either. There are no statistics on the survival rate of alcoholic patients to justify rejecting them as prospective recipients.[27] In fact, studies have shown that when it comes to quality of life and general benefits, a liver transplant has the same effect on alcoholic and non-alcoholic patients; the percentage of recurrence is under 10 percent.[28] Therefore, there is no medical reason for ruling out transplantation for alcoholic patients while emergency and second-transplant patients are receiving organs.

Finally, if the reason for denying organs to alcoholics is ethical, this means that physicians should make a moral assessment of each patient before treatment. However, physicians treat smokers, patients who suffer hypertension because of malnutrition, and people who are erratic about their health care on a daily basis. Those people are not denied treatment on medical or moral grounds. Thus, if surgery is neither life threatening nor redundant, access to transplantation should not be denied to patients who disclose their own illness upon registering on the waiting list; have no alternative treatment; accept responsibility for their treatment; and comply with the minimum conditions for a favorable post-transplant process.

There are no medical, social, or moral reasons for denying access to past alcoholic patients *a priori*. Like other patients, they are ill and need a transplant. We cannot assume that persons choose to be ill or are responsible for their illness. It is unlikely that an alcoholic would have chosen to be so, and suffer accordingly. If the health system and society promote the rejection of alcoholics as candidates for transplantation because they are alcoholics, such denial is a kind of moral punishment that is not grounded on medical variables.

The same can be said of denying transplants to prisoners. Moral punishment through denial is not common when providing primary healthcare to prisoners. Yet, although it contradicts a basic Hippocratic principle, the notion seems to underlie the denial of transplantation to prisoners because they have broken the social contract. Nevertheless, the alleged distinction between different kinds of health care is problematic. There are no degrees in health care.[29]

The restriction in transplant access based on moral or social grounds should not be accepted. Prisoners, including murderers, are not denied medical care when needed, so they should not be denied access to transplantation simply because they are prisoners.

It could be argued that prisoners are in jail precisely to pay for their moral debt to society. Some of those prisoners have minor debts probably related to financial problems. Thus, even if one of them needs a transplant and his medical condition is better than that of a free individual whose morals we know nothing about, we should deny a transplant *a priori* on grounds of social justice. However, before we do that, we must be ready to use health care as an instrument of moral punishment instead of making the best possible use of the organ, and defending fairness.

A different set of issues is raised by the notion of necessity—emergency. This is an ambiguous and relative notion that has been connected to the seriousness of the illness and to the degree of benefit or potential benefit, among others. This category is highly malleable and it must be subject to constant control by limiting the number of times a given patient can be included in the category of urgencies, and by controlling prerequisites.

Although patients with little chances of success are denied access to transplantation, emergency patients with scarce possibilities of survival receive transplants. Complex cases of multiple transplantation or second transplant are also admitted. In these cases, physicians can apply new transplantation techniques and experiment on the patient.

Despite the priority of the efficiency criterion, there is agreement within the medical community that critical patients should receive organs. This causes constant conflict between the notion of need—emergency—and that of maximizing well-being—efficiency. In emergencies, the aim is to help the least advantaged. Efficiency, on the other hand, suggests giving resources to the person with more chances of overcoming his problems through surgery, increasing his life span and expectations.

Second transplants have been defended on account of the suffering caused to the patient by the failure of transplant surgery. According to the argument, physicians have a duty not to abandon their patients. Arguments against second transplants are based on the unfairness of allowing a few individuals to receive multiple transplantation while others on the waiting list have never received an organ. In addition, efficiency is always lower in second transplants.

These considerations lead to the following: second transplants should not be assessed in general terms. Each kind of transplantation requires individual examination. For example, renal-transplants would not entail the death of other people on the waiting list.

Multiple transplantation also means that while some people receive several organs others receive none. In both cases, selection criteria are based on medical training. First, physicians are trained to act in an emergency disregarding any rationing criteria, attempting to save the patient's life in every possible way. Second, medical training requires trying new techniques and working on the most novel and interesting cases from the point of view of the surgeon.

In the case of kidneys, the emergency category, "treating the weakest patient first if he has a chance of survival," is questionable because an alternative method—dialysis—exists. The emergency category is often at odds with the social criterion of a waiting list, "first come, first served," and with the efficiency criterion.

The elimination of the emergency category in kidney distribution protocols, and the introduction of the waiting list as an essential variable in the final stage of organ distribution are indispensable to determine whether the criterion chosen favors fairness in access to transplantation.

B. Rawlsian View: Equality of Opportunity

In Rawls's terms, the notion of justice as fairness is defined through a new formulation of the philosophical tradition of the social contract that starts with a hypothetical situation: the original position. This gathers a group of individuals, placed in reciprocal conditions of equality, who expect to reach an agreement on the most adequate norms to rule the basic institutions of their society. In order to set up a fair procedure, the parties are situated behind a veil of ignorance depriving them of knowledge about their aims, gender, race, place in society, fortune, natural assets, and abilities. The original position is fair because it does not allow the unequal distribution of natural assets or social status to have any weight when discussing issues connected to justice. The aim is to correct inequalities caused by the contingencies of the natural and the social lotteries. Although in themselves the effects caused by such lotteries are neither fair nor unfair, the way society treats them concerns distributive justice.

If each institution sets up different principles for solving local issues, the result may be global unfairness. In this sense, the greatest contribution of the notion of justice as fairness is its concern with defending the rights of the individual, and ensuring an impartial redistribution of goods favoring the less advantaged.

Rawls holds that people in the worst socioeconomic situation would feel even more miserable if they knew that their lot could be improved but it is deliberately left untouched. This leads him to mention the Kantian condition of publicity as a restriction, which holds in any theory of justice: it must admit public broadcasting without diminishing its value or the possibility of carrying it out.

Redistribution would be restricted to the interests of its beneficiaries and not of society. One of Rawls's principles of justice, the difference principle, can be justified as a form of non-envious egalitarianism. Rational individuals would prefer a *maximin* policy, and would therefore choose the difference principle. According to this principle,

> social and economic inequalities must comply with two conditions in order to be justified: a) they must be attached to positions and offices open to all under conditions of fair equality and opportunity, b) they must be to the greatest benefit of the least advantaged members of society.[30]

Justice as fairness demands compensation for the unfairness brought about by the natural and the social lotteries. The aim is to recover the normal functioning of the organism and avoid the perpetuation of unfairness and social inequalities.[31] From a Rawlsian standpoint, no ethical reasons exist for excluding people in need of transplantation on psychosocial grounds—

particularly in the process of access to the waiting list. Thus, it would not be fair to take efficiency as the sole value in organ distribution, overlooking the social significance of medical care.

Rawls's difference principle or, more specifically, his *maximin* criterion, would be an adequate pattern for selecting patients and for allocating organs. This is so because an unequal distribution of those goods is fair only if it complies with the *maximin* rule, namely, if no other way of organizing social institutions that will improve the expectations of the least advantaged group exists.[32]

Morally relevant characteristics for admission to the waiting list and final distribution of organs must not be based on social (status, past moral conduct, finances, geographical location) or natural (gender, race, and age) considerations. However, even if we reject efficiency as a determining factor for distribution, we cannot overlook it when trying to balance fairness and efficiency in organ-allocation. In this sense, the goal is not to favor only the naturally least advantaged, but to find a happy medium and to avoid turning allocation into a futile operation. From a socioeconomic standpoint favoring exclusively the least advantaged would lead to discriminating against other groups.

A central problem in applying the *maximin* criterion is how to define the worst situated. I favor a non-exclusively medical notion of the worst situated, people whose social conditions, illness, and the time spent on the waiting list have diminished their opportunities and their autonomy to carry out their life plan.

In kidney transplants no medical emergency occurs. Although the worst situated is defined by comparison to others, children are favored on the basis of the need to protect their psycho-physical development, and others on the basis of a long record of natural and social unfairness. The goal is to make sure that patients from poor areas in need of a transplant have access to the waiting list and are not left out on account of their socioeconomic situation. This requires some social work. Patients who have received a transplant are immunologically depressed and in need of an adequate social environment to recover from surgery and continue with the appropriate treatment. It is essential that those patients reclaim their autonomy.

However, it has been noted that it is impossible to apply the *maximin* criterion in all cases to guarantee a fair distribution of organs.[33] The danger lies in a strict enforcement of the *maximin* principle that might lead to offer opportunities exclusively to the least advantaged. This would not promote fairness. We should admit then that it is impossible to strike a stable balance in the process of distribution of scarce resources. Choosing one criterion will cause inequalities. Thus, some group will necessarily object to whichever criterion is chosen because it will discriminate against some and favor others.

In short, Rawls's *maximin* principle can be a good guideline in the assessment of categories, both for admission to the waiting list and ultimate distribution of organs. It can help to counterbalance the strong utilitarian rationing model. Yet the principle should not be strictly applied in every situation.

The *maximin* criterion tries to counterbalance the importance given to years of life and patient survival by focusing on fair equality of opportunities. However, regularly favoring the least advantaged would surely bring disadvantages to other patients, whose rights would be affected. At the same time, systematically rejecting the least advantaged and denying them opportunities would only stress natural and social injustice. Rawls's principles are not to be overlooked, but they cannot completely solve the fair distribution of scarce organs.

If we want to find a fair model we must develop new ways of approaching the problem of organ-allocation, even against medical opinion on the subject, to attain a balance between efficiency and fairness. On one hand, people should be able to exercise their autonomy, and this presumes a level of education that will enable them to decide freely about their treatment, and join the waiting list. On the other hand, the state should regulate and control access by establishing non-restrictive or discriminative criteria for admission and for distribution of scarce organs.

Ultimately, the decision about organ-distribution criteria must be based on democratic deliberation guaranteeing impartiality and the legitimacy of the selected criteria.

4. Alternative Proposals to the Medical Model of Patient Selection: Public Consultation or Interdisciplinary Committees?

In order to make sure that the medical expert does not bias selection criteria, some authors have argued that publicity and citizen participation should be the main requisites for admittance to an organ transplantation waiting list.[34] Two models of how social participation can determine criteria have been developed. One is public consultation based on social preferences. The other is through specific interdisciplinary committees.

An example of the first is the criteria for selecting patients for kidney transplant proposed in Alberta, Canada. In the Alberta model, normative and prescriptive criteria are based on social preferences.[35] Each preference represents a social value, identified as operational in the process of selecting patients for admittance to the waiting list for transplants. The main categories employed to represent preferences are self-sufficiency, intelligence, survival probability, and responsibility.

The first category, self-sufficiency, substitutes the criterion of autonomy of the patient assessed in the process of selection of prospective recipients. The Hospital of Alberta drew up a normative scale of medical emergency to be used in organ-distribution. The scale is based on the expected condition of the patient after transplantation. Analysis is not restricted to a common notion of activity but is connected to the future assessment of the patient's contribution to society through production.

The second category is intelligence. Most people would agree that cognitive ability is a criterion for selection. The ethical problem is how to establish appropriate levels in intelligence assessment. Few people would accept giving a transplant to a patient in a vegetative condition. The IQ used as a standard is connected to other items, such as self-sufficiency.

Another factor included in the selection process is survival probability. Nevertheless, this is conditioned by the time spent on the waiting list, since the patient's worsening condition during that period would affect his or her chances of survival. This means that this criterion cannot be considered independently from others, and it is not absolute.

Lastly, the responsibility of prospective recipients and their cooperation with the physician play a significant role in selecting patients. This category would seem to leave out alcoholics and drug addicts, among others.

The Alberta model is hierarchical, based on multiple criteria. The perspectives of both physicians and the community are taken into account. Criteria for selecting patients on the waiting list for transplantation are not assessed individually, but in pairs, to establish their relative importance: conditions of social eligibility for the waiting list, donor-recipient compatibility evaluated together with position on the waiting list, medical emergency, and prospective condition of the patient. Nevertheless, the final list shows that despite the attempt to balance efficiency and fairness, utilitarian criteria have the upper hand even in the community's statements. The aim is to maximize the survival of the organ and the patient.

At present, the value of democratic processes for determining fairness is under discussion. Some people believe that the expression of preferences by the community distorts intuition-based statements, or theories of justice in the distribution of medical resources. The problem is how to assess and weight intuitions, theoretical statements, and stated preferences. Norman Daniels wonders,

> Should we in the end think of the democratic process as a matter of pure procedural justice? If so, we have no way to correct the judgment made through that process, for what it determines to be fair is what counts as fair. Or should we really consider the democratic process as an impure and imperfect form of procedural justice? Then it is one that can be corrected by appeal to some prior notion of what constitutes a fair outcome of rationing.[36]

Similar criticisms apply to other proposals that attempt to justify public policy in terms of social preferences.

I propose the creation of interdisciplinary ethics committees as an alternative to processes of public consultation and to decision making left exclusively in the hands of medical experts. These committees would carry out ethical deliberations on criteria for kidney-distribution, and they would be a forum for democratic deliberation on ethical issues. Democratic deliberation is to be understood as the demand for justification of all collective decisions and actions. In turn, justification requires the production of reasons that those who are affected by such decisions and actions, in our case patients in need of transplantation, may accept.[37] Thus, my proposal is that neither allegedly neutral procedures nor basic constitutional values should determine criteria.

A democracy cannot avoid disagreements among professionals, citizens, and the state, but it does allow for a positive discussion of such disagreements. The basic aims of democratic deliberation are to promote the legitimacy of collective decisions, to foster public spirit, to favor mutual respect, and to correct the mistakes of citizens, professionals, and government. In what follows, I briefly discuss these aims.

First, the problem of the legitimacy of collective decisions arises because organs are scarce. If shortage did not exist, there would be no moral issue. It is true that organ shortage cannot be solved through deliberation. But deliberation helps those who do not receive organs to understand and accept the legitimacy of the decisions made. They can continue trusting the system and working towards a more frequent donation of organs, even if their own needs have not been satisfied. People are more likely to accept their situation if they see that equal treatment is guaranteed, that receiving transplantation is not related to economic considerations, and that relevant demands connected to moral conflict are subsequently analyzed. In this sense, impartiality plays an important role. Morally arbitrary factors such as gender, race, socioeconomic status, and intelligence must not determine organ distribution.

Second, democratic deliberation fosters public spirit, focusing on common interests or the "common good," and encouraging citizen participation and willingness to discuss conflictive ethical issues with no definite solution. Committee members must promote common interests above individual or institutional ones. That is why there should be no institutional administrators and political agents among its members. Securing equal standing among members of the committee is essential. Members should be knowledgeable, possess an adequate level of information, a tolerant disposition, and an open mind.

Third, mutual respect in decisions must be encouraged. This means accepting and analyzing the moral merit of the opponent's views and applying an "economy of moral disagreement," leaving incompatible and polarizing values out of the conflict and the moral debate.

Finally, one of the principal aims of the committee should be to understand decisions on moral problems, and to provide a foundation for those decisions, correcting mistakes. Openness to change is indispensable. The basic notion is still that of Kant and Rawls: publicity or "universalization" of the decision. If the action or decision on organ-distribution criteria can be defended in the public arena, it is morally acceptable.

These committees should be involved in the process of selecting patients for admittance to organ transplantation waiting lists and in determining regulations or protocols for organ distribution. They should also review protocols and regulations on a regular basis.

The need to review criteria for kidney distribution regularly in Argentina leads me to propose the creation of committees inspired on Kantian-Rawlsian principles. However, for them to work and for equal access to transplantation to be secured, patients and physicians must be educated.

Patients must be educated on their own rights and on the process of obtaining an organ and getting a transplant. To see why this is crucial, we can focus on the process of obtaining an organ, when the first studies are carried out to decide the final selection of the recipient. The process begins with the identification of prospective donors, once their death is ascertained, and is followed by a request to the family for the patient's organs. If the family agrees, the ablation and grafting teams are called in, and the process of organ distribution begins. In the case of kidneys, physicians and selected patients are informed in order to carry out the final donor cross-match. If in the course of this process the physician, who must notify the patient about the ongoing process, rejects the organ for transplantation, he must give reasons for his rejection and inform the prospective recipient.

In some cases, physicians have rejected organs without notifying the patient, and have not provided medical reasons to justify their decision. Economic interests or the personal beliefs of the physician may favor keeping the patient in dialysis and rejecting transplantation. This is yet another proof of the discretionary power of physicians still ruling our countries, and of physician's lack of information and education on the rights of prospective recipients. This also illustrates some of the difficulties involved in the process of selection and organ distribution that is shrouded in medical objective opinion. However, the patient is the only person with the right to decide whether to continue with dialysis or to get a transplant.

The selection of patients on the waiting list must guarantee a fair equality of opportunity. Justice requires that upon a serious illness the normal functioning of the organism of a typical member of the species be restored, whenever possible.[38] This does not mean that patients must receive a transplant with the risk and suffering that surgery entails if no reasonable chances of survival exist. It would be wrong to give a transplant or admit this type of patients to a waiting list. But providing information and educating patients on their rights are essential to autonomous action.

In turn, physicians must receive a humanistic and ethical education to help them face the growing ethical conflicts brought about by technological developments. Argentine physicians are trained to act, and they are still inspired by dominant utilitarian notions and the widespread discretionalism of their peers.

Education is an indispensable tool in autonomous decision making, and interdisciplinary ethics committees must foster this. Education and multidisciplinary discussion should be complemented by a stronger policy aimed at shortening waiting lists, which is a responsibility of the state.

5. Summary

Any criterion used to determine how to allocate indivisible and scarce resources such as organs entails that some patients will not receive the needed good. In the case discussed in this chapter, the ethical problem lies in justifying the criteria for determining who is going to receive a needed organ. More specifically, the ethical discussion revolves around the determination of the morally relevant characteristics for accepting or rejecting patients in the two stages of selection for transplantation.

International and national protocols for organ allocation generally use the criterion of medical utility based on medical compatibility. Underlying this criterion is the belief that the success of an organ transplant depends solely on a higher compatibility between the organ donor and the organ recipient. However, medical considerations do not support this argument. In the first place, because the development of immunosuppressant drugs allows for good results with low compatibility. In the second place, because the direct correlation between compatibility and transplant efficiency has not been proven in the case of cadaver transplant where donor and recipient have different genetic characteristics. Moreover, we saw that beyond the purely medical facts, this criterion discriminates against some populations, for example, blacks. Following the publication of statistics and registers of such discrimination, large international centers modified their criteria for renal distribution to alter the unfairness caused by the alleged absolute correlation between compatibility and efficiency.

Yet, in many countries including Argentina, criteria of medical and social utility are overtly or covertly operative. In this chapter, I argued that decisions on who is admitted to a waiting list for transplantation should not be solely determined by medical experts, since no medical and genetic argument to set a rule for organ-rationing exists. Furthermore, selection of patients should not be based on values that discriminate on the basis of morally arbitrary reasons, masking "social utilitarianism" under the guise of "medical utilitarianism." Organ distribution should be based on social decisions ruled by impartial criteria. The Rawls-Daniels theory that defends the right to health is a valuable contribution for grounding equal rights for admission to the waiting list, and yet the *maximin* criterion cannot be used exclusively to favor fairness in every single case. The difference principle cannot be strictly applied because it would only favor the worst situated group (medically and socially) in the process of the final allocation of organs. Fairness and efficiency should be balanced in the distribution of a scarce resource.

The distribution criteria for scarce organs should be justified through processes of democratic deliberation set by interdisciplinary ethics committees. These should aim at establishing public criteria for patient-selection and final allocation of organs, and those criteria should be reviewed regularly.[39]

NOTES

1. John Rawls, *A Theory of Justice* (Cambridge, Mass., Harvard University Press, 1971); Norman Daniels, *Just Health Care* (Cambridge, England: Cambridge University Press, 1985); Ronald Green, "Health Care and Justice in Contract Theory Perspective," *Ethics and Health Policy*, eds. Robert Veatch and Roy Branson (Cambridge, England: Cambridge University Press, 1985).

2. Amy Gutmann and Dennis Thompson, "Deliberating about Bioethics," *Hasting Center Report*, 27:3 (1997), pp. 38-41. See also Carlos Santiago Nino, *La constitución de la democracia deliberativa* (Buenos Aires: Gedisa, 1996), pp. 154-202.

3. Johan De Mester, Guido Persijn, *et al.*, "The New Eurotransplant Kidney Allocation System," *Transplantation*, 66:9 (November 1998), pp. 1154-1159.

4. Eurotransplant Kidney Allocation System—ETKAS Program. Eurotransplant: Austria, Belgium, Germany, Luxembourg, Netherlands.

5. De Mester, *et al.*, "The New Eurotransplant Kidney Allocation System."

6. 1996 Annual Report of the United Network for Organ Sharing Region, UNOS, USA.

7. Francis Delmonico, William Harmon, *et al.*, "A New Allocation Plan for Renal Transplantation," *Transplantation*, 67:2 (January 1999), pp. 303-309.

8. Ronald Guttmann, "Cadaver Kidneys: The Rule of Rationing," *The Lancet*, 348 (1996), p. 456.

9. Ross Isaacs, Steve Nock, *et al.*, "Racial Disparities in Renal Transplant Outcomes," *American Journal of Kidney Diseases*, 34:4 (1999), pp. 706-712. See also Stephen Korbet, David Shih, *et al.*, "Racial Differences in Survival in an Urban Peritoneal Dialysis Program," *American Journal of Kidney Disease*, 34:4 (1999), pp. 713-720.

10. John Ayanian, Paul Cleary, *et al.*, "The Effect of Patients' Preferences on Racial Differences in Access to Renal Transplantation," *The New England Journal of Medicine*, 341:22 (1999), pp. 1661-1669.

11. Robert Wolfe, Valarie Ashby, *et al.*, "Comparison of Mortality in All Patients on Dialysis, Patients on Dialysis Awaiting Transplantation, and Recipients of a First Cadaveric Transplant," *The New England Journal of Medicine*, 341:23 (1999), pp. 1725-1730.

12. *Ley Nacional de Trasplantes de Órganos de la República Argentina*, Nro. 24.193 (1993).

13. Resoluciones del Ministerio de Salud y Acción Social, Instituto Nacional Central Unico Coordinador de Ablación y Transplante, Argentina, No. 363/95, 395/95, 97/95, 286/95.

14. Resolución del Ministerio de Salud y Accion Social, Instituto Nacional Central Unico Coordinador de Ablación y Transplante, Argentina, No. 286/95.

15. INCUCAI: Instituto Nacional Central Único Coordinador de Ablación e Implante, Argentina.

16. Raquel Thevenon, Daniel Capurro, *et al.*, "Análisis de sobrevida de pacientes transplantados bajo el programa de subsidios de la Provincia de Buenos Aires," *Publicación del CUCAIBA*, 2 (1998), pp. 1-9.

17. Thomas Starzl and John Fung, "The Politics of Grafting Cadaver Kidneys," *The Lancet*, 348 (1996), pp. 454-455. See also Paul Terasaki, J. Michael Cecka, *et al.*, "High Survival Rates of Kidney Transplants from Spousal and Living Unrelated Donors," *The New England Journal of Medicine*, 333 (1995), pp. 333-336; Anthony D'Alessandro, Hans W. Sollinger, *et al.*, "Living Related and Unrelated Donors for Kidney Transplantation: A 28-Year Experience," *Annals of Surgery*, 222 (1995), pp. 353-364.

18. Guttmann, "Cadaver Kidneys," p. 457.

19. Ethics committee of a highly complex pediatric hospital in the Province of Buenos Aires, Argentina. For confidentiality reasons, I only make a general reference to the source.

20. Fernando Dapino, Alfredo Casaliba, *et.al.*, "Causas de exclusión de lista de espera en el trasplante renal," *Publicación del CUCAIBA* 2 (1998), p. 62. See also Guillermo Montechia, Hugo Petrone, *et al.*, "Evaluación pre transplante renal. Causas de no aptitud," *Publicación del CUCAIBA* 1 (1997), p. 63.

21. Guttmann, "Cadaver Kidneys," pp. 456-457.

22. *Ibid.*, p. 456.

23. James Childress, *Practical Reasoning in Bioethics* (Indianapolis, Ind.: Indiana University Press, 1997), p. 224.

24. *Ibid.*

25. See Peter Singer, "Utility and Survival Lottery," *Philosophy*, 52 (1977), pp. 218-222; Von Neumann-Morgenstern, *The Theory of Games and Economic Behavior* (Princeton: Princeton University Press, 1947).

26. See María Graciela de Ortúzar, "Etica, transplantes y medios de comunicación," *Actas de AFRA* (UNLP, 1997); María Graciela de Ortúzar, "Bioethics and Organ Transplantation," *Transplantation Proceedings*, The Fourth International Society for Organ Sharing Congress, Washington (1997) pp. 3627-3630; María Graciela de Ortúzar, "Una crítica a la definición esencialista de muerte," *Perspectivas Bioéticas en las Américas*, 4 (1997).

27. Paul McMaster, "Transplantation for Alcoholic Liver Disease in an Era of Organ Shortage," *The Lancet*, 355 (February 2000).

28. *Ibid.*

29. See Graciela Vidiella, *El derecho a la salud* (Buenos Aires, Argentina: Eudeba, 2000).

30. Rawls, *A Theory of Justice*, pp. 83, 13.

31. Daniels, *Just Health Care*, pp. 32-35.

32. Rawls, *A Theory of Justice*.

33. See Francis Kamm, "The Report of the US Task Force on Organ Transplantation: Criticisms and Alternatives," *The Mount Sinai Journal of Medicine*, 56:3 (May 1989).

34. Guttmann, "Cadaver Kidneys."

35. Tom Koch, "Normative and Prescriptive Criteria: the Efficacy of Organ Transplantation Allocation Protocols," *Theoretical Medicine*, 17 (1996), pp. 75-93.

36. Norman Daniels, "Four Unresolved Rationing Problems: A Challenge," *Hasting Center Report*, 24:4 (July-August 1994), p. 29.

37. Gutmann and Thompson, "Deliberating about Bioethics," pp. 38-41. See also Nino, *La constitución de la democracia deliberativa*, pp. 154-202.

38. Daniels, *Just Health Care*, and "Four Unresolved Rationing Problems," pp. 27-42.

39. 1 This chapter has been written thanks to the valuable contribution of ideas and criticisms of María Julia Bertomeu who aroused my concern for applied ethics and for the philosopher's commitment to ethical issues within the community.

NOTES ON CONTRIBUTORS

María Julia Bertomeu is professor of ethics at Universidad Nacional de La Plata, Argentina, and researcher of the National Research Council (CONICET). Among her areas of investigation are theoretical ethics and bioethics. She is co-editor of *Universalismo and Multiculturalismo* (2000). Her most recent articles are "I. Kant en algunas teorías recientes de justicia social" (*Veritas*) and "Comisiones y Comités de Bioética. Una mirada retrospectiva" (*Perspectivas Bioéticas de las Américas.)*

María Victoria Costa is a Ph.D. candidate at the Universidad Nacional de La Plata, Argentina, where she teaches ethics and bioethics. She is Fellow of the National Research Council (CONICET), and has received awards from the Fulbright Commission and the British Council. She has published articles on ethics applied to education, and bioethics.

Paulette Dieterlen (Ph.D.) is professor of philosophy at Universidad Autónoma de México (UNAM) and Research Fellow at Instituto de Investigaciones Filosóficas. Her primary research interests are distributive justice and poverty. She has published numerous articles, and is the author of *Sobre los derechos humanos* (1984), *Ensayos sobre justicia distributiva* (1995); *Marxismo analítico. Explicaciones funcionales e intenciones* (1995); and is the editor of *De la justicia global a la local* (1996).

Martín Diego Farrell is a legal theorist, a judge, and a professor of philosophy of law at the Law School of Universidad Nacional de Buenos Aires and at the Universidad de Palermo. In addition to his many articles on ethics and political philosophy, he has authored several books, including *La ética del aborto y la eutanasia* (1992), and *La filosofía del liberalismo* (1992).

José Roberto Goldim is a biologist with a Ph.D. in bioethics. He wrote his doctoral dissertation on informed consent in research in Brazil. He teaches bioethics at Universidade Federal do Rio Grande do Sul and Pontifícia Universidade Católica do Rio Grande do Sul, Brazil, and is a bioethics consultant in the Hospital de Clínicas de Porto Alegre. He has authored numerous books and articles in journals.

Florencia Luna (Ph.D.) is adjunct researcher of the National Research Council (CONICET) and Board Member of the International Association of Bioethics. She is also temporary advisor of the World Health Organization and the Council for International Organizations of Medical Sciences. She is currently co-directing with Ruth Macklin a research-training grant of the National

Institutes of Health (United States). She is the editor of the journal *Perspectivas bioéticas*, and co-editor of the books *Decisiones de vida y muerte* and *Bioética*.

María Graciela de Ortúzar (MA) is a philosophy teacher and a Ph.D. candidate at the Universidad Nacional de La Plata (UNLP), Argentina. Her dissertation is on the ethical implications of the Human Genome Project. She is also Fellow of the National Research Council (CONICET). Since 1995, she has been doing research on bioethics, participating in Ethics Committees, working as transplant coordinator, and teaching Bioethics at the Law and Medical Schools of UNLP.

Eduardo Rivera López (Ph.D. in Political Sciences, University of Mainz, Germany) is currently professor at the Law School of Universidad Torcuato Di Tella, Argentina. He is author of the forthcoming *Etica y transplantes de órganos* (2001), and has published several articles on liberalism, distributive justice, and bioethics in journals in Argentina, México, Germany, Finland, Spain, and Italy.

Arleen L.F. Salles (Ph.D.) teaches philosophy at Montclair State University, United States, and is a docent in the Master Program in Applied Ethics at the University of Buenos Aires, Argentina. Her research and teaching focus on ethical theory, moral psychology, and bioethical theory. Recent publications center on emotions in ethical theory, ethical issues in cloning, and particularism and emotions in bioethics. She is co-editor of *Decisiones de vida y muerte* (1995), and *Bioética* (1998).

Susana E. Sommer is a biologist. She teaches courses on the ethics of assisted reproduction and genetics at the University of Buenos Aires, Argentina. She is Board member of the Feminist Approaches to Bioethics Network. She is also author of *De la cigüeña a la probeta; Genética, clonación y bioética* and editor of *Reproducción: las nuevas tecnologías: Un enfoque multidisciplinario*. Her articles have appeared in national and international journals and in edited books.

Margarita M. Valdés studied philosophy at Universidad Autónoma de México (UNAM), Smith College, and La Sorbonne (Paris). Her most important publications are on topics concerned with philosophy of language, philosophy of mind, and ethics. She is editor of *Controversias sobre el aborto* to be published by UNAM and Fondo de Cultura Económica in 2001.

Graciela Vidiella (Ph.D) is profesor of ethics and philosophy in the departments of philosophy of the University of Buenos Aires and the

Universidad Nacional de La Plata, Argentina. She is also docent in the Master Program in Applied Ethics at the University of Buenos Aires. She is author of *El derecho a la Salud* (2000), co-editor of *Universalismo and Multiculturalismo* (2000), and author of articles in national and international journals.

INDEX

VIBS

The **Value Inquiry Book Series** is co-sponsored by:

Adler School of Professional Psychology
American Indian Philosophy Association
American Maritain Association
American Society for Value Inquiry
Association for Process Philosophy of Education
Canadian Society for Philosophical Practice
Center for Bioethics, University of Turku
Center for International Partnerships, Rochester Institute of Technology
Center for Professional and Applied Ethics, University of North Carolina at
Charlotte
Centre for Applied Ethics, Hong Kong Baptist University
Centre for Cultural Research, Aarhus University
Centre for the Study of Philosophy and Religion, College of Cape Breton
College of Education and Allied Professions, Bowling Green State University
Concerned Philosophers for Peace
Conference of Philosophical Societies
Department of Moral and Social Philosophy, University of Helsinki
Gannon University
Gilson Society
Global Association for the Study of Persons
Ikeda University
Institute of Philosophy of the High Council of Scientific Research, Spain
International Academy of Philosophy of the Principality of Liechtenstein
International Center for the Arts, Humanities, and Value Inquiry
International Society for Universal Dialogue
Natural Law Society

Philosophical Society of Finland
Philosophy Born of Struggle Association
Philosophy Seminar, University of Mainz
Pragmatism Archive
R.S. Hartman Institute for Formal and Applied Axiology
Research Institute, Lakeridge Health Corporation
Russian Philosophical Society
Society for Iberian and Latin-American Thought
Society for the Philosophic Study of Genocide and the Holocaust
Society for the Philosophy of Sex and Love
Yves R. Simon Institute.

Titles Published

1. Noel Balzer, *The Human Being as a Logical Thinker.*

2. Archie J. Bahm, *Axiology: The Science of Values.*

3. H. P. P. (Hennie) Lötter, *Justice for an Unjust Society.*

4. H. G. Callaway, *Context for Meaning and Analysis: A Critical Study in the Philosophy of Language.*

5. Benjamin S. Llamzon, *A Humane Case for Moral Intuition.*

6. James R. Watson, *Between Auschwitz and Tradition: Postmodern Reflections on the Task of Thinking.* A volume in **Holocaust and Genocide Studies.**

7. Robert S. Hartman, *Freedom to Live: The Robert Hartman Story,* edited by Arthur R. Ellis. A volume in **Hartman Institute Axiology Studies.**

8. Archie J. Bahm, *Ethics: The Science of Oughtness.*

9. George David Miller, *An Idiosyncratic Ethics; Or, the Lauramachean Ethics.*

10. Joseph P. DeMarco, *A Coherence Theory in Ethics.*

11. Frank G. Forrest, *Valuemetrics*^N*: The Science of Personal and Professional Ethics.* A volume in **Hartman Institute Axiology Studies.**

12. William Gerber, *The Meaning of Life: Insights of the World's Great Thinkers.*

13. Richard T. Hull, Editor, *A Quarter Century of Value Inquiry: Presidential Addresses of the American Society for Value Inquiry.* A volume in **Histories and Addresses of Philosophical Societies.**

14. William Gerber, *Nuggets of Wisdom from Great Jewish Thinkers: From Biblical Times to the Present.*

15. Sidney Axinn, *The Logic of Hope: Extensions of Kant's View of Religion.*

16. Messay Kcbede, *Meaning and Development.*

17. Amihud Gilead, *The Platonic Odyssey: A Philosophical-Literary Inquiry into the* Phaedo.

18. Necip Fikri Alican, *Mill's Principle of Utility: A Defense of John Stuart Mill's Notorious Proof.* A volume in **Universal Justice.**

19. Michael H. Mitias, Editor, *Philosophy and Architecture.*

20. Roger T. Simonds, *Rational Individualism: The Perennial Philosophy of Legal Interpretation.* A volume in **Natural Law Studies.**

21. William Pencak, *The Conflict of Law and Justice in the Icelandic Sagas.*

22. Samuel M. Natale and Brian M. Rothschild, Editors, *Values, Work, Education: The Meanings of Work.*

23. N. Georgopoulos and Michael Heim, Editors, *Being Human in the Ultimate: Studies in the Thought of John M. Anderson.*

24. Robert Wesson and Patricia A. Williams, Editors, *Evolution and Human Values.*

25. Wim J. van der Steen, *Facts, Values, and Methodology: A New Approach to Ethics.*

26. Avi Sagi and Daniel Statman, *Religion and Morality.*

27. Albert William Levi, *The High Road of Humanity: The Seven Ethical Ages of Western Man,* edited by Donald Phillip Verene and Molly Black Verene.

28. Samuel M. Natale and Brian M. Rothschild, Editors, *Work Values: Education, Organization, and Religious Concerns.*

29. Laurence F. Bove and Laura Duhan Kaplan, Editors, *From the Eye of the Storm: Regional Conflicts and the Philosophy of Peace.* A volume in **Philosophy of Peace.**

30. Robin Attfield, *Value, Obligation, and Meta-Ethics.*

31. William Gerber, *The Deepest Questions You Can Ask About God: As Answered by the World's Great Thinkers.*

32. Daniel Statman, *Moral Dilemmas.*

33. Rem B. Edwards, Editor, *Formal Axiology and Its Critics.* A volume in **Hartman Institute Axiology Studies.**

34. George David Miller and Conrad P. Pritscher, *On Education and Values: In Praise of Pariahs and Nomads.* A volume in **Philosophy of Education.**

35. Paul S. Penner, *Altruistic Behavior: An Inquiry into Motivation.*

36. Corbin Fowler, *Morality for Moderns.*

37. Giambattista Vico, *The Art of Rhetoric* (*Institutiones Oratoriae,* 1711-1741), from the definitive Latin text and notes, Italian commentary and introduction by Giuliano Crifò, translated and edited by Giorgio A. Pinton and Arthur W. Shippee. A volume in **Values in Italian Philosophy.**

38. W. H. Werkmeister, *Martin Heidegger on the Way,* edited by Richard T. Hull. A volume in **Werkmeister Studies.**

39. Phillip Stambovsky, *Myth and the Limits of Reason.*

40. Samantha Brennan, Tracy Isaacs, and Michael Milde, Editors, *A Question of Values: New Canadian Perspectives in Ethics and Political Philosophy.*

41. Peter A. Redpath, *Cartesian Nightmare: An Introduction to Transcendental Sophistry.* A volume in **Studies in the History of Western Philosophy.**

42. Clark Butler, *History as the Story of Freedom: Philosophy in Intercultural Context,* with Responses by sixteen scholars.

43. Dennis Rohatyn, *Philosophy History Sophistry.*

44. Leon Shaskolsky Sheleff, *Social Cohesion and Legal Coercion: A Critique of Weber, Durkheim, and Marx.* Afterword by Virginia Black.

45. Alan Soble, Editor, *Sex, Love, and Friendship: Studies of the Society for the Philosophy of Sex and Love, 1977-1992.* A volume in **Histories and Addresses of Philosophical Societies.**

46. Peter A. Redpath, *Wisdom's Odyssey: From Philosophy to Transcendental Sophistry.* A volume in **Studies in the History of Western Philosophy.**

47. Albert A. Anderson, *Universal Justice: A Dialectical Approach.* A volume in **Universal Justice.**

48. Pio Colonnello, *The Philosophy of José Gaos.* Translated from Italian by Peter Cocozzella. Edited by Myra Moss. Introduction by Giovanni Gullace. A volume in **Values in Italian Philosophy.**

49. Laura Duhan Kaplan and Laurence F. Bove, Editors, *Philosophical Perspectives on Power and Domination: Theories and Practices.* A volume in **Philosophy of Peace.**

50. Gregory F. Mellema, *Collective Responsibility.*

51. Josef Seifert, *What Is Life? The Originality, Irreducibility, and Value of Life.* A volume in **Central-European Value Studies.**

52. William Gerber, *Anatomy of What We Value Most.*

53. Armando Molina, *Our Ways: Values and Character,* edited by Rem B. Edwards. A volume in **Hartman Institute Axiology Studies.**

69. James W. Vice, *The Reopening of the American Mind: On Skepticism and Constitutionalism.*

70. Sarah Bishop Merrill, *Defining Personhood: Toward the Ethics of Quality in Clinical Care.*

71. Dane R. Gordon, *Philosophy and Vision.*

72. Alan Milchman and Alan Rosenberg, Editors, *Postmodernism and the Holocaust.* A volume in **Holocaust and Genocide Studies.**

73. Peter A. Redpath, *Masquerade of the Dream Walkers: Prophetic Theology from the Cartesians to Hegel.* A volume in **Studies in the History of Western Philosophy.**

74. Malcolm D. Evans, *Whitehead and Philosophy of Education: The Seamless Coat of Learning.* A volume in **Philosophy of Education.**

75. Warren E. Steinkraus, *Taking Religious Claims Seriously: A Philosophy of Religion,* edited by Michael H. Mitias. A volume in **Universal Justice.**

76. Thomas Magnell, Editor, *Values and Education.*

77. Kenneth A. Bryson, *Persons and Immortality.* A volume in **Natural Law Studies.**

78. Steven V. Hicks, *International Law and the Possibility of a Just World Order: An Essay on Hegel's Universalism.* A volume in **Universal Justice.**

79. E. F. Kaelin, *Texts on Texts and Textuality: A Phenomenology of Literary Art,* edited by Ellen J. Burns.

80. Amihud Gilead, *Saving Possibilities: A Study in Philosophical Psychology.* A volume in **Philosophy and Psychology.**

81. André Mineau, *The Making of the Holocaust: Ideology and Ethics in the Systems Perspective.* A volume in **Holocaust and Genocide Studies.**

82. Howard P. Kainz, *Politically Incorrect Dialogues: Topics Not Discussed in Polite Circles.*

83. Veikko Launis, Juhani Pietarinen, and Juha Räikkä, Editors, *Genes and Morality: New Essays.* A volume in **Nordic Value Studies.**

84. Steven Schroeder, *The Metaphysics of Cooperation: The Case of F. D. Maurice.*

85. Caroline Joan ("Kay") S. Picart, *Thomas Mann and Friedrich Nietzsche: Eroticism, Death, Music, and Laughter.* A volume in **Central-European Value Studies.**

86. G. John M. Abbarno, Editor, *The Ethics of Homelessness: Philosophical Perspectives.*

87. James Giles, Editor, *French Existentialism: Consciousness, Ethics, and Relations with Others.* A volume in **Nordic Value Studies.**

88. Deane Curtin and Robert Litke, Editors, *Institutional Violence.* A volume in **Philosophy of Peace.**

89. Yuval Lurie, *Cultural Beings: Reading the Philosophers of Genesis.*

90. Sandra A. Wawrytko, Editor, *The Problem of Evil: An Intercultural Exploration.* A volume in **Philosophy and Psychology.**

91. Gary J. Acquaviva, *Values, Violence, and Our Future.* A volume in **Hartman Institute Axiology Studies.**

92. Michael R. Rhodes, *Coercion: A Nonevaluative Approach.*

93. Jacques Kriel, *Matter, Mind, and Medicine: Transforming the Clinical Method.*

94. Haim Gordon, *Dwelling Poetically: Educational Challenges in Heidegger's Thinking on Poetry.* A volume in **Philosophy of Education.**

95. Ludwig Grünberg, *The Mystery of Values: Studies in Axiology,* edited by Cornelia Grünberg and Laura Grünberg.

96. Gerhold K. Becker, Editor, *The Moral Status of Persons: Perspectives on Bioethics.* A volume in **Studies in Applied Ethics.**

97. Roxanne Claire Farrar, *Sartrean Dialectics: A Method for Critical Discourse on Aesthetic Experience.*

98. Ugo Spirito, *Memoirs of the Twentieth Century.* Translated from Italian and edited by Anthony G. Costantini. A volume in **Values in Italian Philosophy.**

99. Steven Schroeder, *Between Freedom and Necessity: An Essay on the Place of Value.*

100. Foster N. Walker, *Enjoyment and the Activity of Mind: Dialogues on Whitehead and Education.* A volume in **Philosophy of Education.**

101. Avi Sagi, *Kierkegaard, Religion, and Existence: The Voyage of the Self.* Translated from Hebrew by Batya Stein.

102. Bennie R. Crockett, Jr., Editor, *Addresses of the Mississippi Philosophical Association.* A volume in **Histories and Addresses of Philosophical Societies.**

103. Paul van Dijk, *Anthropology in the Age of Technology: The Philosophical Contribution of Günther Anders.*

104. Giambattista Vico, *Universal Right.* Translated from Latin and edited by Giorgio Pinton and Margaret Diehl. A volume in **Values in Italian Philosophy.**

105. Judith Presler and Sally J. Scholz, Editors, *Peacemaking: Lessons from the Past, Visions for the Future.* A volume in **Philosophy of Peace.**

106. Dennis Bonnette, *Origin of the Human Species.* A volume in **Studies in the History of Western Philosophy.**

107. Phyllis Chiasson, *Peirce's Pragmatism: The Design for Thinking.* A volume in **Studies in Pragmatism and Values.**

108. Dan Stone, Editor, *Theoretical Interpretations of the Holocaust.* A volume in **Holocaust and Genocide Studies.**

109. Raymond Angelo Belliotti, *What Is the Meaning of Human Life?*

110. Lennart Nordenfelt, *Health, Science, and Ordinary Language*, with Contributions by George Khushf and K. W. M. Fulford.

111. Daryl Koehn, *Local Insights, Global Ethics for Business.* A volume in **Studies in Applied Ethics.**

112. Matti Häyry and Tuija Takala, Editors, *The Future of Value Inquiry.* A volume in **Nordic Value Studies.**

113. Conrad P. Pritscher, *Quantum Learning: Beyond Duality.*

114. Thomas M. Dicken and Rem B. Edwards, *Dialogues on Values and Centers of Value: Old Friends, New Thoughts.* A volume in **Hartman Institute Axiology Studies.**

115. Rem B. Edwards, *What Caused the Big Bang?* A volume in **Philosophy and Religion.**

116. Jon Mills, Editor, *A Pedagogy of Becoming.* A volume in **Philosophy of Education.**

117. Robert T. Radford, *Cicero: A Study in the Origins of Republican Philosophy.* A volume in **Studies in the History of Western Philosophy.**

118. Arleen L. F. Salles and María Julia Bertomeu, Editors, *Bioethics: Latin American Perspectives.* A volume in **Philosophy in Latin America.**